Student Solutions Manual

to accompany

Investments

Seventh Edition

Zvi Bodie
Boston University

Alex Kane
University of California, San Diego

Alan J. Marcus
Boston College

Prepared by
Bruce Swensen
Adelphi University

Boston   Burr Ridge, IL   Dubuque, IA   Madison, WI   New York   San Francisco   St. Louis
Bangkok   Bogotá   Caracas   Kuala Lumpur   Lisbon   London   Madrid   Mexico City
Milan   Montreal   New Delhi   Santiago   Seoul   Singapore   Sydney   Taipei   Toronto

McGraw-Hill
Irwin

Student Solutions Manual
INVESTMENTS
Bodie, Kane, and Marcus

Published by McGraw-Hill/Irwin, an imprint of The McGraw-Hill Companies, Inc., 1221 Avenue of the Americas, New York, NY 10020. Copyright © 2008 by The McGraw-Hill Companies, Inc. All rights reserved.

1 2 3 4 5 6 7 8 9 0 QPD/QPD 0 9 8 7 6

ISBN: 978-0-07-326970-2
MHID: 0-07-326970-0

www.mhhe.com

Contents

CHAPTER 1: THE INVESTMENT ENVIRONMENT

1. a. Cash is a financial asset because it is the liability of the federal government.

    b. No. The cash does not directly add to the productive capacity of the economy.

    c. Yes.

    d. Society as a whole is worse off, since taxpayers, as a group will make up for the liability.

2. a. The bank loan is a financial liability for Lanni. (Lanni's IOU is the bank's financial asset.) The cash Lanni receives is a financial asset. The new financial asset created is Lanni's promissory note (that is, Lanni's IOU to the bank).

    b. Lanni transfers financial assets (cash) to the software developers. In return, Lanni gets a real asset, the completed software. No financial assets are created or destroyed; cash is simply transferred from one party to another.

    c. Lanni gives the real asset (the software) to Microsoft in exchange for a financial asset, 1,500 shares of Microsoft stock. If Microsoft issues new shares in order to pay Lanni, then this would represent the creation of new financial assets.

    d. Lanni exchanges one financial asset (1,500 shares of stock) for another ($120,000). Lanni gives a financial asset ($50,000 cash) to the bank and gets back another financial asset (its IOU). The loan is "destroyed" in the transaction, since it is retired when paid off and no longer exists.

3. a.

Assets		Liabilities & Shareholders' equity	
Cash	$ 70,000	Bank loan	$ 50,000
Computers	30,000	Shareholders' equity	50,000
Total	$100,000	Total	$100,000

Ratio of real to total assets = $30,000/$100,000 = 0.30

    b.

Assets		Liabilities & Shareholders' equity	
Software product*	$ 70,000	Bank loan	$ 50,000
Computers	30,000	Shareholders' equity	50,000
Total	$100,000	Total	$100,000

*Valued at cost

Ratio of real to total assets = $100,000/$100,000 = 1.0

c.

Assets		Liabilities & Shareholders' equity	
Microsoft shares	$120,000	Bank loan	$ 50,000
Computers	30,000	Shareholders' equity	100,000
Total	$150,000	Total	$150,000

Ratio of real to total assets = $30,000/$150,000 = 0.20

Conclusion: when the firm starts up and raises working capital, it will be characterized by a low ratio of real to total assets. When it is in full production, it will have a high ratio of real assets. When the project "shuts down" and the firm sells it off for cash, financial assets once again replace real assets.

4. Ultimately, it is true that real assets do determine the material well being of an economy. Nevertheless, individuals can benefit when financial engineering creates new products that allow them to manage their portfolios of financial assets more efficiently. Because bundling and unbundling creates financial products with new properties and sensitivities to various sources of risk, it allows investors to hedge particular sources of risk more efficiently.

5. For commercial banks, the ratio is: $94.2/$8,480.5 = 0.011
For non-financial firms, the ratio is: $10,973/$21,851 = 0.502
The difference should be expected primarily because the bulk of the business of financial institutions is to make loans that are financial assets.

6. a. Primary-market transaction

b. Derivative assets.

c. Investors who wish to hold gold without the complication and cost of physical storage.

7. a. A fixed salary means that compensation is (at least in the short run) independent of the firm's success. This salary structure does not tie the manager's immediate compensation to the success of the firm. However, the manager might view this as the safest compensation structure and therefore value it more highly.

b. A salary that is paid in the form of stock in the firm means that the manager earns the most when the shareholders' wealth is maximized. This structure is therefore most likely to align the interests of managers and shareholders. If stock compensation is overdone, however, the manager might view it as overly risky since the manager's career is already linked to the firm, and this undiversified exposure would be exacerbated with a large stock position in the firm.

c.   Call options on shares of the firm create great incentives for managers to contribute to the firm's success. In some cases, however, stock options can lead to other agency problems. For example, a manager with numerous call options might be tempted to take on a very risky investment project, reasoning that if the project succeeds the payoff will be huge, while if it fails, the losses are limited to the lost value of the options. Shareholders, in contrast, bear the losses as well as the gains on the project, and might be less willing to assume that risk.

8.   Even if an individual shareholder could monitor and improve managers' performance, and thereby increase the value of the firm, the payoff would be small, since the ownership share in a large corporation would be very small. For example, if you own $10,000 of GM stock and can increase the value of the firm by 5%, a very ambitious goal, you benefit by only: $0.05 \times \$10,000 = \$500$.

In contrast, a bank that has a multimillion-dollar loan outstanding to the firm has a big stake in making sure that the firm can repay the loan. It is clearly worthwhile for the bank to spend considerable resources to monitor the firm.

9.   Securitization requires access to a large number of potential investors. To attract these investors, the capital market needs:

(1)   a safe system of business laws and low probability of confiscatory taxation/regulation;
(2)   a well-developed investment banking industry;
(3)   a well-developed system of brokerage and financial transactions, and;
(4)   well-developed media, particularly financial reporting.

These characteristics are found in (indeed make for) a well-developed financial market.

10. Securitization leads to disintermediation; that is, securitization provides a means for market participants to bypass intermediaries. For example, mortgage-backed securities channel funds to the housing market without requiring that banks or thrift institutions make loans from their own portfolios. As securitization progresses, financial intermediaries must increase other activities such as providing short-term liquidity to consumers and small business, and financial services.

11. Financial assets make it easy for large firms to raise the capital needed to finance their investments in real assets. If General Motors, for example, could not issue stocks or bonds to the general public, it would have a far more difficult time raising capital. Contraction of the supply of financial assets would make financing more difficult, thereby increasing the cost of capital. A higher cost of capital means less investment and lower real growth.

12. Mutual funds accept funds from small investors and invest, on behalf of these investors, in the national and international securities markets.
Pension funds accept funds and then invest, on behalf of current and future retirees, thereby channeling funds from one sector of the economy to another.

Venture capital firms pool the funds of private investors and invest in start-up firms.

Banks accept deposits from customers and loan those funds to businesses, or use the funds to buy securities of large corporations.

13. Even if the firm does not need to issue stock in any particular year, the stock market is still important to the financial manager. The stock price provides important information about how the market values the firm's investment projects. For example, if the stock price rises considerably, managers might conclude that the market believes the firm's future prospects are bright. This might be a useful signal to the firm to proceed with an investment such as an expansion of the firm's business.

In addition, the fact that shares can be traded in the secondary market makes the shares more attractive to investors since investors know that, when they wish to, they will be able to sell their shares. This in turn makes investors more willing to buy shares in a primary offering, and thus improves the terms on which firms can raise money in the equity market.

14. Treasury bills serve a purpose for investors who prefer a low-risk investment. The lower average rate of return compared to stocks is the price investors pay for predictability of investment performance and portfolio value.

15. With a "top-down" investment strategy, you focus on asset allocation or the broad composition of the entire portfolio, which is the major determinant of overall performance. Moreover, top down management is the natural way to establish a portfolio with a level of risk consistent with your risk tolerance. The disadvantage of an *exclusive* emphasis on top down issues is that you may forfeit the potential high returns that could result from identifying and concentrating in undervalued securities or sectors of the market.

With a "bottom-up" investment strategy, you try to benefit from identifying undervalued securities. The disadvantage is that you tend to overlook the overall composition of your portfolio, which may result in a non-diversified portfolio or a portfolio with a risk level inconsistent with your level of risk tolerance. In addition, this technique tends to require more active management, thus generating more transaction costs. Finally, your analysis may be incorrect, in which case you will have fruitlessly expended effort and money attempting to beat a simple buy-and-hold strategy.

16. You should be skeptical. If the author actually knows how to achieve such returns, one must question why the author would then be so ready to sell the secret to others. Financial markets are very competitive; one of the implications of this fact is that riches do not come easily. High expected returns require bearing some risk, and obvious bargains are few and far between. Odds are that the only one getting rich from the book is its author.

17. a. The SEC website defines the difference between saving and investing in terms of the investment alternatives or the financial assets the individual chooses to acquire. According to the SEC website, saving is the process of acquiring a "safe" financial asset and investing is the process of acquiring "risky" financial assets.

    b. The economist's definition of savings is the difference between income and consumption. Investing is the process of allocating one's savings among available assets, both real assets and financial assets. The SEC definitions actually represent (according the economist's definition) two kinds of investment alternatives.

18. As is the case for the SEC definitions (see Problem 17), the SIA defines saving and investing as acquisition of alternative kinds of financial assets. According to the SIA, saving is the process of acquiring safe assets, generally from a bank, while investing is the acquisition of other financial assets, such as stocks and bonds. On the other hand, the definitions in the chapter indicate that saving means spending less than one's income. Investing is the process of allocating one's savings among financial assets, including savings account deposits and money market accounts ("saving" according to the SIA), other financial assets such as stocks and bonds ("investing" according to the SIA), as well as real assets.

CHAPTER 2: ASSET CLASSES AND FINANCIAL INSTRUMENTS

1.   (d)

2.   The equivalent taxable yield is: $6.75\%/(1 - 0.34) = 10.23\%$

3.   (a)   Writing a call entails unlimited potential losses as the stock price rises.

4.   a.   You would have to pay the asked price of:
            $94:30 = 94.9375\%$ of par $= \$949.375$

      b.   The coupon rate is 3.625% implying coupon payments of \$36.25 annually or, more precisely, \$18.125 semiannually.

      c.   Current yield = (Annual coupon income/price)
            $= \$36.25/\$949.375 = 0.0382 = 3.82\%$

5.   Preferred stock is like long-term debt in that it typically promises a fixed payment each year. In this way, it is a perpetuity. Preferred stock is also like long-term debt in that it does not give the holder voting rights in the firm.

      Preferred stock is like equity in that the firm is under no contractual obligation to make the preferred stock dividend payments. Failure to make payments does not set off corporate bankruptcy. With respect to the priority of claims to the assets of the firm in the event of corporate bankruptcy, preferred stock has a higher priority than common equity but a lower priority than bonds.

6.   Money market securities are called "cash equivalents" because of their great liquidity. The prices of money market securities are very stable, and they can be converted to cash (i.e., sold) on very short notice and with very low transaction costs.

7. $P = \$10,000/1.02 = \$9,803.92$

8. The total before-tax income is $4. After the 70% exclusion for preferred stock dividends, the taxable income is: $0.30 \square \$4 = \$1.20$

    Therefore, taxes are: $0.30 \square \$1.20 = \$0.36$

    After-tax income is: $\$4.00 - \$0.36 = \$3.64$

    Rate of return is: $\$3.64/\$40.00 = 9.10\%$

9. a. General Dynamics closed today at $112.65, which was $1.56 higher than yesterday's price. Yesterday's closing price was: $111.09

    b. You could buy: $\$5,000/\$112.65 = 44.4$ shares

    c. Your annual dividend income would be: $44.4 \times \$1.60 = \$71.04$

    d. The price-to-earnings ratio is 16 and the price is $112.65. Therefore:

    $$\$112.65/\text{Earnings per share} = 16 \Rightarrow \text{Earnings per share} = \$7.04$$

10. a. At $t = 0$, the value of the index is: $(90 + 50 + 100)/3 = 80$

    At $t = 1$, the value of the index is: $(95 + 45 + 110)/3 = 83.333$

    The rate of return is: $(83.333/80) - 1 = 4.17\%$

    b. In the absence of a split, Stock C would sell for 110, so the value of the index would be: $250/3 = 83.333$

    After the split, Stock C sells for 55. Therefore, we need to find the divisor (d) such that:

    $$83.333 = (95 + 45 + 55)/d \Rightarrow d = 2.340$$

    c. The return is zero. The index remains unchanged because the return for each stock separately equals zero.

11. a. Total market value at $t = 0$ is: $(\$9,000 + \$10,000 + \$20,000) = \$39,000$

    Total market value at $t = 1$ is: $(\$9,500 + \$9,000 + \$22,000) = \$40,500$

    Rate of return = $(\$40,500/\$39,000) - 1 = 3.85\%$

    b. The return on each stock is as follows:

    $r_A = (95/90) - 1 = 0.0556$

    $r_B = (45/50) - 1 = -0.10$

    $r_C = (110/100) - 1 = 0.10$

    The equally-weighted average is:

    $[0.0556 + (-0.10) + 0.10]/3 = 0.0185 = 1.85\%$

12. The after-tax yield on the corporate bonds is: $0.09 \times (1 - 0.30) = 0.0630 = 6.30\%$

    Therefore, municipals must offer at least 6.30% yields.

13. a. The taxable bond. With a zero tax bracket, the after-tax yield for the taxable bond is the same as the before-tax yield (5%), which is greater than the yield on the municipal bond.

    b. The taxable bond. The after-tax yield for the taxable bond is:

    $$0.05 \times (1 - 0.10) = 4.5\%$$

    c. You are indifferent. The after-tax yield for the taxable bond is:

    $$0.05 \times (1 - 0.20) = 4.0\%$$

    The after-tax yield is the same as that of the municipal bond.

    d. The municipal bond offers the higher after-tax yield for investors in tax brackets above 20%.

14. Equation (2.5) shows that the equivalent taxable yield is: $r = r_m /(1 - t)$

    a. 4.00%

    b. 4.44%

    c. 5.00%

    d. 5.71%

15. If the after-tax yields are equal, then: $0.056 = 0.08 \; \square \; (1 - t)$

    This implies that $t = 0.30 = 30\%$.

16. a. The higher coupon bond.

    b. The call with the lower exercise price.

    c. The put on the lower priced stock.

17. a. You bought the contract when the futures price was 1687.00 (see Figure 2.12). The contract closes at a price of 1700, which is 13.0 higher than the original futures price. The contract multiplier is $100. Therefore, the profit will be:

$$13.0 \times \$100 = \$1,300$$

b. Open interest is 47,990 contracts.

18. a. Since the stock price exceeds the exercise price, you will exercise the call.

The payoff on the option will be: $37 − $35 = $2

The option originally cost $1.97, so the profit is: $2.00 − $1.97 = $0.03

Rate of return = $0.03/$1.97 = 0.0152 = 1.52%

b. If the exercise price were $32.50, you would exercise the call.
The payoff on the option will be: $37.00 − $32.50 = $4.50
The option originally cost $3.70 so the profit is: $4.50 − $3.70 = $0.80
Rate of return = $0.80/$3.70 = 0.2162 = 21.62%

c. If the put has an exercise price of $35, you would not exercise for any stock price of $35 or above. The loss on the put would be the initial cost, $1.30.

19. There is always a possibility that the option will be in-the-money at some time prior to expiration. Investors will pay something for this possibility of a positive payoff.

20.

	Value of call at expiration	Initial Cost	Profit
a.	0	4	-4
b.	0	4	-4
c.	0	4	-4
d.	5	4	1
e.	10	4	6

	Value of put at expiration	Initial Cost	Profit
a.	10	6	4
b.	5	6	-1
c.	0	6	-6
d.	0	6	-6
e.	0	6	-6

21. A put option conveys the *right* to sell the underlying asset at the exercise price. A short position in a futures contract carries an *obligation* to sell the underlying asset at the futures price.

22. A call option conveys the *right* to buy the underlying asset at the exercise price. A long position in a futures contract carries an *obligation* to buy the underlying asset at the futures price.

23. The spread will widen. Deterioration of the economy increases credit risk, that is, the likelihood of default. Investors will demand a greater premium on debt securities subject to default risk.

24. On the day we tried this experiment, 36 of the 50 stocks met this criterion, leading us to conclude that returns on stock investments can be quite volatile.

CHAPTER 3: HOW SECURITIES ARE TRADED

1. a. In addition to the explicit fees of $70,000, FBN appears to have paid an implicit price in underpricing of the IPO. The underpricing is $3 per share, or a total of $300,000, implying total costs of $370,000.

   b. No. The underwriters do not capture the part of the costs corresponding to the underpricing. The underpricing may be a rational marketing strategy. Without it, the underwriters would need to spend more resources in order to place the issue with the public. The underwriters would then need to charge higher explicit fees to the issuing firm. The issuing firm may be just as well off paying the implicit issuance cost represented by the underpricing.

2. a. In principle, potential losses are unbounded, growing directly with increases in the price of IBM.

   b. If the stop-buy order can be filled at $128, the maximum possible loss per share is $8. If the price of IBM shares go above $128, then the stop-buy order would be executed, limiting the losses from the short sale.

3. a. The stock is purchased for: $300 \times \$40 = \$12,000$

      The amount borrowed is $4,000. Therefore, the investor put up equity, or margin, of $8,000.

   b. If the share price falls to $30, then the value of the stock falls to $9,000. By the end of the year, the amount of the loan owed to the broker grows to:

      $\$4,000 \times 1.08 = \$4,320$

      Therefore, the remaining margin in the investor's account is:

      $\$9,000 - \$4,320 = \$4,680$

      The percentage margin is now: $\$4,680/\$9,000 = 0.52 = 52\%$

      Therefore, the investor will not receive a margin call.

   c. The rate of return on the investment over the year is:

      (Ending equity in the account − Initial equity)/Initial equity

      $= (\$4,680 - \$8,000)/\$8,000 = -0.415 = -41.5\%$

4. a. The initial margin was: $0.50 \times 1,000 \times \$40 = \$20,000$
   As a result of the increase in the stock price Old Economy Traders loses:

   $$\$10 \times 1,000 = \$10,000$$

   Therefore, margin decreases by $10,000. Moreover, Old Economy Traders must pay the dividend of $2 per share to the lender of the shares, so that the margin in the account decreases by an additional $2,000. Therefore, the remaining margin is:

   $$\$20,000 - \$10,000 - \$2,000 = \$8,000$$

   b. The percentage margin is: $\$8,000/\$50,000 = 0.16 = 16\%$

   So there will be a margin call.

   c. The equity in the account decreased from $20,000 to $8,000 in one year, for a rate of return of: $(-\$12,000/\$20,000) = -0.60 = -60\%$

5. Much of what the specialist does (e.g., crossing orders and maintaining the limit order book) can be accomplished by a computerized system. In fact, some exchanges use an automated system for night trading. A more difficult issue to resolve is whether the more discretionary activities of specialists involving trading for their own accounts (e.g., maintaining an orderly market) can be replicated by a computer system.

6. a. The buy order will be filled at the best limit-sell order price: $50.25

   b. The next market buy order will be filled at the next-best limit-sell order price: $51.50

   c. You would want to increase your inventory. There is considerable buying demand at prices just below $50, indicating that downside risk is limited. In contrast, limit sell orders are sparse, indicating that a moderate buy order could result in a substantial price increase.

7. a. You buy 200 shares of Telecom for $10,000. These shares increase in value by 10%, or $1,000. You pay interest of: $0.08 \times 5,000 = \$400$
   The rate of return will be:

   $$\frac{\$1,000 - \$400}{\$5,000} = 0.12 = 12\%$$

b.   The value of the 200 shares is 200P. Equity is (200P – $5,000). You will receive a margin call when:

$$\frac{200P - \$5,000}{200P} = 0.30 \Rightarrow \text{when } P = \$35.71 \text{ or lower}$$

8.   a.   Initial margin is 50% of $5,000 or $2,500.

   b.   Total assets are $7,500 ($5,000 from the sale of the stock and $2,500 put up for margin). Liabilities are 100P. Therefore, net worth is ($7,500 – 100P). A margin call will be issued when:

$$\frac{\$7,500 - 100P}{100P} = 0.30 \Rightarrow \text{when } P = \$57.69 \text{ or higher}$$

9.   The total cost of the purchase is: $40 × 500 = $20,000
You borrow $5,000 from your broker, and invest $15,000 of your own funds.
Your margin account starts out with net worth of $15,000.

   a.   (i)   Net worth increases to: ($44 × 500) – $5,000 = $17,000

      Percentage gain = $2,000/$15,000 = 0.1333 = 13.33%

      (ii)   With price unchanged, net worth is unchanged.

      Percentage gain = zero

      (iii)   Net worth falls to ($36 × 500) – $5,000 = $13,000

      Percentage gain = (–$2,000/$15,000) = –0.1333 = –13.33%

   The relationship between the percentage return and the percentage change in the price of the stock is given by:

$$\% \text{ return} = \% \text{ change in price} \times \frac{\text{Total investment}}{\text{Investor's initial equity}} = \% \text{ change in price} \times 1.333$$

   For example, when the stock price rises from $40 to $44, the percentage change in price is 10%, while the percentage gain for the investor is:

$$\% \text{ return} = 10\% \times \frac{\$20,000}{\$15,000} = 13.33\%$$

   b.   The value of the 500 shares is 500P. Equity is (500P – $5,000). You will receive a margin call when:

$$\frac{500P - \$5,000}{500P} = 0.25 \Rightarrow \text{when } P = \$13.33 \text{ or lower}$$

c. The value of the 500 shares is 500P. But now you have borrowed $10,000 instead of $5,000. Therefore, equity is (500P − $10,000). You will receive a margin call when:

$$\frac{500P - \$10,000}{500P} = 0.25 \Rightarrow \text{when } P = \$26.67$$

With less equity in the account, you are far more vulnerable to a margin call.

d. By the end of the year, the amount of the loan owed to the broker grows to:

$$\$5,000 \times 1.08 = \$5,400$$

The equity in your account is (500P − $5,400). Initial equity was $15,000. Therefore, your rate of return after one year is as follows:

(i) $$\frac{(500 \times \$44) - \$5,400 - \$15,000}{\$15,000} = 0.1067 = 10.67\%$$

(ii) $$\frac{(500 \times \$40) - \$5,400 - \$15,000}{\$15,000} = -0.0267 = -2.67\%$$

(iii) $$\frac{(500 \times \$36) - \$5,400 - \$15,000}{\$15,000} = -0.1600 = -16.00\%$$

The relationship between the percentage return and the percentage change in the price of Intel is given by:

$$\% \text{ return} = \left(\% \text{ change in price} \times \frac{\text{Total investment}}{\text{Investor's initial equity}} \right) - \left(8\% \times \frac{\text{Funds borrowed}}{\text{Investor's initial equity}} \right)$$

For example, when the stock price rises from $40 to $44, the percentage change in price is 10%, while the percentage gain for the investor is:

$$\left(10\% \times \frac{\$20,000}{\$15,000} \right) - \left(8\% \times \frac{\$5,000}{\$15,000} \right) = 10.67\%$$

e. The value of the 500 shares is 500P. Equity is (500P − $5,400). You will receive a margin call when:

$$\frac{500P - \$5,400}{500P} = 0.25 \Rightarrow \text{when } P = \$14.40 \text{ or lower}$$

10. a. The gain or loss on the short position is: $(-500 \times \Delta P)$
Invested funds = \$15,000

Therefore: rate of return = $(-500 \times \Delta P)/15,000$

The rate of return in each of the three scenarios is:

(i) rate of return = $(-500 \times \$4)/\$15,000 = -0.1333 = -13.33\%$

(ii) rate of return = $(-500 \times \$0)/\$15,000 = 0\%$

(iii) rate of return = $[-500 \times (-\$4)]/\$15,000 = +0.1333 = +13.33\%$

b. Total assets in the margin account are:

\$20,000 (from the sale of the stock) + \$15,000 (the initial margin) = \$35,000

Liabilities are 500P. A margin call will be issued when:

$$\frac{\$35,000 - 500P}{500P} = 0.25 \Rightarrow \text{when P = \$56 or higher}$$

c. With a \$1 dividend, the short position must now pay on the borrowed shares: (\$1/share × 500 shares) = \$500. Rate of return is now:

$$[(-500 \times \Delta P) - 500]/15,000$$

(i) rate of return = $[(-500 \times \$4) - \$500]/\$15,000 = -0.1667 = -16.67\%$

(ii) rate of return = $[(-500 \times \$0) - \$500]/\$15,000 = -0.0333 = -3.33\%$

(iii) rate of return = $[(-500) \times (-\$4) - \$500]/\$15,000 = +0.1000 = +10.00\%$

Total assets are \$35,000, and liabilities are (500P + 500). A margin call will be issued when:

$$\frac{35,000 - 500P - 500}{500P} = 0.25 \Rightarrow \text{when P = \$55.20 or higher}$$

11. Answers to this problem will vary.

12. The broker is instructed to attempt to sell your Marriott stock as soon as the Marriott stock trades at a bid price of \$38 or less. Here, the broker will attempt to execute, but may not be able to sell at \$38, since the bid price is now \$37.85. The price at which you sell may be more or less than \$38 because the stop-loss becomes a market order to sell at current market prices.

13. a. 55.50

  b. 55.25

  c. The trade will not be executed because the bid price is lower than the price specified in the limit sell order.

  d. The trade will not be executed because the asked price is greater than the price specified in the limit buy order.

14. a. In an exchange market, there can be price improvement in the two market orders. Brokers for each of the market orders (i.e., the buy and the sell orders) can agree to execute a trade inside the quoted spread. For example, they can trade at $55.37, thus improving the price for both customers by $0.12 or $0.13 relative to the quoted bid and asked prices. The buyer gets the stock for $0.13 less than the quoted asked price, and the seller receives $0.12 more for the stock than the quoted bid price.

  b. Whereas the limit order to buy at $55.37 would not be executed in a dealer market (since the asked price is $55.50), it could be executed in an exchange market. A broker for another customer with an order to sell at market would view the limit buy order as the best bid price; the two brokers could agree to the trade and bring it to the specialist, who would then execute the trade.

15. The SuperDot system expedites the flow of orders from exchange members to the specialists. It allows members to send computerized orders directly to the floor of the exchange, which allows the nearly simultaneous sale of each stock in a large portfolio. This capability is necessary for program trading.

16. The dealer sets the bid and asked price. Spreads should be higher on inactively traded stocks and lower on actively traded stocks.

17. a. You will not receive a margin call. You borrowed $20,000 and with another $20,000 of your own equity you bought 1,000 shares of Disney at $40 per share. At $35 per share, the market value of the stock is $35,000, your equity is $15,000, and the percentage margin is: $15,000/$35,000 = 42.9%
Your percentage margin exceeds the required maintenance margin.

  b. You will receive a margin call when:

$$\frac{1,000P - \$20,000}{1,000P} = 0.35 \Rightarrow \text{when } P = \$30.77 \text{ or lower}$$

18. a. Over short periods of time, the price of an exchange membership generally increases with increases in trading activity. This makes sense because trading commissions depend on trading volume.

    b. The price of an exchange membership has risen far less in percentage terms than trading volume. This suggests that the commissions charged to traders on "typical" trades have fallen over time.

19. The proceeds from the short sale (net of commission) were: $(\$14 \times 100) - \$50 = \$1,350$

    A dividend payment of $200 was withdrawn from the account. Covering the short sale at $9 per share cost you (including commission): $\$900 + \$50 = \$950$

    Therefore, the value of your account is equal to the net profit on the transaction:

    $\$1350 - \$200 - \$950 = \$200$

    Note that your profit ($200) equals (100 shares × profit per share of $2). Your net proceeds per share was:

$14	selling price of stock
−$ 9	repurchase price of stock
−$ 2	dividend per share
−$ 1	2 trades × $0.50 commission per share
$ 2	

20. (d) The broker will sell, at current market price, after the first transaction at $55 or less.

21. (b)

22. (d)

CHAPTER 4: MUTUAL FUNDS AND OTHER INVESTMENT COMPANIES

1. The unit investment trust should have lower operating expenses. Because the investment trust portfolio is fixed once the trust is established, it does not have to pay portfolio managers to constantly monitor and rebalance the portfolio as perceived needs or opportunities change. Because the portfolio is fixed, the unit investment trust also incurs virtually no trading costs.

2. The offering price includes a 6% front-end load, or sales commission, meaning that every dollar paid results in only $0.94 going toward purchase of shares. Therefore:

$$\text{Offering price} = \frac{\text{NAV}}{1-\text{load}} = \frac{\$10.70}{1-0.06} = \$11.38$$

3. $\text{NAV} = \text{offering price} \times (1 - \text{load}) = \$12.30 \times 0.95 = \$11.69$

4.

Stock	Value held by fund
A	$ 7,000,000
B	12,000,000
C	8,000,000
D	15,000,000
Total	$42,000,000

$$\text{Net asset value} = \frac{\$42,000,000 - \$30,000}{4,000,000} = \$10.49$$

5. Value of stocks sold and replaced = $15,000,000

$$\text{Turnover rate} = \frac{\$15,000,000}{\$42,000,000} = 0.357 = 35.7\%$$

6. a. $$\text{NAV} = \frac{\$200,000,000 - \$3,000,000}{5,000,000} = \$39.40$$

   b. $$\text{Premium (or discount)} = \frac{\text{Price} - \text{NAV}}{\text{NAV}} = \frac{\$36 - \$39.40}{\$39.40} = -0.086 = -8.6\%$$

   The fund sells at an 8.6% discount from NAV.

7. Rate of return =

$$\frac{NAV_1 - NAV_0 + \text{distributions}}{NAV_0} = \frac{\$12.10 - \$12.50 + \$1.50}{\$12.50} = 0.088 = 8.8\%$$

8. a. Start-of-year price: $P_0 = \$12.00 \times 1.02 = \$12.24$

   End-of-year price: $P_1 = \$12.10 \times 0.93 = \$11.25$

   Although NAV increased by \$0.10, the price of the fund decreased by \$0.99.

   $$\text{Rate of return} = \frac{P_1 - P_0 + \text{Distributions}}{P_0} = \frac{\$11.25 - \$12.24 + \$1.50}{\$12.24} = 0.042 = 4.2\%$$

   b. An investor holding the same portfolio as the manager would have earned a rate of return based on the increase in the NAV of the portfolio:

   Rate of return =

   $$\frac{NAV_1 - NAV_0 + \text{distributions}}{NAV_0} = \frac{\$12.10 - \$12.00 + \$1.50}{\$12.00} = 0.133 = 13.3\%$$

9. a. *Unit investment trusts*: diversification from large-scale investing, lower transaction costs associated with large-scale trading, low management fees, predictable portfolio composition, guaranteed low portfolio turnover rate.

   b. *Open-end funds*: diversification from large-scale investing, lower transaction costs associated with large-scale trading, professional management that may be able to take advantage of buy or sell opportunities as they arise, record keeping.

   c. *Individual stocks and bonds*: No management fee, realization of capital gains or losses can be coordinated with investor's personal tax situation, portfolio can be designed to investor's specific risk profile.

10. Open-end funds are obligated to redeem investor's shares at net asset value, and thus must keep cash or cash-equivalent securities on hand in order to meet potential redemptions. Closed-end funds do not need the cash reserves because there are no redemptions for closed-end funds. Investors in closed-end funds sell their shares when they wish to cash out.

11. Balanced funds keep relatively stable proportions of funds invested in each asset class. They are meant as convenient instruments to provide participation in a range of asset classes. Life-cycle funds are balanced funds whose asset mix generally depends on the age of the investor. Aggressive life-cycle funds, with larger investments in equities, are marketed to younger investors, while conservative life-cycle funds, with larger investments in fixed-income securities, are designed for older investors. Asset allocation funds, in contrast, may vary the proportions invested in each asset class by large amounts as predictions of relative performance across classes vary. Asset allocation funds therefore engage in more aggressive market timing.

12. a.   Empirical research indicates that past performance of mutual funds is not highly predictive of future performance, especially for better-performing funds. While there *may* be some tendency for the fund to be an above average performer next year, it is unlikely to once again be a top 10% performer.

     b.   On the other hand, the evidence is more suggestive of a tendency for poor performance to persist. This tendency is probably related to fund costs and turnover rates. Thus if the fund is among the poorest performers, investors would be concerned that the poor performance will persist.

13. $NAV_0 = \$200,000,000/10,000,000 = \$20$

     Dividends per share = $\$2,000,000/10,000,000 = \$0.20$

     NAV_1 is based on the 8% price gain, less the 1% 12b-1 fee:

     $NAV_1 = \$20 \times 1.08 \times (1 - 0.01) = \$21.384$

     Rate of return = $\dfrac{\$21.384 - \$20 + \$0.20}{\$20} = 0.0792 = 7.92\%$

14. The excess of purchases over sales must be due to new inflows into the fund. Therefore, $400 million of stock previously held by the fund was replaced by new holdings. So turnover is: $400/$2,200 = 0.182 = 18.2%

15. Fees paid to investment managers were: $(0.007 \times \$2.2 \text{ billion}) = \$15.4$ million Since the total expense ratio was 1.1% and the management fee was 0.7%, we conclude that 0.4% must be for other expenses. Therefore, other administrative expenses were: $(0.004 \times \$2.2 \text{ billion}) = \$8.8$ million

16. As an initial approximation, your return equals the return on the shares minus the total of the expense ratio and purchase costs: $(12\% - 1.2\% - 4\%) = 6.8\%$
But the precise return is less than this because the 4% load is paid up front, not at the end of the year.

To purchase the shares, you would have had to invest: $\$20,000/(1 - 0.04) = \$20,833$

The shares increase in value from \$20,000 to: $\$20,000 \times (1.12 - 0.012) = \$22,160$

The rate of return is: $(\$22,160 - \$20,833)/\$20,833 = 6.37\%$

17. Suppose you have \$1,000 to invest. The initial investment in Class A shares is \$940 net of the front-end load. After four years, your portfolio will be worth:

$$\$940 \times (1.10)^4 = \$1,376.25$$

Class B shares allow you to invest the full \$1,000, but your investment performance net of 12b-1 fees will be only 9.5%, and you will pay a 1% back-end load fee if you sell after four years. Your portfolio value after four years will be:

$$\$1,000 \times (1.095)^4 = \$1,437.66$$

After paying the back-end load fee, your portfolio value will be:

$$\$1,437.66 \times 0.99 = \$1,423.28$$

Class B shares are the better choice if your horizon is four years.

With a fifteen-year horizon, the Class A shares will be worth:

$$\$940 \times (1.10)^{15} = \$3,926.61$$

For the Class B shares, there is no back-end load in this case since the horizon is greater than five years. Therefore, the value of the Class B shares will be:

$$\$1,000 \times (1.095)^{15} = \$3,901.32$$

At this longer horizon, Class B shares are no longer the better choice. The effect of Class B's 0.5% 12b-1 fees accumulates over time and finally overwhelms the 6% load charged to Class A investors.

18. Suppose that finishing in the top half of all portfolio managers is purely luck, and that the probability of doing so in any year is exactly ½. Then the probability that any particular manager would finish in the top half of the sample five years in a row is $(\frac{1}{2})^5 = 1/32$. We would then expect to find that $[350 \times (1/32)] = 11$ managers finish in the top half for each of the five consecutive years. This is precisely what we found. Thus, we should not conclude that the consistent performance after five years is proof of skill. We would expect to find eleven managers exhibiting precisely this level of "consistency" even if performance is due solely to luck.

19.　a.　After two years, each dollar invested in a fund with a 4% load and a portfolio return equal to r will grow to: $0.96 \times (1 + r - 0.005)^2$

Each dollar invested in the bank CD will grow to: 1×1.06^2

If the mutual fund is to be the better investment, then the portfolio return (r) must satisfy:

$$0.96 \times (1 + r - 0.005)^2 > 1.06^2$$
$$0.96 \times (1 + r - 0.005)^2 > 1.1236$$
$$(1 + r - 0.005)^2 > 1.1704$$
$$1 + r - 0.005 > 1.0819$$
$$1 + r > 1.0869$$

Therefore: $r > 0.0869 = 8.69\%$

b.　If you invest for six years, then the portfolio return must satisfy:

$$0.96 \times (1 + r - 0.005)^6 > 1.06^6 = 1.4185$$
$$(1 + r - 0.005)^6 > 1.4776$$
$$1 + r - 0.005 > 1.0672$$
$$1 + r > 1.0722$$
$$r > 7.22\%$$

The cutoff rate of return is lower for the six-year investment because the "fixed cost" (i.e., the one-time front-end load) is spread out over a greater number of years.

c.　With a 12b-1 fee instead of a front-end load, the portfolio must earn a rate of return (r) that satisfies:

$$1 + r - 0.005 - 0.0075 > 1.06$$

In this case, r must exceed 7.25% regardless of the investment horizon.

20.　The turnover rate is 50%. This means that, on average, 50% of the portfolio is sold and replaced with other securities each year. Trading costs on the sell orders are 0.4%; and the buy orders to replace those securities entail another 0.4% in trading costs. Total trading costs will reduce portfolio returns by: $2 \times 0.4\% \times 0.50 = 0.4\%$

21. For the bond fund, the fraction of portfolio income given up to fees is:

$$\frac{0.6\%}{4.0\%} = 0.150 = 15.0\%$$

For the equity fund, the fraction of investment earnings given up to fees is:

$$\frac{0.6\%}{12.0\%} = 0.050 = 5.0\%$$

Fees are a much higher fraction of expected earnings for the bond fund, and therefore may be a more important factor in selecting the bond fund.

This may help to explain why unmanaged unit investment trusts are concentrated in the fixed income market. The advantages of unit investment trusts are low turnover and low trading costs and management fees. This is a more important concern to bond-market investors.

CHAPTER 5: LEARNING ABOUT RETURN AND RISK FROM THE HISTORICAL RECORD

1.   For the money market fund, your holding period return for the next year depends on the level of 30-day interest rates each month when the fund rolls over maturing securities. The one-year savings deposit offers a 7.5% holding period return for the year. If you forecast that the rate on money market instruments will increase significantly above the current 6% yield, then the money market fund might result in a higher HPR than the savings deposit. The 20-year Treasury bond offers a yield to maturity of 9% per year, which is 150 basis points higher than the rate on the one-year savings deposit; however, you could earn a one-year HPR much less than 7.5% on the bond if long-term interest rates increase during the year. If Treasury bond yields rise above 9%, then the price of the bond will fall, and the resulting capital loss will wipe out some or all of the 9% return you would have earned if bond yields had remained unchanged over the course of the year.

2.   a.   If businesses reduce their capital spending, then they are likely to decrease their demand for funds. This will shift the demand curve in Figure 5.1 to the left and reduce the equilibrium real rate of interest.

      b.   Increased household saving will shift the supply of funds curve to the right and cause real interest rates to fall.

      c.   Open market purchases of U.S. Treasury securities by the Federal Reserve Board is equivalent to an increase in the supply of funds (a shift of the supply curve to the right). The equilibrium real rate of interest will fall.

3.   a.   The "Inflation-Plus" CD is the safer investment because it guarantees the purchasing power of the investment. Using the approximation that the real rate equals the nominal rate minus the inflation rate, the CD provides a real rate of 3.5% regardless of the inflation rate.

      b.   The expected return depends on the expected rate of inflation over the next year. If the expected rate of inflation is less than 3.5% then the conventional CD offers a higher real return than the Inflation-Plus CD; if the expected rate of inflation is greater than 3.5%, then the opposite is true.

c.   If you expect the rate of inflation to be 3% over the next year, then the conventional CD offers you an expected real rate of return of 4%, which is 0.5% higher than the real rate on the inflation-protected CD. But unless you know that inflation will be 3% with certainty, the conventional CD is also riskier. The question of which is the better investment then depends on your attitude towards risk versus return. You might choose to diversify and invest part of your funds in each.

d.   No. We cannot assume that the entire difference between the risk-free nominal rate (on conventional CDs) of 7% and the real risk-free rate (on inflation-protected CDs) of 3.5% is the expected rate of inflation. Part of the difference is probably a risk premium associated with the uncertainty surrounding the real rate of return on the conventional CDs. This implies that the expected rate of inflation is less than 3.5% per year.

4. $E(r) = [0.35 \times 44.5\%] + [0.30 \times 14.0\%] + [0.35 \times (-16.5\%)] = 14\%$

$\sigma^2 = [0.35 \times (44.5 - 14)^2] + [0.30 \times (14 - 14)^2] + [0.35 \times (-16.5 - 14)^2] = 630$

$\sigma = 25.52\%$

The mean is unchanged, but the standard deviation has increased, as the probabilities of the high and low returns have increased.

5.   Probability distribution of price and one-year holding period return for a 30-year U.S. Treasury bond (which will have 29 years to maturity at year's end):

Economy	Probability	YTM	Price	Capital Gain	Coupon Interest	HPR
Boom	0.20	11.0%	$ 74.05	−$25.95	$8.00	−17.95%
Normal Growth	0.50	8.0%	$100.00	$ 0.00	$8.00	8.00%
Recession	0.30	7.0%	$112.28	$12.28	$8.00	20.28%

6.   From Table 5.3, the average risk premium for large-capitalization U.S. stocks for the period 1926-2005 was: (12.15% − 3.75%) = 8.40% per year
Adding 8.40% to the 6% risk-free interest rate, the expected annual HPR for the S&P 500 stock portfolio is: 6.00% + 8.40% = 14.40%

7. The average rates of return and standard deviations are quite different in the sub periods:

STOCKS

	Mean	Standard Deviation	Skewness	Kurtosis
1926 – 2005	12.15%	20.26%	-0.3605	-0.0673
1976 – 2005	13.85%	15.68%	-0.4575	-0.6489
1926 – 1941	6.39%	30.33%	-0.0022	-1.0716

BONDS

	Mean	Standard Deviation	Skewness	Kurtosis
1926 – 2005	5.68%	8.09%	0.9903	1.6314
1976 – 2005	9.57%	10.32%	0.3772	-0.0329
1926 – 1941	4.42%	4.32%	-0.5036	0.5034

The most relevant statistics to use for projecting into the future would seem to be the statistics estimated over the period 1976-2005, because this later period seems to have been a different economic regime. After 1955, the U.S. economy entered the Keynesian era, when the Federal government actively attempted to stabilize the economy and to prevent extremes in boom and bust cycles. Note that the standard deviation of stock returns has decreased substantially in the later period while the standard deviation of bond returns has increased.

8. a $r = \dfrac{1+R}{1+i} - 1 = \dfrac{R-i}{1+i} = \dfrac{0.80 - 0.70}{1.70} = 0.0588 = 5.88\%$

    b. $r \approx R - i = 80\% - 70\% = 10\%$

    Clearly, the approximation gives a real HPR that is too high.

9. From Table 5.2, the average real rate on T-bills has been: 0.72%

    a.   T-bills: 0.72% real rate + 3% inflation = 3.72%

    b.   Expected return on large stocks:

    3.72% T-bill rate + 8.40% historical risk premium = 12.12%

    c.   The risk premium on stocks remains unchanged. A premium, the difference between two rates, is a real value, unaffected by inflation.

10. Real interest rates are expected to rise. The investment activity will shift the demand for funds curve (in Figure 5.1) to the right. Therefore the equilibrium real interest rate will increase.

11. The expected dollar return on the investment in equities is $18,000 compared to the $5,000 expected return for T-bills. Therefore, the expected risk premium is $13,000.

12. $E(r) = [0.2 \times (-25\%)] + [0.3 \times 10\%] + [0.5 \times 24\%] = 10\%$

13. $E(r_X) = [0.2 \times (-20\%)] + [0.5 \times 18\%] + [0.3 \times 50\%] = 20\%$
    $E(r_Y) = [0.2 \times (-15\%)] + [0.5 \times 20\%] + [0.3 \times 10\%] = 10\%$

14. $\sigma_X^2 = [0.2 \times (-20 - 20)^2] + [0.5 \times (18 - 20)^2] + [0.3 \times (50 - 20)^2] = 592$
    $\sigma_X = 24.33\%$
    $\sigma_Y^2 = [0.2 \times (-15 - 10)^2] + [0.5 \times (20 - 10)^2] + [0.3 \times (10 - 10)^2] = 175$
    $\sigma_X = 13.23\%$

15. $E(r) = (0.9 \times 20\%) + (0.1 \times 10\%) = 19\%$

16. The probability that the economy will be neutral is 0.50, or 50%. *Given* a neutral economy, the stock will experience poor performance 30% of the time. The probability of both poor stock performance and a neutral economy is therefore:
    $0.30 \times 0.50 = 0.15 = 15\%$

17. $E(r) = (0.1 \times 15\%) + (0.6 \times 13\%) + (0.3 \times 7\%) = 11.4\%$

18. a. Probability Distribution of the HPR on the Stock Market and Put:

State of the Economy	Probability	STOCK		PUT	
		Ending Price + Dividend	HPR	Ending Value	HPR
Boom	0.30	$134	34%	$ 0.00	−100%
Normal Growth	0.50	$114	14%	$ 0.00	−100%
Recession	0.20	$ 84	−16%	$ 29.50	146%

Remember that the cost of the index fund is $100 per share, and the cost of the put option is $12.

b. The cost of one share of the index fund plus a put option is $112. The probability distribution of the HPR on the portfolio is:

State of the Economy	Probability	Ending Price + Put + $4 Dividend	HPR	
Boom	0.30	$134.00	19.6%	= (134 − 112)/112
Normal Growth	0.50	$114.00	1.8%	= (114 − 112)/112
Recession	0.20	$113.50	1.3%	= (113.50 − 112)/112

c. Buying the put option guarantees the investor a minimum HPR of 1.3% regardless of what happens to the stock's price. Thus, it offers insurance against a price decline.

19. The probability distribution of the dollar return on CD plus call option is:

State of the Economy	Probability	Ending Value of CD	Ending Value of Call	Combined Value
Boom	0.30	$114.00	$19.50	$133.50
Normal Growth	0.50	$114.00	$ 0.00	$114.00
Recession	0.20	$114.00	$ 0.00	$114.00

CHAPTER 6: RISK AVERSION AND CAPITAL ALLOCATION TO RISKY ASSETS

1. a. The expected cash flow is: $(0.5 \times \$70,000) + (0.5 \times 200,000) = \$135,000$

    With a risk premium of 8% over the risk-free rate of 6%, the required rate of return is 14%. Therefore, the present value of the portfolio is:

    $$\$135,000/1.14 = \$118,421$$

   b. If the portfolio is purchased for \$118,421, and provides an expected cash inflow of \$135,000, then the expected rate of return [E(r)] is derived as follows:

    $$\$118,421 \times [1 + E(r)] = \$135,000$$

    Therefore, $E(r) = 14\%$. The portfolio price is set to equate the expected rate or return with the required rate of return.

   c. If the risk premium over T-bills is now 12%, then the required return is:

    $$6\% + 12\% = 18\%$$

    The present value of the portfolio is now:

    $$\$135,000/1.18 = \$114,407$$

   d. For a given expected cash flow, portfolios that command greater risk premia must sell at lower prices. The extra discount from expected value is a penalty for risk.

2. When we specify utility by $U = E(r) - 0.5A\sigma^2$, the utility level for T-bills is: 0.07

   The utility level for the risky portfolio is: $U = 0.12 - 0.5A(0.18)^2 = 0.12 - 0.0162A$

   In order for the risky portfolio to be preferred to bills, the following inequality must hold:

   $$0.12 - 0.0162A > 0.07 \Rightarrow A < 0.05/0.0162 = 3.09$$

   A must be less than 3.09 for the risky portfolio to be preferred to bills.

3. Points on the curve are derived by solving for $E(r)$ in the following equation:

$$U = 0.05 = E(r) - 0.5A\sigma^2 = E(r) - 1.5\sigma^2$$

The values of $E(r)$, given the values of σ^2, are therefore:

σ	σ^2	$E(r)$
0.00	0.0000	0.05000
0.05	0.0025	0.05375
0.10	0.0100	0.06500
0.15	0.0225	0.08375
0.20	0.0400	0.11000
0.25	0.0625	0.14375

The bold line in the following graph (labeled Q3, for Question 3) depicts the indifference curve.

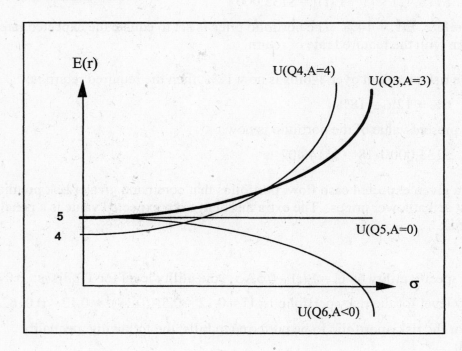

4. Repeating the analysis in Problem 3, utility is now:

$$U = E(r) - 0.5A\sigma^2 = E(r) - 2.0\sigma^2 = 0.04$$

The equal-utility combinations of expected return and standard deviation are presented in the table below. The indifference curve is the upward sloping line in the graph above, labeled Q4 (for Question 4).

σ	σ^2	$E(r)$
0.00	0.0000	0.0400
0.05	0.0025	0.0450
0.10	0.0100	0.0600
0.15	0.0225	0.0850
0.20	0.0400	0.1200
0.25	0.0625	0.1650

The indifference curve in Problem 4 differs from that in Problem 3 in both slope and intercept. When A increases from 3 to 4, the increased risk aversion results in a greater slope for the indifference curve since more expected return is needed in order to compensate for additional σ. The lower level of utility assumed for Problem 4 (0.04 rather than 0.05) shifts the vertical intercept down by 1%.

5. The coefficient of risk aversion for a risk neutral investor is zero. Therefore, the corresponding utility is equal to the portfolio's expected return. The corresponding indifference curve in the expected return-standard deviation plane is a horizontal line, labeled Q5 in the graph above (see Problem 3).

6. A risk lover, rather than penalizing portfolio utility to account for risk, derives greater utility as variance increases. This amounts to a negative coefficient of risk aversion. The corresponding indifference curve is downward sloping in the graph above (see Problem 3), and is labeled Q6.

7. Utility for each investment $= E(r) - 0.5 \times 4 \times \sigma^2$

    We choose the investment with the highest utility value.

Investment	Expected return $E(r)$	Standard deviation σ	Utility U
1	0.12	0.30	-0.0600
2	0.15	0.50	-0.3500
3	0.21	0.16	0.1588
4	0.24	0.21	0.1518

8. When investors are risk neutral, then $A = 0$; the investment with the highest utility is Investment 4 because it has the highest expected return.

9. b

10. The portfolio expected return and variance are computed as follows:

(1) W_{Bills}	(2) r_{Bills}	(3) W_{Index}	(4) r_{Index}	$r_{Portfolio}$ (1)×(2)+(3)×(4)	$\sigma_{Portfolio}$ (3) × 20%	$\sigma^2{}_{Portfolio}$
0.0	5%	1.0	13.5%	13.5% = 0.135	20% = 0.20	0.0400
0.2	5%	0.8	13.5%	11.8% = 0.118	16% = 0.16	0.0256
0.4	5%	0.6	13.5%	10.1% = 0.101	12% = 0.12	0.0144
0.6	5%	0.4	13.5%	8.4% = 0.084	8% = 0.08	0.0064
0.8	5%	0.2	13.5%	6.7% = 0.067	4% = 0.04	0.0016
1.0	5%	0.0	13.5%	5.0% = 0.050	0% = 0.00	0.0000

11. Computing utility from $U = E(r) - 0.5 \times A\sigma^2 = E(r) - 1.5\sigma^2$, we arrive at the values in the column labeled U(A = 3) in the following table:

W_{Bills}	W_{Index}	$r_{Portfolio}$	$\sigma_{Portfolio}$	$\sigma^2{}_{Portfolio}$	U(A = 3)	U(A = 5)
0.0	1.0	0.135	0.20	0.0400	0.0750	0.0350
0.2	0.8	0.118	0.16	0.0256	0.0796	0.0540
0.4	0.6	0.101	0.12	0.0144	0.0794	0.0650
0.6	0.4	0.084	0.08	0.0064	0.0744	0.0680
0.8	0.2	0.067	0.04	0.0016	0.0646	0.0630
1.0	0.0	0.050	0.00	0.0000	0.0500	0.0500

The column labeled U(A = 3) implies that investors with A = 3 prefer a portfolio that is invested 80% in the market index and 20% in T-bills to any of the other portfolios in the table.

12. The column labeled U(A = 5) in the table above is computed from:

$$U = E(r) - 0.5A\sigma^2 = E(r) - 2.5\sigma^2$$

The more risk averse investors prefer the portfolio that is invested 40% in the market index, rather than the 80% market weight preferred by investors with A = 3.

13. Expected return = $(0.7 \times 18\%) + (0.3 \times 8\%) = 15\%$

Standard deviation = $0.7 \times 28\% = 19.6\%$

14. Investment proportions: 30.0% in T-bills
    $0.7 \times 25\% =$ 17.5% in Stock A
    $0.7 \times 32\% =$ 22.4% in Stock B
    $0.7 \times 43\% =$ 30.1% in Stock C

15. Your reward-to-variability ratio: $S = \dfrac{18-8}{28} = 0.3571$

Client's reward-to-variability ratio: $S = \dfrac{15-8}{19.6} = 0.3571$

16.

17. a. $E(r_C) = r_f + y[E(r_P) - r_f] = 8 + y(18 - 8)$

If the expected return for the portfolio is 16%, then:

$16 = 8 + 10\,y \Rightarrow y = \dfrac{16-8}{10} = 0.8$

Therefore, in order to have a portfolio with expected rate of return equal to 16%, the client must invest 80% of total funds in the risky portfolio and 20% in T-bills.

b.

Client's investment proportions:		20.0% in T-bills
	$0.8 \times 25\% =$	20.0% in Stock A
	$0.8 \times 32\% =$	25.6% in Stock B
	$0.8 \times 43\% =$	34.4% in Stock C

c. $\sigma_C = 0.8 \times \sigma_P = 0.8 \times 28\% = 22.4\%$

18. a. $\sigma_C = y \times 28\%$

       If your client prefers a standard deviation of at most 18%, then:

       $y = 18/28 = 0.6429 = 64.29\%$ invested in the risky portfolio

   b. $E(r_C) = 8 + 10y = 8 + (0.6429 \times 10) = 8 + 6.429 = 14.429\%$

19. a. $y^* = \dfrac{E(r_P) - r_f}{A\sigma_P^2} = \dfrac{0.18 - 0.08}{3.5 \times 0.28^2} = \dfrac{0.10}{0.2744} = 0.3644$

       Therefore, the client's optimal proportions are: 36.44% invested in the risky portfolio and 63.56% invested in T-bills.

   b. $E(r_C) = 8 + 10y^* = 8 + (0.3644 \times 10) = 11.644\%$

       $\sigma_C = 0.3644 \times 28 = 10.203\%$

20. a.   Slope of the CML $= \dfrac{13 - 8}{25} = 0.20$

       The diagram follows.

   b.   My fund allows an investor to achieve a higher mean for any given standard deviation than would a passive strategy, i.e., a higher expected return for any given level of risk.

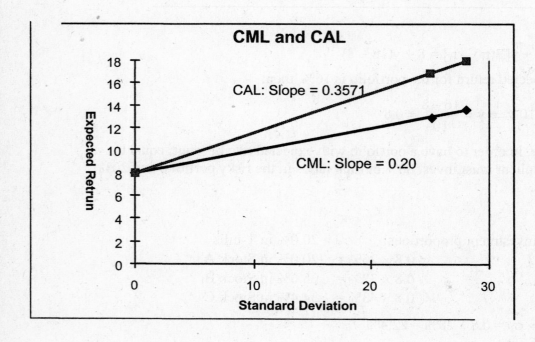

21.   a.   With 70% of his money invested in my fund's portfolio, the client's expected return is 15% per year and standard deviation is 19.6% per year. If he shifts that money to the passive portfolio (which has an expected return of 13% and standard deviation of 25%), his overall expected return becomes:

$$E(r_C) = r_f + 0.7[E(r_M) - r_f] = 8 + [0.7 \times (13 - 8)] = 11.5\%$$

The standard deviation of the complete portfolio using the passive portfolio would be:

$$\sigma_C = 0.7 \times \sigma_M = 0.7 \times 25\% = 17.5\%$$

Therefore, the shift entails a decrease in mean from 14% to 11.5% and a decrease in standard deviation from 19.6% to 17.5%. Since both mean return *and* standard deviation decrease, it is not yet clear whether the move is beneficial. The disadvantage of the shift is that, if the client is willing to accept a mean return on his total portfolio of 11.5%, he can achieve it with a lower standard deviation using my fund rather than the passive portfolio.

To achieve a target mean of 11.5%, we first write the mean of the complete portfolio as a function of the proportion invested in my fund (*y*):

$$E(r_C) = 8 + y(18 - 8) = 8 + 10y$$

Our target is: $E(r_C) = 11.5\%$. Therefore, the proportion that must be invested in my fund is determined as follows:

$$11.5 = 8 + 10y \Rightarrow y = \frac{11.5 - 8}{10} = 0.35$$

The standard deviation of this portfolio would be:

$$\sigma_C = y \times 28\% = 0.35 \times 28\% = 9.8\%$$

Thus, by using my portfolio, the same 11.5% expected return can be achieved with a standard deviation of only 9.8% as opposed to the standard deviation of 17.5% using the passive portfolio.

   b.   The fee would reduce the reward-to-variability ratio, i.e., the slope of the CAL. The client will be indifferent between my fund and the passive portfolio if the slope of the after-fee CAL and the CML are equal. Let f denote the fee:

$$\text{Slope of CAL with fee } = \frac{18 - 8 - f}{28} = \frac{10 - f}{28}$$

$$\text{Slope of CML (which requires no fee)} = \frac{13 - 8}{25} = 0.20$$

Setting these slopes equal we have:

$$\frac{10 - f}{28} = 0.20 \Rightarrow 10 - f = 28 \times 0.20 = 5.6 \Rightarrow f = 10 - 5.6 = 4.4\% \text{ per year}$$

22.   a.   The formula for the optimal proportion to invest in the passive portfolio is:

$$y* = \frac{E(r_M) - r_f}{A\sigma_M^2}$$

Substitute the following: $E(r_M) = 13\%$; $r_f = 8\%$; $\sigma_M = 25\%$; $A = 3.5$:

$$y* = \frac{0.13 - 0.08}{3.5 \times 0.25^2} = 0.2286$$

     b.   The answer here is the same as the answer to Problem 21(b). The fee that you can charge a client is the same regardless of the asset allocation mix of the client's portfolio. You can charge a fee that will equate the reward-to-variability *ratio* of your portfolio to that of your competition.

23.   a.   If the period 1926 - 2005 is assumed to be representative of future expected performance, then we use the following data to compute the fraction allocated to equity: $A = 4$, $E(r_M) - r_f = 8.39\%$, $\sigma_M = 20.54\%$ (we use the standard deviation of the risk premium from Table 6.8). Then y^* is given by:

$$y* = \frac{E(r_M) - r_f}{A\sigma_M^2} = \frac{0.0839}{4 \times 0.2054^2} = 0.4972$$

That is, 49.72% of the portfolio should be allocated to equity and 50.28% should be allocated to T-bills.

     b.   If the period 1986 - 2005 is assumed to be representative of future expected performance, then we use the following data to compute the fraction allocated to equity: $A = 4$, $E(r_M) - r_f = 8.60\%$, $\sigma_M = 16.24\%$ and $y*$ is given by:

$$y* = \frac{E(r_M) - r_f}{A\sigma_M^2} = \frac{0.0860}{4 \times 0.1624^2} = 0.8152$$

Therefore, 81.52% of the complete portfolio should be allocated to equity and 18.48% should be allocated to T-bills.

     c.   In part (b), the market risk premium is expected to be higher than in part (a) and market risk is lower. Therefore, the reward-to-variability *ratio* is expected to be higher in part (b), which explains the greater proportion invested in equity.

24.   Assuming no change in risk tolerance, that is, an unchanged risk aversion coefficient (A), then higher perceived volatility increases the denominator of the equation for the optimal investment in the risky portfolio (Equation 6.12). The proportion invested in the risky portfolio will therefore decrease.

25. a. $E(r_C) = 8\% = 5\% + y(11\% - 5\%) \Rightarrow y = \dfrac{8-5}{11-5} = 0.5$

b. $\sigma_C = y\sigma_P = 0.50 \times 15\% = 7.5\%$

c. The first client is more risk averse, allowing a smaller standard deviation.

26. Data: $r_f = 5\%$, $E(r_M) = 13\%$, $\sigma_M = 25\%$, and $r_f^B = 9\%$

The CML and indifference curves are as follows:

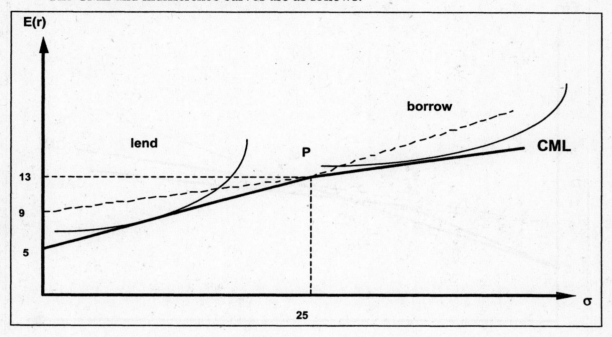

27. For y to be less than 1.0 (so that the investor is a lender), risk aversion (A) must be large enough such that:

$$y = \frac{E(r_M) - r_f}{A\sigma_M^2} < 1 \Rightarrow A > \frac{0.13 - 0.05}{0.25^2} = 1.28$$

For y to be greater than 1.0 (so that the investor is a borrower), risk aversion must be small enough such that:

$$y = \frac{E(r_M) - r_f}{A\sigma_M^2} > 1 \Rightarrow A < \frac{0.13 - 0.09}{0.25^2} = 0.64$$

For values of risk aversion within this range, the client will neither borrow nor lend, but instead will hold a complete portfolio comprised only of the optimal risky portfolio:

$$y = 1 \text{ for } 0.64 \le A \le 1.28$$

28. a. The graph for Problem 26 has to be redrawn here, with:
$E(r_P) = 11\%$ and $\sigma_P = 15\%$

b. For a lending position: $A > \dfrac{0.11 - 0.05}{0.15^2} = 2.67$

For a borrowing position: $A < \dfrac{0.11 - 0.09}{0.15^2} = 0.89$

Therefore, $y = 1$ for $0.89 \le A \le 2.67$

29. The maximum feasible fee, denoted f, depends on the reward-to-variability ratio. For $y < 1$, the lending rate, 5%, is viewed as the relevant risk-free rate, and we solve for f as follows:

$$\frac{11 - 5 - f}{15} = \frac{13 - 5}{25} \Rightarrow f = 6 - \frac{15 \times 8}{25} = 1.2\%$$

For $y > 1$, the borrowing rate, 9%, is the relevant risk-free rate. Then we notice that, even without a fee, the active fund is inferior to the passive fund because:

$$\frac{11 - 9}{15} = 0.13 < \frac{13 - 9}{25} = 0.16$$

More risk tolerant investors (who are more inclined to borrow) will not be clients of the fund even without a fee. (If you solved for the fee that would make investors who borrow indifferent between the active and passive portfolio, as we did above for lending investors, you would find that f is negative: that is, you would need to *pay* investors to choose your active fund.) These investors desire higher risk-higher return complete portfolios and thus are in the borrowing range of the relevant CAL. In this range, the reward-to-variability ratio of the index (the passive fund) is better than that of the managed fund.

30. Indifference curve 2

31. Point E

32. $(0.6 \times \$50,000) + [0.4 \times (-\$30,000)] - \$5,000 = \$13,000$

33. b

34. Expected return for equity fund = T-bill rate + risk premium = 6% + 10% = 16%

Expected return of client's overall portfolio = $(0.6 \times 16\%) + (0.4 \times 6\%) = 12\%$

Standard deviation of client's overall portfolio = $0.6 \times 14\% = 8.4\%$

35. Reward to variability ratio = $\dfrac{10}{14} = 0.71$

CHAPTER 6: APPENDIX

1. By year end, the $50,000 investment will grow to: $50,000 \times 1.06 = $53,000
   Without insurance, the probability distribution of end-of-year wealth is:

	Probability	Wealth
No fire	0.999	$253,000
Fire	0.001	$ 53,000

   For this distribution, expected utility is computed as follows:

   $$E[U(W)] = [0.999 \times \ln(253,000)] + [0.001 \times \ln(53,000)] = 12.439582$$

   The certainty equivalent is:

   $$W_{CE} = e^{12.439582} = \$252,604.85$$

   With fire insurance, at a cost of $P, the investment in the risk-free asset is:

   $$\$(50,000 - P)$$

   Year-end wealth will be certain (since you are fully insured) and equal to:

   $$[\$(50,000 - P) \times 1.06] + \$200,000$$

   Solve for P in the following equation:

   $$[\$(50,000 - P) \times 1.06] + \$200,000 = \$252,604.85 \Rightarrow P = \$372.78$$

   This is the most you are willing to pay for insurance. Note that the expected loss is "only" $200, so you are willing to pay a substantial risk premium over the expected value of losses. The primary reason is that the value of the house is a large proportion of your wealth.

2. a. With insurance coverage for one-half the value of the house, the premium is $100, and the investment in the safe asset is $49,900. By year end, the investment of $49,900 will grow to: $49,900 \times 1.06 = $52,894
   If there is a fire, your insurance proceeds will be $100,000, and the probability distribution of end-of-year wealth is:

	Probability	Wealth
No fire	0.999	$252,894
Fire	0.001	$152,894

   For this distribution, expected utility is computed as follows:

   $$E[U(W)] = [0.999 \times \ln(252,894)] + [0.001 \times \ln(152,894)] = 12.4402225$$

   The certainty equivalent is:

   $$W_{CE} = e^{12.4402225} = \$252,766.77$$

b. With insurance coverage for the full value of the house, costing $200, end-of-year wealth is certain, and equal to:

$$[(\$50,000 - \$200) \times 1.06] + \$200,000 = \$252,788$$

Since wealth is certain, this is also the certainty equivalent wealth of the fully insured position.

c. With insurance coverage for 1½ times the value of the house, the premium is $300, and the insurance pays off $300,000 in the event of a fire. The investment in the safe asset is $49,700. By year end, the investment of $49,700 will grow to: $49,700 × 1.06 = $52,682

The probability distribution of end-of-year wealth is:

	Probability	Wealth
No fire	0.999	$252,682
Fire	0.001	$352,682

For this distribution, expected utility is computed as follows:

$$E[U(W)] = [0.999 \times \ln(252,682)] + [0.001 \times \ln(352,682)] = 12.4402205$$

The certainty equivalent is:

$$W_{CE} = e^{12.440222} = \$252,766.27$$

Therefore, full insurance dominates both over- and under-insurance. Over-insuring creates a gamble (you actually gain when the house burns down). Risk is minimized when you insure exactly the value of the house.

CHAPTER 7: OPTIMAL RISKY PORTFOLIOS

1.   The parameters of the opportunity set are:

$$E(r_S) = 20\%, \ E(r_B) = 12\%, \ \sigma_S = 30\%, \ \sigma_B = 15\%, \ \rho = 0.10$$

From the standard deviations and the correlation coefficient we generate the covariance matrix [note that $Cov(r_S, r_B) = \rho\sigma_S\sigma_B$]:

	Bonds	Stocks
Bonds	225	45
Stocks	45	900

The minimum-variance portfolio is computed as follows:

$$w_{Min}(S) = \frac{\sigma_B^2 - Cov(r_S, r_B)}{\sigma_S^2 + \sigma_B^2 - 2Cov(r_S, r_B)} = \frac{225 - 45}{900 + 225 - (2 \times 45)} = 0.1739$$

$$w_{Min}(B) = 1 - 0.1739 = 0.8261$$

The minimum variance portfolio mean and standard deviation are:

$$E(r_{Min}) = (0.1739 \times 20) + (0.8261 \times 12) = 13.39\%$$

$$\sigma_{Min} = [w_S^2 \sigma_S^2 + w_B^2 \sigma_B^2 + 2w_S w_B Cov(r_S, r_B)]^{1/2}$$

$$= [(0.1739^2 \times 900) + (0.8261^2 \times 225) + (2 \times 0.1739 \times 0.8261 \times 45)]^{1/2}$$

$$= 13.92\%$$

2.

Proportion in stock fund	Proportion in bond fund	Expected return	Standard Deviation	
0.00%	100.00%	12.00%	15.00%	
17.39%	82.61%	13.39%	13.92%	minimum variance
20.00%	80.00%	13.60%	13.94%	
40.00%	60.00%	15.20%	15.70%	
45.16%	54.84%	15.61%	16.54%	tangency portfolio
60.00%	40.00%	16.80%	19.53%	
80.00%	20.00%	18.40%	24.48%	
100.00%	0.00%	20.00%	30.00%	

Graph shown on next page.

3.

INVESTMENT OPPORTUNITY SET

CML

Tangency Portfolio

Efficient frontier of risky assets

Minimum Variance Portfolio

The graph indicates that the optimal portfolio is the tangency portfolio with expected return approximately 15.6% and standard deviation approximately 16.5%.

4. The proportion of the optimal risky portfolio invested in the stock fund is given by:

$$w_S = \frac{[E(r_S) - r_f]\sigma_B^2 - [E(r_B) - r_f]Cov(r_S, r_B)}{[E(r_S) - r_f]\sigma_B^2 + [E(r_B) - r_f]\sigma_S^2 - [E(r_S) - r_f + E(r_B) - r_f]Cov(r_S, r_B)}$$

$$= \frac{[(20-8) \times 225] - [(12-8) \times 45]}{[(20-8) \times 225] + [(12-8) \times 900] - [(20-8+12-8) \times 45]} = 0.4516$$

$w_B = 1 - 0.4516 = 0.5484$

The mean and standard deviation of the optimal risky portfolio are:

$E(r_P) = (0.4516 \times 20) + (0.5484 \times 12) = 15.61\%$

$\sigma_P = [(0.4516^2 \times 900) + (0.5484^2 \times 225) + (2 \times 0.4516 \times 0.5484 \times 45)]^{1/2}$

$= 16.54\%$

5. The reward-to-variability ratio of the optimal CAL is:

$$\frac{E(r_p) - r_f}{\sigma_p} = \frac{15.61 - 8}{16.54} = 0.4601$$

6. a. If you require that your portfolio yield an expected return of 14%, then you can find the corresponding standard deviation from the optimal CAL. The equation for this CAL is:

$$E(r_C) = r_f + \frac{E(r_p) - r_f}{\sigma_P} \sigma_C = 8 + 0.4601\sigma_C$$

Setting $E(r_C)$ equal to 14%, we find that the standard deviation of the optimal portfolio is 13.04%.

b. To find the proportion invested in the T-bill fund, remember that the mean of the complete portfolio (i.e., 14%) is an average of the T-bill rate and the optimal combination of stocks and bonds (P). Let y be the proportion invested in the portfolio P. The mean of any portfolio along the optimal CAL is:

$$E(r_C) = (1 - y)r_f + yE(r_P) = r_f + y[E(r_P) - r_f] = 8 + y(15.61 - 8)$$

Setting $E(r_C) = 14\%$ we find: y = 0.7884 and (1 − y) = 0.2116 (the proportion invested in the T-bill fund).

To find the proportions invested in each of the funds, multiply 0.7884 times the respective proportions of stocks and bonds in the optimal risky portfolio:

Proportion of stocks in complete portfolio = 0.7884 × 0.4516 = 0.3560

Proportion of bonds in complete portfolio = 0.7884 × 0.5484 = 0.4324

7. Using only the stock and bond funds to achieve a portfolio expected return of 14%, we must find the appropriate proportion in the stock fund (w_S) and the appropriate proportion in the bond fund ($w_B = 1 - w_S$) as follows:

$$14 = 20w_S + 12(1 - w_S) = 12 + 8w_S \Rightarrow w_S = 0.25$$

So the proportions are 25% invested in the stock fund and 75% in the bond fund. The standard deviation of this portfolio will be:

$$\sigma_P = [(0.25^2 \times 900) + (0.75^2 \times 225) + (2 \times 0.25 \times 0.75 \times 45)]^{1/2} = 14.13\%$$

This is considerably greater than the standard deviation of 13.04% achieved using T-bills and the optimal portfolio.

8.   a.

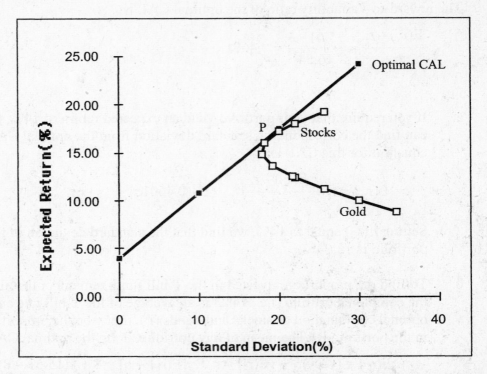

Even though it seems that gold is dominated by stocks, gold might still be an attractive asset to hold as a *part* of a portfolio. If the correlation between gold and stocks is sufficiently low, gold will be held as a component in a portfolio, specifically, the optimal tangency portfolio.

b.   If the correlation between gold and stocks equals +1, then no one would hold gold. The optimal CAL would be comprised of bills and stocks only. Since the set of risk/return combinations of stocks and gold would plot as a straight line with a negative slope (see the following graph), these combinations would be dominated by the stock portfolio. Of course, this situation could not persist. If no one desired gold, its price would fall and its expected rate of return would increase until it became sufficiently attractive to include in a portfolio.

9. Since Stock A and Stock B are perfectly negatively correlated, a risk-free portfolio can be created and the rate of return for this portfolio, in equilibrium, will be the risk-free rate. To find the proportions of this portfolio [with the proportion w_A invested in Stock A and $w_B = (1 - w_A)$ invested in Stock B], set the standard deviation equal to zero. With perfect negative correlation, the portfolio standard deviation is:

$$\sigma_P = \text{Absolute value } [w_A\sigma_A - w_B\sigma_B]$$

$$0 = 5w_A - [10 \times (1 - w_A)] \Rightarrow w_A = 0.6667$$

The expected rate of return for this risk-free portfolio is:

$$E(r) = (0.6667 \times 10) + (0.3333 \times 15) = 11.667\%$$

Therefore, the risk-free rate is 11.667%.

10. False. If the borrowing and lending rates are not identical, then, depending on the tastes of the individuals (that is, the shape of their indifference curves), borrowers and lenders could have different optimal risky portfolios.

11. False. The portfolio standard deviation equals the weighted average of the component-asset standard deviations *only* in the special case that all assets are perfectly positively correlated. Otherwise, as the formula for portfolio standard deviation shows, the portfolio standard deviation is *less* than the weighted average of the component-asset standard deviations. The portfolio *variance* is a weighted *sum* of the elements in the covariance matrix, with the products of the portfolio proportions as weights.

12. The probability distribution is:

Probability	Rate of Return
0.7	100%
0.3	−50%

Mean = $[0.7 \times 100] + [0.3 \times (−50)] = 55\%$

Variance = $[0.7 \times (100 − 55)^2] + [0.3 \times (−50 − 55)^2] = 4725$

Standard deviation = $4725^{1/2} = 68.74\%$

13. $\sigma_P = 30 = y\sigma = 40y \Rightarrow y = 0.75$

$E(r_P) = 12 + 0.75(30 − 12) = 25.5\%$

14. a. Restricting the portfolio to 20 stocks, rather than 40 to 50 stocks, will increase the risk of the portfolio, but it is possible that the increase in risk will be minimal. Suppose that, for instance, the 50 stocks in a universe have the same standard deviation (σ) and the correlations between each pair are identical, with correlation coefficient ρ. Then, the covariance between each pair of stocks would be $\rho\sigma^2$, and the variance of an equally weighted portfolio would be:

$$\sigma_P^2 = \frac{1}{n}\sigma^2 + \frac{n-1}{n}\rho\sigma^2$$

The effect of the reduction in n on the second term on the right-hand side would be relatively small (since 49/50 is close to 19/20 and $\rho\sigma^2$ is smaller than σ^2), but the denominator of the first term would be 20 instead of 50. For example, if $\sigma = 45\%$ and $\rho = 0.2$, then the standard deviation with 50 stocks would be 20.91%, and would rise to 22.05% when only 20 stocks are held. Such an increase might be acceptable if the expected return is increased sufficiently.

b.   Hennessy could contain the increase in risk by making sure that he maintains reasonable diversification among the 20 stocks that remain in his portfolio. This entails maintaining a low correlation among the remaining stocks. For example, in part (a), with $\rho = 0.2$, the increase in portfolio risk was minimal. As a practical matter, this means that Hennessy would have to spread his portfolio among many industries; concentrating on just a few industries would result in higher correlations among the included stocks.

15.   Risk reduction benefits from diversification are not a linear function of the number of issues in the portfolio. Rather, the incremental benefits from additional diversification are most important when you are least diversified. Restricting Hennesey to 10 instead of 20 issues would increase the risk of his portfolio by a greater amount than would a reduction in the size of the portfolio from 30 to 20 stocks. In our example, restricting the number of stocks to 10 will increase the standard deviation to 23.81%. The 1.76% increase in standard deviation resulting from giving up 10 of 20 stocks is greater than the 1.14% increase that results from giving up 30 of 50 stocks.

16.   The point is well taken because the committee should be concerned with the volatility of the entire portfolio. Since Hennessy's portfolio is only one of six well-diversified portfolios and is smaller than the average, the concentration in fewer issues might have a minimal effect on the diversification of the total fund. Hence, unleashing Hennessy to do stock picking may be advantageous.

17.   The correct choice is c. Intuitively, we note that since all stocks have the same expected rate of return and standard deviation, we choose the stock that will result in lowest risk. This is the stock that has the lowest correlation with Stock A.

More formally, we note that when all stocks have the same expected rate of return, the optimal portfolio for any risk-averse investor is the global minimum variance portfolio (G). When the portfolio is restricted to Stock A and one additional stock, the objective is to find G for any pair that includes Stock A, and then select the combination with the lowest variance. With two stocks, I and J, the formula for the weights in G is:

$$w_{Min}(I) = \frac{\sigma_J^2 - Cov(r_I, r_J)}{\sigma_I^2 + \sigma_J^2 - 2Cov(r_I, r_J)}$$

$$w_{Min}(J) = 1 - w_{Min}(I)$$

Since all standard deviations are equal to 20%:

$$\text{Cov}(r_I, r_J) = \rho\sigma_I\sigma_J = 400\rho \text{ and } w_{Min}(I) = w_{Min}(J) = 0.5$$

This intuitive result is an implication of a property of any efficient frontier, namely, that the covariances of the global minimum variance portfolio with all other assets on the frontier are identical and equal to its own variance. (Otherwise, additional diversification would further reduce the variance.) In this case, the standard deviation of G(I, J) reduces to:

$$\sigma_{Min}(G) = [200(1 + \rho_{I\,J})]^{1/2}$$

This leads to the intuitive result that the desired addition would be the stock with the lowest correlation with Stock A, which is Stock D. The optimal portfolio is equally invested in Stock A and Stock D, and the standard deviation is 17.03%.

18. No, the answer to Problem 17 would not change, at least as long as investors are not risk lovers. Risk neutral investors would not care which portfolio they held since all portfolios have an expected return of 8%.

19. No, the answers to Problems 17 and 18 would not change. The efficient frontier of risky assets is horizontal at 8%, so the optimal CAL runs from the risk-free rate through G. The best Portfolio G is, again, the one with the lowest variance. The optimal complete portfolio depends on risk aversion.

20. d. Portfolio Y cannot be efficient because it is dominated by another portfolio. For example, Portfolio X has both higher expected return and lower standard deviation.

21. c.

22. d.

23. b.

24. a.

25. c.

26. Since we do not have any information about expected returns, we focus exclusively on reducing variability. Stocks A and C have equal standard deviations, but the correlation of Stock B with Stock C (0.10) is less than that of Stock A with Stock B (0.90). Therefore, a portfolio comprised of Stocks B and C will have lower total risk than a portfolio comprised of Stocks A and B.

27. Rearranging the table (converting rows to columns), and computing serial correlation results in the following table:

Nominal Rates

	Small company stocks	Large company stocks	Long-term government bonds	Intermed-term government bonds	Treasury bills	Inflation
1920s	-3.72	18.36	3.98	3.77	3.56	-1.00
1930s	7.28	-1.25	4.60	3.91	0.30	-2.04
1940s	20.63	9.11	3.59	1.70	0.37	5.36
1950s	19.01	19.41	0.25	1.11	1.87	2.22
1960s	13.72	7.84	1.14	3.41	3.89	2.52
1970s	8.75	5.90	6.63	6.11	6.29	7.36
1980s	12.46	17.60	11.50	12.01	9.00	5.10
1990s	13.84	18.20	8.60	7.74	5.02	2.93
Serial Correlation	0.46	-0.22	0.60	0.59	0.63	0.23

For example: to compute serial correlation in decade nominal returns for large-company stocks, we set up the following two columns in an Excel spreadsheet. Then, use the Excel function "CORREL" to calculate the correlation for the data.

	Decade	Previous
1930s	-1.25%	18.36%
1940s	9.11%	-1.25%
1950s	19.41%	9.11%
1960s	7.84%	19.41%
1970s	5.90%	7.84%
1980s	17.60%	5.90%
1990s	18.20%	17.60%

Note that each correlation is based on only seven observations, so we cannot arrive at any statistically significant conclusions. Looking at the results, however, it appears that, with the exception of large-company stocks, there is persistent serial correlation. (This conclusion changes when we turn to real rates in the next problem.)

28. The table for real rates (using the approximation of subtracting a decade's average inflation from the decade's average nominal return) is:

Real Rates

	Small company stocks	Large company stocks	Long-term government bonds	Intermed-term government bonds	Treasury bills
1920s	-2.72	19.36	4.98	4.77	4.56
1930s	9.32	0.79	6.64	5.95	2.34
1940s	15.27	3.75	-1.77	-3.66	-4.99
1950s	16.79	17.19	-1.97	-1.11	-0.35
1960s	11.20	5.32	-1.38	0.89	1.37
1970s	1.39	-1.46	-0.73	-1.25	-1.07
1980s	7.36	12.50	6.40	6.91	3.90
1990s	10.91	15.27	5.67	4.81	2.09
Serial Correlation	0.29	-0.27	0.38	0.11	0.00

While the serial correlation in decade *nominal* returns seems to be positive, it appears that real rates are serially uncorrelated. The decade time series (although again too short for any definitive conclusions) suggest that real rates of return are independent from decade to decade.

29. Fund D represents the single *best* addition to complement Stephenson's current portfolio, given his selection criteria. First, Fund D's expected return (14.0 percent) has the potential to increase the portfolio's return somewhat. Second, Fund D's relatively low correlation with his current portfolio (+0.65) indicates that Fund D will provide greater diversification benefits than any of the other alternatives except Fund B. The result of adding Fund D should be a portfolio with approximately the same expected return and somewhat lower volatility compared to the original portfolio.

The other three funds have shortcomings in terms of either expected return enhancement or volatility reduction through diversification benefits. Fund A offers the potential for increasing the portfolio's return, but is too highly correlated to provide substantial volatility reduction benefits through diversification. Fund B provides substantial volatility reduction through diversification benefits, but is expected to generate a return well below the current portfolio's return. Fund C has the greatest potential to increase the portfolio's return, but is too highly correlated to provide substantial volatility reduction benefits through diversification.

30. a. Subscript OP refers to the original portfolio, ABC to the new stock, and NP to the new portfolio.

   i. $E(r_{NP}) = w_{OP} E(r_{OP}) + w_{ABC} E(r_{ABC}) = (0.9 \times 0.67) + (0.1 \times 1.25) = 0.728\%$

   ii. $Cov = r \times \sigma_{OP} \times \sigma_{ABC} = 0.40 \times 2.37 \times 2.95 = 2.7966 \cong 2.80$

   iii. $\sigma_{NP} = [w_{OP}^2 \sigma_{OP}^2 + w_{ABC}^2 \sigma_{ABC}^2 + 2 w_{OP} w_{ABC} (Cov_{OP, ABC})]^{1/2}$

   $= [(0.9^2 \times 2.37^2) + (0.1^2 \times 2.95^2) + (2 \times 0.9 \times 0.1 \times 2.80)]^{1/2}$

   $= 2.2673\% \cong 2.27\%$

   b. Subscript OP refers to the original portfolio, GS to government securities, and NP to the new portfolio.

   i. $E(r_{NP}) = w_{OP} E(r_{OP}) + w_{GS} E(r_{GS}) = (0.9 \times 0.67) + (0.1 \times 0.042) = 0.645\%$

   ii. $Cov = r \times \sigma_{OP} \times \sigma_{GS} = 0 \times 2.37 \times 0 = 0$

   iii. $\sigma_{NP} = [w_{OP}^2 \sigma_{OP}^2 + w_{GS}^2 \sigma_{GS}^2 + 2 w_{OP} w_{GS} (Cov_{OP, GS})]^{1/2}$

   $= [(0.9^2 \times 2.37^2) + (0.1^2 \times 0) + (2 \times 0.9 \times 0.1 \times 0)]^{1/2}$

   $= 2.133\% \cong 2.13\%$

   c. Adding the risk-free government securities would result in a lower beta for the new portfolio. The new portfolio beta will be a weighted average of the individual security betas in the portfolio; the presence of the risk-free securities would lower that weighted average.

   d. The comment is not correct. Although the respective standard deviations and expected returns for the two securities under consideration are equal, the covariances between each security and the original portfolio are unknown, making it impossible to draw the conclusion stated. For instance, if the covariances are different, selecting one security over the other may result in a lower standard deviation for the portfolio as a whole. In such a case, that security would be the preferred investment, assuming all other factors are equal.

   e. i. Grace clearly expressed the sentiment that the risk of loss was more important to her than the opportunity for return. Using variance (or standard deviation) as a measure of risk in her case has a serious limitation because standard deviation does not distinguish between positive and negative price movements.

ii. Two alternative risk measures that could be used instead of variance are:

Range of Returns, which considers the highest and lowest expected returns in the future period, with a larger range being a sign of greater variability and therefore of greater risk.

Semivariance, which can be used to measure expected deviations of returns below the mean, or some other benchmark, such as zero.

Either of these measures would potentially be superior to variance for Grace. Range of returns would help to highlight the full spectrum of risk she is assuming, especially the downside portion of the range about which she is so concerned. Semivariance would also be effective, because it implicitly assumes that the investor wants to minimize the likelihood of returns falling below some target rate; in Grace's case, the target rate would be set at zero (to protect against negative returns).

31. a. Systematic risk refers to fluctuations in asset prices caused by macroeconomic factors that are common to all risky assets; hence systematic risk is often referred to as market risk. Examples of systematic risk factors include the business cycle, inflation, monetary policy and technological changes.

Firm-specific risk refers to fluctuations in asset prices caused by factors that are independent of the market such as industry characteristics or firm characteristics. Examples of firm-specific risk factors include litigation, patents, management, and financial leverage.

b. Trudy should explain to the client that picking only the top five best ideas would most likely result in the client holding a much more risky portfolio. The total risk of a portfolio, or portfolio variance, is the combination of systematic risk and firm-specific risk.

The systematic component depends on the sensitivity of the individual assets to market movements as measured by beta. Assuming the portfolio is well diversified, the number of assets will not affect the systematic risk component of portfolio variance. The portfolio beta depends on the individual security betas and the portfolio weights of those securities.

On the other hand, the components of firm-specific risk (sometimes called nonsystematic risk) are not perfectly positively correlated with each other and, as more assets are added to the portfolio, those additional assets tend to reduce portfolio risk. Hence, increasing the number of securities in a portfolio reduces firm-specific risk. For example, a patent expiration for one company would not affect the other securities in the portfolio. An increase in oil prices might hurt an airline stock but aid an energy stock. As the number of randomly selected securities increases, the total risk (variance) of the portfolio approaches its systematic variance.

CHAPTER 8: INDEX MODELS

1.   a.   To optimize this portfolio one would need:

       $n = 60$ estimates of means

       $n = 60$ estimates of variances

$$\frac{n^2 - n}{2} = 1{,}770 \text{ estimates of covariances}$$

Therefore, in total: $\dfrac{n^2 + 3n}{2} = 1{,}890$ estimates

     b.   In a single index model: $r_i - r_f = \alpha_i + \beta_i(r_M - r_f) + e_i$

Equivalently, using excess returns: $R_i = \alpha_i + \beta_i R_M + e_i$

The variance of the rate of return on each stock can be decomposed into the components:

(1)   The variance due to the common market factor: $\beta_i^2 \sigma_M^2$

(2)   The variance due to firm specific unanticipated events: $\sigma^2(e_i)$

In this model: $Cov(r_i, r_j) = \beta_i \beta_j \sigma$

The number of parameter estimates is:

     $n = 60$ estimates of the mean $E(r_i)$

     $n = 60$ estimates of the sensitivity coefficient β_i

     $n = 60$ estimates of the firm-specific variance $\sigma^2(e_i)$

     1 estimate of the market mean $E(r_M)$

     1 estimate of the market variance σ_M^2

Therefore, in total, 182 estimates.

Thus, the single index model reduces the total number of required parameter estimates from 1,890 to 182. In general, the number of parameter estimates is reduced from:

$$\left(\frac{n^2 + 3n}{2}\right) \text{ to } (3n + 2)$$

2.   a.   The standard deviation of each individual stock is given by:

$$\sigma_i = [\beta_i^2 \sigma_M^2 + \sigma^2(e_i)]^{1/2}$$

Since $\beta_A = 0.8$, $\beta_B = 1.2$, $\sigma(e_A) = 30\%$, $\sigma(e_B) = 40\%$, and $\sigma_M = 22\%$, we get:

$$\sigma_A = (0.8^2 \times 22^2 + 30^2)^{1/2} = 34.78\%$$

$$\sigma_B = (1.2^2 \times 22^2 + 40^2)^{1/2} = 47.93\%$$

    b.   The expected rate of return on a portfolio is the weighted average of the expected returns of the individual securities:

$$E(r_P) = w_A E(r_A) + w_B E(r_B) + w_f r_f$$

where w_A, w_B, and w_f are the portfolio weights for Stock A, Stock B, and T-bills, respectively.

Substituting in the formula we get:

$$E(r_P) = (0.30 \times 13) + (0.45 \times 18) + (0.25 \times 8) = 14\%$$

The beta of a portfolio is similarly a weighted average of the betas of the individual securities:

$$\beta_P = w_A \beta_A + w_B \beta_B + w_f \beta_f$$

The beta for T-bills (β_f) is zero. The beta for the portfolio is therefore:

$$\beta_P = (0.30 \times 0.8) + (0.45 \times 1.2) + 0 = 0.78$$

The variance of this portfolio is:

$$\sigma_P^2 = \beta_P^2 \sigma_M^2 + \sigma^2(e_P)$$

where $\beta_P^2 \sigma_M^2$ is the systematic component and $\sigma^2(e_P)$ is the nonsystematic component. Since the residuals (e_i) are uncorrelated, the non-systematic variance is:

$$\sigma^2(e_P) = w_A^2 \sigma^2(e_A) + w_B^2 \sigma^2(e_B) + w_f^2 \sigma^2(e_f)$$

$$= (0.30^2 \times 30^2) + (0.45^2 \times 40^2) + (0.25^2 \times 0) = 405$$

where $\sigma^2(e_A)$ and $\sigma^2(e_B)$ are the firm-specific (nonsystematic) variances of Stocks A and B, and $\sigma^2(e_f)$, the nonsystematic variance of T-bills, is zero. The residual standard deviation of the portfolio is thus:

$$\sigma(e_P) = (405)^{1/2} = 20.12\%$$

The total variance of the portfolio is then:

$$\sigma_P^2 = (0.78^2 \times 22^2) + 405 = 699.47$$

The standard deviation is 26.45%.

3. a. The two figures depict the stocks' security characteristic lines (SCL). Stock A has higher firm-specific risk because the deviations of the observations from the SCL are larger for Stock A than for Stock B. Deviations are measured by the vertical distance of each observation from the SCL.

b. Beta is the slope of the SCL, which is the measure of systematic risk. The SCL for Stock B is steeper; hence Stock B's systematic risk is greater.

c. The R^2 (or squared correlation coefficient) of the SCL is the ratio of the explained variance of the stock's return to total variance, and the total variance is the sum of the explained variance plus the unexplained variance (the stock's residual variance):

$$R^2 = \frac{\beta_i^2 \sigma_M^2}{\beta_i^2 \sigma_M^2 + \sigma^2(e_i)}$$

Since the explained variance for Stock B is greater than for Stock A (the explained variance is $\beta_B^2 \sigma_M^2$, which is greater since its beta is higher), *and* its residual variance $\sigma^2(e_B)$ is smaller, its R^2 is higher than Stock A's.

d. Alpha is the intercept of the SCL with the expected return axis. Stock A has a small positive alpha whereas Stock B has a negative alpha; hence, Stock A's alpha is larger.

e. The correlation coefficient is simply the square root of R^2, so Stock B's correlation with the market is higher.

4. a. Firm-specific risk is measured by the residual standard deviation. Thus, stock A has more firm-specific risk: 10.3% > 9.1%

b. Market risk is measured by beta, the slope coefficient of the regression. A has a larger beta coefficient: 1.2 > 0.8

c. R^2 measures the fraction of total variance of return explained by the market return. A's R^2 is larger than B's: 0.576 > 0.436

d. Rewriting the SCL equation in terms of total return (r) rather than excess return (R):

$$r_A - r_f = \alpha + \beta(r_M - r_f) \Rightarrow r_A = \alpha + r_f(1 - \beta) + \beta r_M$$

The intercept is now equal to:

$$\alpha + r_f(1 - \beta) = 1 + r_f(1 - 1.2)$$

Since $r_f = 6\%$, the intercept would be: $1 - 1.2 = -0.2\%$

5. The standard deviation of each stock can be derived from the following equation for R^2:

$$R_i^2 = \frac{\beta_i^2 \sigma_M^2}{\sigma_i^2} = \frac{\text{Explained variance}}{\text{Total variance}}$$

Therefore:

$$\sigma_A^2 = \frac{\beta_A^2 \sigma_M^2}{R_A^2} = \frac{0.7^2 \times 20^2}{0.20} = 980$$

$$\sigma_A = 31.30\%$$

For stock B:

$$\sigma_B^2 = \frac{1.2^2 \times 20^2}{0.12} = 4,800$$

$$\sigma_B = 69.28\%$$

6. The systematic risk for A is:

$$\beta_A^2 \sigma_M^2 = 0.70^2 \times 20^2 = 196$$

The firm-specific risk of A (the residual variance) is the difference between A's total risk and its systematic risk:

$$980 - 196 = 784$$

The systematic risk for B is:

$$\beta_B^2 \sigma_M^2 = 1.20^2 \times 20^2 = 576$$

B's firm-specific risk (residual variance) is:

$$4800 - 576 = 4224$$

7. The covariance between the returns of A and B is (since the residuals are assumed to be uncorrelated):

$$\text{Cov}(r_A, r_B) = \beta_A \beta_B \sigma_M^2 = 0.70 \times 1.20 \times 400 = 336$$

The correlation coefficient between the returns of A and B is:

$$\rho_{AB} = \frac{\text{Cov}(r_A, r_B)}{\sigma_A \sigma_B} = \frac{336}{31.30 \times 69.28} = 0.155$$

8. Note that the correlation is the square root of R^2: $\rho = \sqrt{R^2}$

$$\text{Cov}(r_A, r_M) = \rho\sigma_A\sigma_M = 0.20^{1/2} \times 31.30 \times 20 = 280$$

$$\text{Cov}(r_B, r_M) = \rho\sigma_B\sigma_M = 0.12^{1/2} \times 69.28 \times 20 = 480$$

9. For portfolio P we can compute:

$$\sigma_P = [(0.6^2 \times 980) + (0.4^2 \times 4800) + (2 \times 0.4 \times 0.6 \times 336]^{1/2} = [1282.08]^{1/2} = 35.81\%$$

$$\beta_P = (0.6 \times 0.7) + (0.4 \times 1.2) = 0.90$$

$$\sigma^2(e_P) = \sigma_P^2 - \beta_P^2\sigma_M^2 = 1282.08 - (0.90^2 \times 400) = 958.08$$

$$\text{Cov}(r_P, r_M) = \beta_P\sigma_M^2 = 0.90 \times 400 = 360$$

This same result can also be attained using the covariances of the individual stocks with the market:

$$\text{Cov}(r_P, r_M) = \text{Cov}(0.6r_A + 0.4r_B, r_M) = 0.6\text{Cov}(r_A, r_M) + 0.4\text{Cov}(r_B, r_M)$$
$$= (0.6 \times 280) + (0.4 \times 480) = 360$$

10. Note that the variance of T-bills is zero, and the covariance of T-bills with any asset is zero. Therefore, for portfolio Q:

$$\sigma_Q = \left[w_P^2\sigma_P^2 + w_M^2\sigma_M^2 + 2 \times w_P \times w_M \times \text{Cov}(r_P, r_M)\right]^{1/2}$$
$$= \left[(0.5^2 \times 1{,}282.08) + (0.3^2 \times 400) + (2 \times 0.5 \times 0.3 \times 360)\right]^{1/2} = 21.55\%$$

$$\beta_Q = w_P\beta_P + w_M\beta_M = (0.5 \times 0.90) + (0.3 \times 1) + 0 = 0.75$$

$$\sigma^2(e_Q) = \sigma_Q^2 - \beta_Q^2\sigma_M^2 = 464.52 - (0.75^2 \times 400) = 239.52$$

$$\text{Cov}(r_Q, r_M) = \beta_Q\sigma_M^2 = 0.75 \times 400 = 300$$

11. a. Merrill Lynch adjusts beta by taking the sample estimate of beta and averaging it with 1.0, using the weights of 2/3 and 1/3, as follows:

$$\text{adjusted beta} = [(2/3) \times 1.24] + [(1/3) \times 1.0] = 1.16$$

b. If you use your current estimate of beta to be $\beta_{t-1} = 1.24$, then

$$\beta_t = 0.3 + (0.7 \times 1.24) = 1.168$$

12. The regression results provide quantitative measures of return and risk based on monthly returns over the five-year period.

β for ABC was 0.60, considerably less than the average stock's β of 1.0. This indicates that, when the S&P 500 rose or fell by 1 percentage point, ABC's return on average rose or fell by only 0.60 percentage point. Therefore, ABC's systematic risk (or market risk) was low relative to the typical value for stocks. ABC's alpha (the intercept of the regression) was –3.2%, indicating that when the market return was 0%, the average return on ABC was –3.2%. ABC's unsystematic risk (or residual risk), as measured by $\sigma(e)$, was 13.02%. For ABC, R^2 was 0.35, indicating closeness of fit to the linear regression greater than the value for a typical stock.

β for XYZ was somewhat higher, at 0.97, indicating XYZ's return pattern was very similar to the β for the market index. Therefore, XYZ stock had average systematic risk for the period examined. Alpha for XYZ was positive and quite large, indicating a return of almost 7.3%, on average, for XYZ independent of market return. Residual risk was 21.45%, half again as much as ABC's, indicating a wider scatter of observations around the regression line for XYZ. Correspondingly, the fit of the regression model was considerably less than that of ABC, consistent with an R^2 of only 0.17.

The effects of including one or the other of these stocks in a diversified portfolio may be quite different. If it can be assumed that both stocks' betas will remain stable over time, then there is a large difference in systematic risk level. The betas obtained from the two brokerage houses may help the analyst draw inferences for the future. The three estimates of ABC's β are similar, regardless of the sample period of the underlying data. The range of these estimates is 0.60 to 0.71, well below the market average β of 1.0. The three estimates of XYZ's β vary significantly among the three sources, ranging as high as 1.45 for the weekly data over the most recent two years. One could infer that XYZ's β for the future might be well above 1.0, meaning it might have somewhat greater systematic risk than was implied by the monthly regression for the five-year period.

These stocks appear to have significantly different systematic risk characteristics. If these stocks are added to a diversified portfolio, XYZ will add more to total volatility.

13. For Stock A:

$$\alpha_A = r_A - [r_f + \beta_A(r_M - r_f)] = 11 - [6 + 0.8(12 - 6)] = 0.2\%$$

For stock B:

$$\alpha_B = 14 - [6 + 1.5(12 - 6)] = -1\%$$

Stock A would be a good addition to a well-diversified portfolio. A short position in Stock B may be desirable.

14. The R^2 of the regression is: $0.70^2 = 0.49$

Therefore, 51% of total variance is unexplained by the market; this is nonsystematic risk.

15. $9 = 3 + \beta (11 - 3) \Rightarrow \beta = 0.75$

16. d.

17. b.

18. a.

Alpha (α) $\alpha_i = r_i - [r_f + \beta_i(r_M - r_f)]$	Expected excess return $E(r_i) - r_f$
$\alpha_A = 20\% - [8\% + 1.3(16\% - 8\%)] = 1.6\%$	$20\% - 8\% = 12\%$
$\alpha_B = 18\% - [8\% + 1.8(16\% - 8\%)] = -4.4\%$	$18\% - 8\% = 10\%$
$\alpha_C = 17\% - [8\% + 0.7(16\% - 8\%)] = 3.4\%$	$17\% - 8\% = 9\%$
$\alpha_D = 12\% - [8\% + 1.0(16\% - 8\%)] = -4.0\%$	$12\% - 8\% = 4\%$

Stocks A and C have positive alphas, whereas stocks B and D have negative alphas.

The residual variances are:

$$\sigma^2(e_A) = 58^2 = 3{,}364$$

$$\sigma^2(e_B) = 71^2 = 5{,}041$$

$$\sigma^2(e_C) = 60^2 = 3{,}600$$

$$\sigma^2(e_D) = 55^2 = 3{,}025$$

b. To construct the optimal risky portfolio, we first determine the optimal active portfolio. Using the Treynor-Black technique, we construct the active portfolio:

	$\dfrac{\alpha}{\sigma^2(e)}$	$\dfrac{\alpha / \sigma^2(e)}{\Sigma \alpha / \sigma^2(e)}$
A	0.000476	−0.6142
B	−0.000873	1.1265
C	0.000944	−1.2181
D	−0.001322	1.7058
Total	−0.000775	1.0000

Do not be concerned that the positive alpha stocks have negative weights and vice versa. We will see that the entire position in the active portfolio will be negative, returning everything to good order.

With these weights, the forecast for the active portfolio is:

$\alpha = [-0.6142 \times 1.6] + [1.1265 \times (-4.4)] - [1.2181 \times 3.4] + [1.7058 \times (-4.0)]$

$\quad = -16.90\%$

$\beta = [-0.6142 \times 1.3] + [1.1265 \times 1.8] - [1.2181 \times 0.70] + [1.7058 \times 1] = 2.08$

The high beta (higher than any individual beta) results from the short positions in the relatively low beta stocks and the long positions in the relatively high beta stocks.

$\sigma^2(e) = [(-0.6142)^2 \times 3364] + [1.1265^2 \times 5041] + [(-1.2181)^2 \times 3600] + [1.7058^2 \times 3025]$

$\quad = 21,809.6$

$\sigma(e) = 147.68\%$

Here, again, the levered position in stock B [with high $\sigma^2(e)$] overcomes the diversification effect, and results in a high residual standard deviation. The optimal risky portfolio has a proportion w^* in the active portfolio, computed as follows:

$$w_0 = \frac{\alpha / \sigma^2(e)}{[E(r_M) - r_f] / \sigma_M^2} = \frac{-16.90 / 21,809.6}{8 / 23^2} = -0.05124$$

The negative position is justified for the reason stated earlier.

The adjustment for beta is:

$$w^* = \frac{w_0}{1+(1-\beta)w_0} = \frac{-0.05124}{1+(1-2.08)(-0.05124)} = -0.0486$$

Since w* is negative, the result is a positive position in stocks with positive alphas and a negative position in stocks with negative alphas. The position in the index portfolio is:

$$1 - (-0.0486) = 1.0486$$

c.   To calculate Sharpe's measure for the optimal risky portfolio, we compute the information ratio for the active portfolio and Sharpe's measure for the market portfolio. The information ratio for the active portfolio is computed as follows:

$$A = \alpha / \sigma(e) = -16.90/147.68 = -0.1144$$

$$A^2 = 0.0131$$

Hence, the square of Sharpe's measure (S) of the optimized risky portfolio is:

$$S^2 = S_M^2 + A^2 = \left(\frac{8}{23}\right)^2 + 0.0131 = 0.1341$$

$$S = 0.3662$$

Compare this to the market's Sharpe measure:

$$S_M = 8/23 = 0.3478$$

The difference is: 0.0184

Note that the only-moderate improvement in performance results from the fact that only a small position is taken in the active portfolio A because of its large residual variance.

d.   To calculate the exact makeup of the complete portfolio, we first compute `the mean excess return of the optimal risky portfolio and its variance. The risky portfolio beta is given by:

$$\beta_P = w_M + (w_A \times \beta_A) = 1.0486 + [(-0.0486) \times 2.08] = 0.95$$

$$E(R_P) = \alpha_P + \beta_P E(R_M) = [(-0.0486) \times (-16.90\%)] + (0.95 \times 8\%) = 8.42\%$$

$$\sigma_P^2 = \beta_P^2 \sigma_M^2 + \sigma^2(e_P) = (0.95 \times 23)^2 + \left((-0.0486^2) \times 21,809.6\right) = 528.94$$

$$\sigma_P = 23.00\%$$

Since A = 2.8, the optimal position in this portfolio is:

$$y = \frac{8.42}{0.01 \times 2.8 \times 528.94} = 0.5685$$

In contrast, with a passive strategy:

$$y = \frac{8}{0.01 \times 2.8 \times 23^2} = 0.5401$$

This is a difference of: 0.0284

The final positions of the complete portfolio are:

Bills	1 − 0.5685 =	43.15%
M	0.5685 × 1.0486 =	59.61%
A	0.5685 × (−0.0486) × (−0.6142) =	1.70%
B	0.5685 × (−0.0486) × 1.1265 =	− 3.11%
C	0.5685 × (−0.0486) × (−1.2181) =	3.37%
D	0.5685 × (−0.0486) × 1.7058 =	− 4.71%
		100.00%

[sum is subject to rounding error]

Note that M may include positive proportions of stocks A through D.

19. a.   If a manager is not allowed to sell short he will not include stocks with negative alphas in his portfolio, so he will consider only A and C:

	α	$\sigma^2(e)$	$\dfrac{\alpha}{\sigma^2(e)}$	$\dfrac{\alpha / \sigma^2(e)}{\Sigma\alpha / \sigma^2(e)}$
A	1.6	3,364	0.000476	0.3352
C	3.4	3,600	0.000944	0.6648
			0.001420	1.0000

The forecast for the active portfolio is:

$\alpha = (0.3352 \times 1.6) + (0.6648 \times 3.4) = 2.80\%$

$\beta = (0.3352 \times 1.3) + (0.6648 \times 0.7) = 0.90$

$\sigma^2(e) = (0.3352^2 \times 3,364) + (0.6648^2 \times 3,600) = 1,969.03$

$\sigma(e) = 44.37\%$

The weight in the active portfolio is:

$$w_0 = \frac{\alpha/\sigma^2(e)}{E(R_M)/\sigma_M^2} = \frac{2.80/1,969.03}{8/23^2} = 0.0940$$

Adjusting for beta:

$$w^* = \frac{w_0}{1+(1-\beta)w_0} = \frac{0.094}{1+[(1-0.90)\times 0.094]} = 0.0931$$

The information ratio of the active portfolio is:

$$A = \alpha/\sigma(e) = 2.80/44.37 = 0.0631$$

Hence, the square of Sharpe's measure is:

$$S^2 = (8/23)^2 + 0.0631^2 = 0.1250$$

Therefore: S = 0.3535

The market's Sharpe measure is: $S_M = 0.3478$

When short sales are allowed (Problem 18), the manager's Sharpe measure is higher (0.3662). The reduction in the Sharpe measure is the cost of the short sale restriction.

The characteristics of the optimal risky portfolio are:

$$\beta_P = w_M + w_A \times \beta_A = (1 - 0.0931) + (0.0931 \times 0.9) = 0.99$$

$$E(R_P) = \alpha_P + \beta_P E(R_M) = (0.0931 \times 2.8\%) + (0.99 \times 8\%) = 8.18\%$$

$$\sigma_P^2 = \beta_P^2 \sigma_M^2 + \sigma^2(e_P) = (0.99 \times 23)^2 + (0.0931^2 \times 1,969.03) = 535.54$$

$$\sigma_P = 23.14\%$$

With A = 2.8, the optimal position in this portfolio is:

$$y = \frac{8.18}{0.01 \times 2.8 \times 535.54} = 0.5455$$

The final positions in each asset are:

Bills	1 − 0.5455 =	45.45%
M	0.5455 × (1 − 0.0931) =	49.47%
A	0.5455 × 0.0931 × 0.3352 =	1.70%
C	0.5455 × 0.0931 × 0.6648 =	3.38%
		100.00%

b. The mean and variance of the optimized complete portfolios in the unconstrained and short-sales constrained cases, and for the passive strategy are:

	$E(R_C)$	σ_C^2
Unconstrained	$0.5685 \times 8.42 = 4.79$	$0.5685^2 \times 528.94 = 170.95$
Constrained	$0.5455 \times 8.18 = 4.46$	$0.5455^2 \times 535.54 = 159.36$
Passive	$0.5401 \times 8.00 = 4.32$	$0.5401^2 \times 529.00 = 154.31$

The utility levels below are computed using the formula: $E(r_C) - 0.005A\sigma_C^2$

Unconstrained $8 + 4.79 - (0.005 \times 2.8 \times 170.95) = 10.40$

Constrained $8 + 4.46 - (0.005 \times 2.8 \times 159.36) = 10.23$

Passive $8 + 4.32 - (0.005 \times 2.8 \times 154.31) = 10.16$

20. All alphas are reduced to 0.3 times their values in the original case. Therefore, the relative weights of each security in the active portfolio are unchanged, but the alpha of the active portfolio is only 0.3 times its previous value: $0.3 \times -16.90\% = -5.07\%$ The investor will take a smaller position in the active portfolio. The optimal risky portfolio has a proportion w^* in the active portfolio as follows:

$$w_0 = \frac{\alpha / \sigma^2(e)}{E(r_M - r_f)/\sigma_M^2} = \frac{-5.07/21,809.6}{8/23^2} = -0.01537$$

The negative position is justified for the reason given earlier.
The adjustment for beta is:

$$w^* = \frac{w_0}{1 + (1-\beta)w_0} = \frac{-0.01537}{1 + [(1-2.08) \times (-0.01537)]} = -0.0151$$

Since w^* is negative, the result is a positive position in stocks with positive alphas and a negative position in stocks with negative alphas. The position in the index portfolio is:

$1 - (-0.0151) = 1.0151$

To calculate Sharpe's measure for the optimal risky portfolio we compute the information ratio for the active portfolio and Sharpe's measure for the market portfolio. The information ratio of the *active portfolio* is 0.3 times its previous value:

$A = \alpha / \sigma(e) = -5.07/147.68 = -0.0343$ and $A^2 = 0.00118$

Hence, the square of Sharpe's measure of the *optimized risky portfolio* is:

$$S^2 = S^2_M + A^2 = (8/23)^2 + 0.00118 = 0.1222$$
$$S = 0.3495$$

Compare this to the market's Sharpe measure: $S_M = 8/23 = 0.3478$

The difference is: 0.0017

Note that the reduction of the forecast alphas by a factor of 0.3 reduced the squared information ratio and the improvement in the squared Sharpe ratio by a factor of:

$$0.3^2 = 0.09$$

CHAPTER 9: THE CAPITAL ASSET PRICING MODEL

1. $E(r_P) = r_f + \beta_P [E(r_M) - r_f]$

    $18 = 6 + \beta_P(14 - 6) \Rightarrow \beta_P = 12/8 = 1.5$

2. If the security's correlation coefficient with the market portfolio doubles (with all other variables such as variances unchanged), then beta, and therefore the risk premium, will also double. The current risk premium is: $14 - 6 = 8\%$
    The new risk premium would be 16%, and the new discount rate for the security would be: $16 + 6 = 22\%$

    If the stock pays a constant perpetual dividend, then we know from the original data that the dividend (D) must satisfy the equation for the present value of a perpetuity:

    > Price = Dividend/Discount rate

    > $50 = D/0.14 \Rightarrow D = 50 \times 0.14 = \$7.00$

    At the new discount rate of 22%, the stock would be worth: $\$7/0.22 = \$31.82$
    The increase in stock risk has lowered its value by 36.36%.

3. The appropriate discount rate for the project is:

    > $r_f + \beta[E(r_M) - r_f] = 8 + [1.8 \times (16 - 8)] = 22.4\%$

    Using this discount rate:

    $$\text{NPV} = -\$40 + \sum_{t=1}^{10} \frac{\$15}{1.224^t} = -\$40 + [\$15 \times \text{Annuity factor (22.4\%, 10 years)}] = \$18.09$$

    The internal rate of return (IRR) for the project is 35.73%. Recall from your introductory finance class that NPV is positive if IRR > discount rate (or, equivalently, hurdle rate). The highest value that beta can take before the hurdle rate exceeds the IRR is determined by:

    > $35.73 = 8 + \beta(16 - 8) \Rightarrow \beta = 27.73/8 = 3.47$

4. a. False. $\beta = 0$ implies $E(r) = r_f$, not zero.

    b. False. Investors require a risk premium only for bearing systematic (undiversifiable or market) risk. Total volatility includes diversifiable risk.

    c. False. Your portfolio should be invested 75% in the market portfolio and 25% in T-bills. Then:

    > $\beta_P = (0.75 \times 1) + (0.25 \times 0) = 0.75$

5. a. Call the aggressive stock A and the defensive stock D. Beta is the sensitivity of the stock's return to the market return, i.e., the change in the stock return per unit change in the market return. Therefore, we compute each stock's beta by calculating the difference in its return across the two scenarios divided by the difference in the market return:

$$\beta_A = \frac{-2-38}{5-25} = 2.00$$

$$\beta_D = \frac{6-12}{5-25} = 0.30$$

   b. With the two scenarios equally likely, the expected return is an average of the two possible outcomes:

$$E(r_A) = 0.5 \times (-2 + 38) = 18\%$$

$$E(r_D) = 0.5 \times (6 + 12) = 9\%$$

   c. The SML is determined by the market expected return of $[0.5(25 + 5)] = 15\%$, with a beta of 1, and the T-bill return of 6% with a beta of zero. See the following graph.

The equation for the security market line is:

$$E(r) = 6 + \beta(15 - 6)$$

d. Based on its risk, the aggressive stock has a required expected return of:

$$E(r_A) = 6 + 2.0(15 - 6) = 24\%$$

The analyst's forecast of expected return is only 18%. Thus the stock's alpha is:

$$\alpha_A = \text{actually expected return} - \text{required return (given risk)}$$

$$= 18\% - 24\% = -6\%$$

Similarly, the required return for the defensive stock is:

$$E(r_D) = 6 + 0.3(15 - 6) = 8.7\%$$

The analyst's forecast of expected return for D is 9%, and hence, the stock has a positive alpha:

$$\alpha_D = \text{actually expected return} - \text{required return (given risk)}$$

$$= 9 - 8.7 = +0.3\%$$

The points for each stock plot on the graph as indicated above.

e. The hurdle rate is determined by the project beta (0.3), not the firm's beta. The correct discount rate is 8.7%, the fair rate of return for stock D.

6. Not possible. Portfolio A has a higher beta than Portfolio B, but the expected return for Portfolio A is lower than the expected return for Portfolio B. Thus, these two portfolios cannot exist in equilibrium.

7. Possible. If the CAPM is valid, the expected rate of return compensates only for systematic (market) risk, represented by beta, rather than for the standard deviation, which includes nonsystematic risk. Thus, Portfolio A's lower rate of return can be paired with a higher standard deviation, as long as A's beta is less than B's.

8. Not possible. The reward-to-variability ratio for Portfolio A is better than that of the market. This scenario is impossible according to the CAPM because the CAPM predicts that the market is the most efficient portfolio. Using the numbers supplied:

$$S_A = \frac{16 - 10}{12} = 0.5$$

$$S_M = \frac{18 - 10}{24} = 0.33$$

Portfolio A provides a better risk-reward tradeoff than the market portfolio.

9. Not possible. Portfolio A clearly dominates the market portfolio. Portfolio A has both a lower standard deviation and a higher expected return.

10. Not possible. The SML for this scenario is: $E(r) = 10 + \beta(18 - 10)$

Portfolios with beta equal to 1.5 have an expected return equal to:

$$E(r) = 10 + [1.5 \times (18 - 10)] = 22\%$$

The expected return for Portfolio A is 16%; that is, Portfolio A plots below the SML ($\alpha_A = -6\%$), and hence, is an overpriced portfolio. This is inconsistent with the CAPM.

11. Not possible. The SML is the same as in Problem 10. Here, Portfolio A's required return is: $10 + (0.9 \times 8) = 17.2\%$

This is greater than 16%. Portfolio A is overpriced with a negative alpha:
$\alpha_A = -1.2\%$

12. Possible. The CML is the same as in Problem 8. Portfolio A plots below the CML, as any asset is expected to. This scenario is not inconsistent with the CAPM.

13. Since the stock's beta is equal to 1.2, its expected rate of return is:

$$6 + [1.2 \times (16 - 6)] = 18\%$$

$$E(r) = \frac{D_1 + P_1 - P_0}{P_0}$$

$$0.18 = \frac{6 + P_1 - 50}{50} \Rightarrow P_1 = \$53$$

14. The series of $1,000 payments is a perpetuity. If beta is 0.5, the cash flow should be discounted at the rate:

$$6 + [0.5 \times (16 - 6)] = 11\%$$
$$PV = \$1,000/0.11 = \$9,090.91$$

If, however, beta is equal to 1, then the investment should yield 16%, and the price paid for the firm should be:

$$PV = \$1,000/0.16 = \$6,250$$

The difference, $2,840.91, is the amount you will overpay if you erroneously assume that beta is 0.5 rather than 1.

15. Using the SML: $4 = 6 + \beta(16 - 6) \Rightarrow \beta = -2/10 = -0.2$

16. $r_1 = 19\%$; $r_2 = 16\%$; $\beta_1 = 1.5$; $\beta_2 = 1$

    a.   To determine which investor was a better selector of individual stocks we look at abnormal return, which is the ex-post alpha; that is, the abnormal return is the difference between the actual return and that predicted by the SML. Without information about the parameters of this equation (risk-free rate and market rate of return) we cannot determine which investor was more accurate.

    b.   If $r_f = 6\%$ and $r_M = 14\%$, then (using the notation alpha for the abnormal return):

$$\alpha_1 = 19 - [6 + 1.5(14 - 6)] = 19 - 18 = 1\%$$

$$\alpha_2 = 16 - [6 + 1(14 - 6)] = 16 - 14 = 2\%$$

Here, the second investor has the larger abnormal return and thus appears to be the superior stock selector. By making better predictions, the second investor appears to have tilted his portfolio toward underpriced stocks.

    c.   If $r_f = 3\%$ and $r_M = 15\%$, then:

$$\alpha_1 = 19 - [3 + 1.5(15 - 3)] = 19 - 21 = -2\%$$

$$\alpha_2 = 16 - [3 + 1(15 - 3)] = 16 - 15 = 1\%$$

Here, not only does the second investor appear to be the superior stock selector, but the first investor's predictions appear valueless (or worse).

17.   a.   Since the market portfolio, by definition, has a beta of 1, its expected rate of return is 12%.

    b. $\beta = 0$ means no systematic risk. Hence, the stock's expected rate of return in market equilibrium is the risk-free rate, 5%.

    c.   Using the SML, the *fair* expected rate of return for a stock with $\beta = -0.5$ is:

$$E(r) = 5 + [(-0.5)(12 - 5)] = 1.5\%$$

The *actually* expected rate of return, using the expected price and dividend for next year is:

$$E(r) = [(\$41 + \$1)/40] - 1 = 0.10 = 10\%$$

Because the actually expected return exceeds the fair return, the stock is underpriced.

18. a. Agree; Regan's conclusion is correct. By definition, the market portfolio lies on the capital market line (CML). Under the assumptions of capital market theory, all portfolios on the CML dominate, in a risk-return sense, portfolios that lie on the Markowitz efficient frontier because, given that leverage is allowed, the CML creates a portfolio possibility line that is higher than all points on the efficient frontier except for the market portfolio, which is Rainbow's portfolio. Because Eagle's portfolio lies on the Markowitz efficient frontier at a point other than the market portfolio, Rainbow's portfolio dominates Eagle's portfolio.

   b. Unsystematic risk is the unique risk of individual stocks in a portfolio that is diversified away by holding a well-diversified portfolio. Total risk is composed of systematic (market) risk and unsystematic (firm-specific) risk.

   Disagree; Wilson's remark is incorrect. Because both portfolios lie on the Markowitz efficient frontier, neither Eagle nor Rainbow has any unsystematic risk. Therefore, unsystematic risk does not explain the different expected returns. The determining factor is that Rainbow lies on the (straight) line (the CML) connecting the risk-free asset and the market portfolio (Rainbow), at the point of tangency to the Markowitz efficient frontier having the highest return per unit of risk. Wilson's remark is also countered by the fact that, since unsystematic risk can be eliminated by diversification, the expected return for bearing unsystematic is zero. This is a result of the fact that well-diversified investors bid up the price of every asset to the point where only systematic risk earns a positive return (unsystematic risk earns no return).

19. $E(r) = r_f + \beta \times [E(r_M) - r_f]$

   Fuhrman Labs: $E(r) = 5 + 1.5 \times [11.5 - 5.0] = 14.75\%$

   Garten Testing: $E(r) = 5 + 0.8 \times [11.5 - 5.0] = 10.20\%$

   If the forecast rate of return is less than (greater than) the required rate of return, then the security is overvalued (undervalued).

   Fuhrman Labs: Forecast return – Required return = $13.25\% - 14.75\% = -1.50\%$

   Garten Testing: Forecast return – Required return = $11.25\% - 10.20\% = 1.05\%$

   Therefore, Fuhrman Labs is overvalued and Garten Testing is undervalued.

20. In the zero-beta CAPM the zero-beta portfolio replaces the risk-free rate, and thus:

   $E(r) = 8 + 0.6(17 - 8) = 13.4\%$

21. a.

22. d. From CAPM, the fair expected return = 8 + 1.25(15 − 8) = 16.75%
Actually expected return = 17%

$\alpha = 17 - 16.75 = 0.25\%$

23. d.

24. c.

25. d.

26. d. [You need to know the risk-free rate]

27. d. [You need to know the risk-free rate]

28. Under the CAPM, the only risk that investors are compensated for bearing is the risk that cannot be diversified away (systematic risk). Because systematic risk (measured by beta) is equal to 1.0 for both portfolios, an investor would expect the same rate of return from both portfolios A and B. Moreover, since both portfolios are well diversified, it doesn't matter if the specific risk of the individual securities is high or low. The firm-specific risk has been diversified away for both portfolios.

29. a. McKay should borrow funds and invest those funds proportionately in Murray's existing portfolio (i.e., buy more risky assets on margin). In addition to increased expected return, the alternative portfolio on the capital market line will also have increased risk, which is caused by the higher proportion of risky assets in the total portfolio.

   b. McKay should substitute low beta stocks for high beta stocks in order to reduce the overall beta of York's portfolio. By reducing the overall portfolio beta, McKay will reduce the systematic risk of the portfolio, and therefore reduce its volatility relative to the market. The security market line (SML) suggests such action (i.e., moving down the SML), even though reducing beta may result in a slight loss of portfolio efficiency unless full diversification is maintained. York's primary objective, however, is not to maintain efficiency, but to reduce risk exposure; reducing portfolio beta meets that objective. Because York does not want to engage in borrowing or lending, McKay cannot reduce risk by selling equities and using the proceeds to buy risk-free assets (i.e., lending part of the portfolio).

30. a. $E(r_P) = r_f + \beta_P [E(r_M) - r_f] = 5\% + 0.8 (15\% - 5\%) = 13\%$

   $\alpha = 14\% - 13\% = 1\%$

   You should invest in this fund because alpha is positive.

   b.   The passive portfolio with the same beta as the fund should be invested 80%
   in the market-index portfolio and 20% in the money market account. For this
   portfolio:

   $E(r_P) = (0.8 \times 15\%) + (0.2 \times 5\%) = 13\%$

   $14\% - 13\% = 1\% = \alpha$

31. a.

	Expected Return	Alpha
Stock X	$5\% + 0.8(14\% - 5\%) = 12.2\%$	$14.0\% - 12.2\% = 1.8\%$
Stock Y	$5\% + 1.5(14\% - 5\%) = 18.5\%$	$17.0\% - 18.5\% = -1.5\%$

   b.   i. Kay should recommend Stock X because of its positive alpha, compared to
   Stock Y, which has a negative alpha. In graphical terms, the expected
   return/risk profile for Stock X plots above the security market line (SML),
   while the profile for Stock Y plots below the SML. Also, depending on the
   individual risk preferences of Kay's clients, the lower beta for Stock X may
   have a beneficial effect on overall portfolio risk.

   ii. Kay should recommend Stock Y because it has higher forecasted return and
   lower standard deviation than Stock X. The respective Sharpe ratios for
   Stocks X and Y and the market index are:

   Stock X: $(14\% - 5\%)/36\% = 0.25$

   Stock Y: $(17\% - 5\%)/25\% = 0.48$

   Market index: $(14\% - 5\%)/15\% = 0.60$

   The market index has an even more attractive Sharpe ratio than either of the
   individual stocks, but, given the choice between Stock X and Stock Y, Stock
   Y is the superior alternative.

   When a stock is held as a single stock portfolio, standard deviation is the
   relevant risk measure. For such a portfolio, beta as a risk measure is
   irrelevant. Although holding a single asset is not a typically recommended
   investment strategy, some investors may hold what is essentially a single-asset
   portfolio when they hold the stock of their employer company. For such
   investors, the relevance of standard deviation versus beta is an important
   issue.

CHAPTER 10: ARBITRAGE PRICING THEORY
AND MULTIFACTOR MODELS OF RISK AND RETURN

1. The revised estimate of the expected rate of return on the stock would be the old estimate plus the sum of the products of the unexpected change in each factor times the respective sensitivity coefficient:

    revised estimate = 12% + [(1 × 2%) + (0.5 × 3%)] = 15.5%

2. Equation 10.9 applies here:

    $$E(r_p) = r_f + \beta_{P1}[E(r_1) - r_f] + \beta_{P2}[E(r_2) - r_f]$$

    We need to find the risk premium (RP) for each of the two factors:

    $$RP_1 = [E(r_1) - r_f] \text{ and } RP_2 = [E(r_2) - r_f]$$

    In order to do so, we solve the following system of two equations with two unknowns:

    $$31 = 6 + (1.5 × RP_1) + (2.0 × RP_2)$$
    $$27 = 6 + (2.2 × RP_1) + [(-0.2) × RP_2]$$

    The solution to this set of equations is:

    $$RP_1 = 10\% \text{ and } RP_2 = 5\%$$

    Thus, the expected return-beta relationship is:

    $$E(r_P) = 6\% + (\beta_{P1} × 10\%) + (\beta_{P2} × 5\%)$$

3. The expected return for Portfolio F equals the risk-free rate since its beta equals 0.

    For Portfolio A, the ratio of risk premium to beta is: (12 – 6)/1.2 = 5

    For Portfolio E, the ratio is lower at: (8 – 6)/0.6 = 3.33

    This implies that an arbitrage opportunity exists. For instance, you can create a Portfolio G with beta equal to 0.6 (the same as E's) by combining Portfolio A and Portfolio F in equal weights. The expected return and beta for Portfolio G are then:

    $$E(r_G) = (0.5 × 12\%) + (0.5 × 6\%) = 9\%$$

    $$\beta_G = (0.5 × 1.2) + (0.5 × 0) = 0.6$$

    Comparing Portfolio G to Portfolio E, G has the same beta and higher return. Therefore, an arbitrage opportunity exists by buying Portfolio G and selling an equal amount of Portfolio E. The profit for this arbitrage will be:

    $$r_G - r_E = [9\% + (0.6 × F)] - [8\% + (0.6 × F)] = 1\%$$

    That is, 1% of the funds (long or short) in each portfolio.

4.   a.   This statement is incorrect. The CAPM requires a mean-variance efficient market portfolio, but APT does not.

      b.   This statement is incorrect. The CAPM assumes normally distributed security returns, but APT does not.

      c.   This statement is correct.

5.   Substituting the portfolio returns and betas in the expected return-beta relationship, we obtain two equations with two unknowns, the risk-free rate (r_f) and the factor risk premium (RP):

$$12 = r_f + (1.2 \times RP)$$
$$9 = r_f + (0.8 \times RP)$$

Solving these equations, we obtain:

$$r_f = 3\% \text{ and } RP = 7.5\%$$

6.   a.   Shorting an equally-weighted portfolio of the ten negative-alpha stocks and investing the proceeds in an equally-weighted portfolio of the ten positive-alpha stocks eliminates the market exposure and creates a zero-investment portfolio. Denoting the systematic market factor as R_M, the expected dollar return is (noting that the expectation of non-systematic risk, e, is zero):

$$\$1,000,000 \times [0.02 + (1.0 \times R_M)] - \$1,000,000 \times [(-0.02) + (1.0 \times R_M)]$$
$$= \$1,000,000 \times 0.04 = \$40,000$$

The sensitivity of the payoff of this portfolio to the market factor is zero because the exposures of the positive alpha and negative alpha stocks cancel out. (Notice that the terms involving R_M sum to zero.) Thus, the systematic component of total risk is also zero. The variance of the analyst's profit is not zero, however, since this portfolio is not well diversified.

For n = 20 stocks (i.e., long 10 stocks and short 10 stocks) the investor will have a $100,000 position (either long or short) in each stock. Net market exposure is zero, but firm-specific risk has not been fully diversified. The variance of dollar returns from the positions in the 20 stocks is:

$$20 \times [(100,000 \times 0.30)^2] = 18,000,000,000$$

The standard deviation of dollar returns is $134,164.

b. If n = 50 stocks (25 stocks long and 25 stocks short), the investor will have a $40,000 position in each stock, and the variance of dollar returns is:

$$50 \times [(40,000 \times 0.30)^2] = 7,200,000,000$$

The standard deviation of dollar returns is $84,853.

Similarly, if n = 100 stocks (50 stocks long and 50 stocks short), the investor will have a $20,000 position in each stock, and the variance of dollar returns is:

$$100 \times [(20,000 \times 0.30)^2] = 3,600,000,000$$

The standard deviation of dollar returns is $60,000.

Notice that, when the number of stocks increases by a factor of 5 (i.e., from 20 to 100), standard deviation decreases by a factor of $\sqrt{5} = 2.23607$ (from $134,164 to $60,000).

7 a. $\sigma^2 = \beta^2 \sigma_M^2 + \sigma^2(e)$

$\sigma_A^2 = (0.8^2 \times 20^2) + 25^2 = 881$

$\sigma_B^2 = (1.0^2 \times 20^2) + 10^2 = 500$

$\sigma_C^2 = (1.2^2 \times 20^2) + 20^2 = 976$

b. If there are an infinite number of assets with identical characteristics, then a well-diversified portfolio of each type will have only systematic risk since the non-systematic risk will approach zero with large n. The mean will equal that of the individual (identical) stocks.

c. There is no arbitrage opportunity because the well-diversified portfolios all plot on the security market line (SML). Because they are fairly priced, there is no arbitrage.

8. a. A long position in a portfolio (P) comprised of Portfolios A and B will offer an expected return-beta tradeoff lying on a straight line between points A and B. Therefore, we can choose weights such that $\beta_P = \beta_C$ but with expected return higher than that of Portfolio C. Hence, combining P with a short position in C will create an arbitrage portfolio with zero investment, zero beta, and positive rate of return.

b. The argument in part (a) leads to the proposition that the coefficient of β^2 must be zero in order to preclude arbitrage opportunities.

9. The APT factors must correlate with major sources of uncertainty, i.e., sources of uncertainty that are of concern to many investors. Researchers should investigate factors that correlate with uncertainty in consumption and investment opportunities. GDP, the inflation rate, and interest rates are among the factors that can be expected to determine risk premiums. In particular, industrial production (IP) is a good indicator of changes in the business cycle. Thus, IP is a candidate for a factor that is highly correlated with uncertainties that have to do with investment and consumption opportunities in the economy.

10. Any pattern of returns can be "explained" if we are free to choose an indefinitely large number of explanatory factors. If a theory of asset pricing is to have value, it must explain returns using a reasonably limited number of explanatory variables (i.e., systematic factors).

11. a. $E(r) = 6 + (1.2 \times 6) + (0.5 \times 8) + (0.3 \times 3) = 18.1\%$

    b. Surprises in the macroeconomic factors will result in surprises in the return of the stock:

    Unexpected return from macro factors =

    $$[1.2(4 - 5)] + [0.5(6 - 3)] + [0.3(0 - 2)] = -0.3\%$$
    $$E(r) = 18.1\% - 0.3\% = 17.8\%$$

12. The APT *required* (i.e., equilibrium) rate of return on the stock based on r_f and the factor betas is:

    required $E(r) = 6 + (1 \times 6) + (0.5 \times 2) + (0.75 \times 4) = 16\%$

    According to the equation for the return on the stock, the actually expected return on the stock is 15% (because the *expected* surprises on all factors are zero by definition). Because the actually expected return based on risk is less than the equilibrium return, we conclude that the stock is overpriced.

13. b. Since Portfolio X has $\beta = 1.0$, then X is the market portfolio and $E(R_M) = 16\%$. Using $E(R_M) = 16\%$ and $r_f = 8\%$, the expected return for portfolio Y is not consistent.

14. d.

15. c.

16. d.

17. c. Investors will take on as large a position as possible only if the mispricing opportunity is an arbitrage. Otherwise, considerations of risk and diversification will limit the position they attempt to take in the mispriced security.

18. d.

19. d.

20. The first two factors seem promising with respect to the likely impact on the firm's cost of capital. Both are macro factors that would elicit hedging demands across broad sectors of investors. The third factor, while important to Pork Products, is a poor choice for a multifactor SML because the price of hogs is of minor importance to most investors and is therefore highly unlikely to be a priced risk factor. Better choices would focus on variables that investors in aggregate might find more important to their welfare. Examples include: inflation uncertainty, short-term interest-rate risk, energy price risk, or exchange rate risk. The important point here is that, in specifying a multifactor SML, we not confuse risk factors that are important to a particular investor with factors that are important to investors in general; only the latter are likely to command a risk premium in the capital markets.

CHAPTER 11: THE EFFICIENT MARKET HYPOTHESIS

1.   The correlation coefficient between stock returns for two non-overlapping periods should be zero. If not, one could use returns from one period to predict returns in later periods and make abnormal profits.

2.   c.   This is a predictable pattern in returns which should not occur if the weak-form EMH is valid.

3.   c.   This is a classic filter rule which should not produce superior returns in an efficient market.

4.   b.   This is the definition of an efficient market.

5.   c.   The P/E ratio is public information and should not be predictive of abnormal security returns.

6.   b.   Semi-strong form efficiency implies that market prices reflect all *publicly available* information concerning past trading history as well as fundamental aspects of the firm.

7.   a.   The full price adjustment should occur just as the news about the dividend becomes publicly available.

8.   d.   If low P/E stocks tend to have positive abnormal returns, this would represent an unexploited profit opportunity that would provide evidence that investors are not using all available information to make profitable investments.

9.   c.   In an efficient market, no securities are consistently overpriced or underpriced. While some securities will turn out after any investment period to have provided positive alphas (i.e., risk-adjusted abnormal returns) and some negative alphas, these past returns are not predictive of future returns.

10.   c.   A random walk implies that stock price changes are unpredictable, using past price changes or any other data.

11. d.   A gradual adjustment to fundamental value would allow for the use of strategies based on past price movements in order to generate abnormal profits.

12. a.

13. b.   The contrarian technical analyst would notice that other investors have become deeply pessimistic about prices, and therefore would take this as a *bullish* indicator, reasoning that market sentiment swings too widely and that stock prices reflect a too-pessimistic view of the economy.

14. No. Microsoft's continuing profitability does not imply that stock market investors who purchased Microsoft shares after its success was already evident would have earned an exceptionally high return on their investments.

15. The question regarding market efficiency is whether investors can earn abnormal risk-adjusted profits. If the stock price run-up occurs when only insiders are aware of the coming dividend increase, then it is a violation of strong-form, but not semistrong-form, efficiency. If the public already knows of the increase, then it is a violation of semistrong-form efficiency.

16. While positive beta stocks respond well to favorable new information about the economy's progress through the business cycle, they should not show abnormal returns around already anticipated events. If a recovery, for example, is already anticipated, the actual recovery is not news. The stock price already should reflect the coming recovery.

17. a.   Consistent. Based on pure luck, half of all managers should beat the market in any year.

    b.   Inconsistent. This would be the basis of an "easy money" rule: simply invest with last year's best managers.

    c.   Consistent. In contrast to predictable returns, predictable *volatility* does not convey a means to earn abnormal returns.

    d.   Inconsistent. The abnormal performance ought to occur in January when earnings are announced.

    e.   Inconsistent. Reversals offer a means to earn easy money: just buy last week's losers.

18. Expected rates of return will differ because of differential risk premiums.

19. The return on the market is 8%. Therefore, the forecast monthly return for GM is:

    $$0.10\% + (1.1 \times 8\%) = 8.9\%$$

    GM's actual return was 7%, so the abnormal return was −1.9%.

20. a. Based on broad market trends, the CAPM indicates that AmbChaser stock should have increased by: $1.0\% + 2.0(1.5\% - 1.0\%) = 2.0\%$
    Its firm-specific (nonsystematic) return due to the lawsuit is $1 million per $100 million initial equity, or 1%. Therefore, the total return should be 3%. (It is assumed here that the outcome of the lawsuit had a zero expected value.)

    b. If the settlement was expected to be $2 million, then the actual settlement was a "$1 million disappointment," and so the firm-specific return would be −1%, for a total return of $2\% - 1\% = 1\%$.

21. Given market performance, predicted returns on the two stocks would be:

    Apex: $0.2\% + (1.4 \times 3\%) = 4.4\%$

    Bpex: $-0.1\% + (0.6 \times 3\%) = 1.7\%$

    Apex underperformed this prediction; Bpex outperformed the prediction. We conclude that Bpex won the lawsuit.

22. a. $E(r_M) = 12\%$, $r_f = 4\%$ and $\beta = 0.5$

    Therefore, the expected rate of return is:

    $$4\% + 0.5(12\% - 4\%) = 8\%$$

    If the stock is fairly priced, then $E(r) = 8\%$.

    b. If r_M falls short of your expectation by 2% (that is, $10\% - 12\%$) then you would expect the return for Changing Fortunes Industries to fall short of your original expectation by: $\beta \times 2\% = 1\%$
    Therefore, you would forecast a "revised" expectation for Changing Fortunes of: $8\% - 1\% = 7\%$

    c. Given a market return of 10%, you would forecast a return for Changing Fortunes of 7%. The actual return is 10%. Therefore, the surprise due to firm-specific factors is $10\% - 7\% = 3\%$ which we attribute to the settlement. Because the firm is initially worth $100 million, the surprise amount of the settlement is 3% of $100 million, or $3 million, implying that the prior expectation for the settlement was only $2 million.

23. Implicit in the dollar-cost averaging strategy is the notion that stock prices fluctuate around a "normal" level. Otherwise, there is no meaning to statements such as: "when the price is high." How do we know, for example, whether a price of $25 today will turn out to be viewed as high or low compared to the stock price six months from now?

24. No. The value of dividend predictability would be already reflected in the stock price.

25. The market responds positively to *new* news. If the eventual recovery is anticipated, then the recovery is already reflected in stock prices. Only a better-than-expected recovery should affect stock prices.

26. Over the long haul, there is an expected upward drift in stock prices based on their fair expected rates of return. The fair expected return over any single day is very small (e.g., 12% per year is only about 0.03% per day), so that on any day the price is virtually equally likely to rise or fall. However, over longer periods, the small expected daily returns accumulate, and upward moves are indeed more likely than downward ones.

27. Buy. In your view, the firm is not as bad as everyone else believes it to be. Therefore, you view the firm as undervalued by the market. You are less pessimistic about the firm's prospects than the beliefs built into the stock price.

28. The negative abnormal returns (downward drift in CAR) just prior to stock purchases suggest that insiders deferred their purchases until *after* bad news was released to the public. This is evidence of valuable inside information. The positive abnormal returns after purchase suggest insider purchases in anticipation of good news. The analysis is symmetric for insider sales.

29. Here we need a two-factor model relating Ford's return to those of both the broad market and the auto industry. If we call r_I the industry return, then we would first estimate parameters a,b,c in the following regression:

$$r_{FORD} = a + br_M + cr_I + e$$

Given these estimates we would calculate Ford's firm-specific return as:

$$r_{FORD} - [a + br_M + cr_I + e]$$

This estimate of firm-specific news would measure the market's assessment of the potential profitability of Ford's new model.

30. The market may have anticipated even greater earnings. *Compared to prior expectations,* the announcement was a disappointment.

31. a. Some empirical evidence that supports the EMH is:

    (i) professional money managers do not typically earn higher returns than comparable risk, passive index strategies;

    (ii) event studies typically show that stocks respond immediately to the public release of relevant news;

    (iii) most tests of technical analysis find that it is difficult to identify price trends that can be exploited to earn superior risk-adjusted investment returns.

    b. Some evidence that is difficult to reconcile with the EMH concerns simple portfolio strategies that apparently would have provided high risk-adjusted returns in the past. Some examples of portfolios with attractive historical returns:

    (i) low P/E stocks;

    (ii) high book-to-market ratio stocks;

    (iii) small firms in January;

    (iv) firms with very poor stock price performance in the last few months.

    Other evidence concerns post-earnings-announcement stock price drift and intermediate-term price momentum.

    c. An investor might choose not to index even if markets are efficient because he or she may want to tailor a portfolio to specific tax considerations or to specific risk management issues, for example, the need to hedge (or at least not add to) exposure to a particular source of risk (e.g., industry exposure).

32. a. The efficient market hypothesis (EMH) states that a market is efficient if security prices immediately and fully reflect all available relevant information. If the market fully reflects information, the knowledge of that information would not allow an investor to profit from the information because stock prices already incorporate the information.

    i. The *weak form* of the EMH asserts that stock prices reflect all the information that can be derived by examining market trading data such as the history of past prices and trading volume.

    A strong body of evidence supports weak-form efficiency in the major U.S. securities markets. For example, test results suggest that technical trading rules do not produce superior returns after adjusting for transaction costs and taxes.

ii. The *semistrong form* states that a firm's stock price reflects all publicly available information about a firm's prospects. Examples of publicly available information are company annual reports and investment advisory data.

Evidence strongly supports the notion of semistrong efficiency, but occasional studies (e.g., those identifying market anomalies such as the small-firm-in-January or book-to-market effects) and events (such as the stock market crash of October 19, 1987) are inconsistent with this form of market efficiency. However, there is a question concerning the extent to which these "anomalies" result from data mining.

iii. The *strong form* of the EMH holds that current market prices reflect *all* information (whether publicly available or privately held) that can be relevant to the valuation of the firm.

Empirical evidence suggests that strong-form efficiency does not hold. If this form were correct, prices would fully reflect all information. Therefore even insiders could not earn excess returns. But the evidence is that corporate officers do have access to pertinent information long enough before public release to enable them to profit from trading on this information.

b. i. *Technical analysis* involves the search for recurrent and predictable patterns in stock prices in order to enhance returns. The EMH implies that technical analysis is without value. If past prices contain no useful information for predicting future prices, there is no point in following any technical trading rule.

ii. *Fundamental analysis* uses earnings and dividend prospects of the firm, expectations of future interest rates, and risk evaluation of the firm to determine proper stock prices. The EMH predicts that most fundamental analysis is doomed to failure. According to semistrong-form efficiency, no investor can earn excess returns from trading rules based on publicly available information. Only analysts with unique insight achieve superior returns.

In summary, the EMH holds that the market appears to adjust so quickly to information about both individual stocks and the economy as a whole that no technique of selecting a portfolio using either technical or fundamental analysis can consistently outperform a strategy of simply buying and holding a diversified portfolio of securities, such as those comprising the popular market indexes.

c. Portfolio managers have several roles and responsibilities even in perfectly efficient markets. The most important responsibility is to identify the risk/return objectives for a portfolio given the investor's constraints. In an efficient market, portfolio managers are responsible for tailoring the portfolio to meet the investor's needs, rather than to beat the market, which requires identifying the client's return requirements and risk tolerance. Rational portfolio management also requires examining the investor's constraints, including liquidity, time horizon, laws and regulations, taxes, and unique preferences and circumstances such as age and employment.

33. a. The earnings (and dividend) growth rate of growth stocks may be consistently overestimated by investors. Investors may extrapolate recent growth too far into the future and thereby downplay the inevitable slowdown. At any given time, growth stocks are likely to revert to (lower) mean returns and value stocks are likely to revert to (higher) mean returns, often over an extended future time horizon.

   b. In efficient markets, the current prices of stocks already reflect all known relevant information. In this situation, growth stocks and value stocks provide the same risk-adjusted expected return.

CHAPTER 12: BEHAVIORAL FINANCE
AND TECHNICAL ANALYSIS

1. i. Mental accounting is best illustrated by Statement #3. Sampson's requirement that his income needs be met via interest income and stock dividends is an example of mental accounting. Mental accounting holds that investors segregate funds into mental accounts (e.g., dividends and capital gains), maintain a set of separate mental accounts, and do not combine outcomes; a loss in one account is treated separately from a loss in another account. Mental accounting leads to an investor preference for dividends over capital gains and to an inability or failure to consider total return.

    ii. Overconfidence (illusion of control) is best illustrated by Statement #6. Sampson's desire to select investments that are inconsistent with his overall strategy indicates overconfidence. Overconfident individuals often exhibit risk-seeking behavior. People are also more confident in the validity of their conclusions than is justified by their success rate. Causes of overconfidence include the illusion of control, self-enhancement tendencies, insensitivity to predictive accuracy, and misconceptions of chance processes.

    iii. Reference dependence is best illustrated by Statement #5. Sampson's desire to retain poor performing investments and to take quick profits on successful investments suggests reference dependence. Reference dependence holds that investment decisions are critically dependent on the decision-maker's reference point. In this case, the reference point is the original purchase price. Alternatives are evaluated not in terms of final outcomes but rather in terms of gains and losses relative to this reference point. Thus, preferences are susceptible to manipulation simply by changing the reference point.

2. a. Frost's statement is an example of reference dependence. His inclination to sell the international investments once prices return to the original cost depends not only on the terminal wealth value, but also on where he is now, that is, his reference point. This reference point, which is below the original cost, has become a critical factor in Frost's decision.

    In standard finance, alternatives are evaluated in terms of terminal wealth values or final outcomes, not in terms of gains and losses relative to some reference point such as original cost.

b. Frost's statement is an example of susceptibility to cognitive error, in at least two ways. First, he is displaying the behavioral flaw of overconfidence. He likely is more confident about the validity of his conclusion than is justified by his rate of success. He is very confident that the past performance of Country XYZ indicates future performance. Behavioral investors could, and often do, conclude that a five-year record is ample evidence to suggest future performance. Second, by choosing to invest in the securities of only Country XYZ, Frost is also exemplifying the behavioral finance phenomenon of asset segregation. That is, he is evaluating Country XYZ investment in terms of its anticipated gains or losses viewed in isolation.

Individuals are typically more confident about the validity of their conclusions than is justified by their success rate or by the principles of standard finance, especially with regard to relevant time horizons. In standard finance, investors know that five years of returns on Country XYZ securities relative to all other markets provide little information about future performance. A standard finance investor would not be fooled by this "law of small numbers." In standard finance, investors evaluate performance in portfolio terms, in this case defined by combining the Country XYZ holding with all other securities held. Investments in Country XYZ, like all other potential investments, should be evaluated in terms of the anticipated contribution to the risk- reward profile of the entire portfolio.

c. Frost's statement is an example of mental accounting. Mental accounting holds that investors segregate money into mental accounts (e.g., safe versus speculative), maintain a set of separate mental accounts, and do not combine outcomes; a loss in one account is treated separately from a loss in another account. One manifestation of mental accounting, in which Frost is engaging, is building a portfolio as a pyramid of assets, layer by layer, with the retirement account representing a layer separate from the "speculative" fund. Each layer is associated with different goals and attitudes toward risk. He is more risk averse with respect to the retirement account than he is with respect to the "speculative" fund account. The money in the retirement account is a down side protection layer, designed to avoid future poverty. The money in the "speculative" fund account is the upside potential layer, designed for a chance at being rich.

In standard finance, decisions consider the risk and return profile of the entire portfolio rather than anticipated gains or losses on any particular account, investment, or class of investments. Alternatives should be considered in terms of final outcomes in a total portfolio context rather than in terms of contributions to a "safe" or a "speculative" account. Standard finance investors seek to maximize the mean-variance structure of the portfolio as a whole and consider covariances between assets as they construct their portfolios. Standard finance investors have consistent attitudes toward risk across their entire portfolio.

3.   a.   *Illusion of knowledge*: Maclin believes he is an expert on, and can make accurate forecasts about, the real estate market solely because he has studied housing market data on the Internet. He may have access to a large amount of real estate-related information, but he may not understand how to analyze the information nor have the ability to apply it to a proposed investment.

Overconfidence: Overconfidence causes us to misinterpret the accuracy of our information and our skill in analyzing it. Maclin has assumed that the information he collected on the internet is accurate without attempting to verify it or consult other sources. He also assumes he has skill in evaluating and analyzing the real estate-related information he has collected, although there is no information in the question that suggests he possesses such ability.

   b.   *Reference point*: Maclin's reference point for his bond position is the purchase price, as evidenced by the fact that he will not sell a position for less than he paid for it. This fixation on a reference point, and the subsequent waiting for the price of the security to move above that reference point before selling the security, prevents Maclin from undertaking a risk/return-based analysis of his portfolio position.

   c.   *Familiarity*: Maclin is evaluating his holding of company stock based on his familiarity with the company rather than on sound investment and portfolio principles. Company employees, because of this familiarity, may have a distorted perception of their own company, assuming a "good company" will also be a good investment. Irrational investors believe an investment in a company with which they are familiar will produce higher returns and have less risk than non-familiar investments.

Representativeness: Maclin is confusing his company (which may well be a good company) with the company's stock (which may or may not be an appropriate holding for his portfolio and/or a good investment) and its future performance. This can result in employees' overweighting their company stock, resulting in an under-diversified portfolio

4.   a.   The behavioral finance principle of biased expectations/overconfidence is most consistent with the investor's first statement. Petrie stock provides a level of confidence and comfort for the investor because of the circumstances in which she acquired the stock and her recent history with the returns and income from the stock. However, the investor exhibits overconfidence in the stock given the needs of the Trust and the brevity of the recent performance history. Maintaining a 15 percent position in a single stock is inconsistent with the overall strategy of the Trust, and the investor's level of confidence should reflect the stock's overall record, not just the past two years.

b. The behavioral finance principle of mental accounting is most consistent with the investor's second statement. The investor has segregated the monies distributed from the Trust into two "accounts": the returns the Trust receives from the Petrie stock, and the remaining funds that the Trust receives for her benefit. She is maintaining a separate set of mental accounts with regard to the total funds distributed. The investor's "specific uses" should be viewed in the overall context of the spending needs of the Trust and should consider the risk and return profile of the entire Trust.

5. i. *Overconfidence (Biased Expectations and Illusion of Control)*: Pierce is basing her investment strategy for supporting her parents on her confidence in the economic forecasts. This is a cognitive error reflecting overconfidence in the form of both biased expectations and an illusion of control. Pierce is likely more confident in the validity of those forecasts than is justified by the accuracy of prior forecasts. Analysts' consensus forecasts have proven routinely and widely inaccurate. Pierce also appears to be overly confident that the recent performance of the Pogo Island economy is a good indicator of future performance. Behavioral investors often conclude that a short track record is ample evidence to suggest future performance.

Standard finance investors understand that individuals typically have greater confidence in the validity of their conclusions than is justified by their success rate. The calibration paradigm, which compares confidence to predictive ability, suggests that there is significantly lower probability of success than the confidence levels reported by individuals. In addition, standard finance investors know that recent performance provides little information about future performance and are not deceived by this "law of small numbers."

ii. *Loss Aversion (Risk Seeking)*: Pierce is exhibiting *risk aversion* in deciding to sell the Core Bond Fund despite its gains and favorable prospects. She prefers a certain gain over a possibly larger gain coupled with a smaller chance of a loss. Pierce is exhibiting *loss aversion* (risk seeking) by holding the High Yield Bond Fund despite its uncertain prospects. She prefers the modest possibility of recovery coupled with the chance of a larger loss over a certain loss. People tend to exhibit risk seeking, rather than risk aversion, behavior when the probability of loss is large. There is considerable evidence indicating that risk aversion holds for gains and risk seeking behavior holds for losses, and that attitudes toward risk vary depending on particular goals and circumstances.

Standard finance investors are consistently risk averse, and systematically prefer a certain outcome over a gamble with the same expected value. Such investors also take a symmetrical view of gains and losses of the same magnitude, and their sensitivity (aversion) to changes in value is not a function of a specified value reference point.

iii. *Reference Dependence:* Pierce's inclination to sell her Small Company Fund once it returns to her original cost is an example of *reference dependence*. Her sell decision is predicated on the current value as related to original cost, her reference point. Her decision does not consider any analysis of expected terminal value or the impact of this sale on her total portfolio. This reference point of original cost has become a critical but inappropriate factor in Pierce's decision.

In standard finance, alternatives are evaluated in terms of terminal wealth values or final outcomes, not in terms of gains and losses relative to a reference point such as original cost. Standard finance investors also consider the risk and return profile of the entire portfolio rather than anticipated gains or losses on any particular investment or asset class.

6. $$\text{Trin} = \frac{\text{Volume declining} / \text{Number declining}}{\text{Volume advancing} / \text{Number advancing}} = \frac{354{,}280 / 950}{1{,}256{,}091 / 2{,}352} = 0.698$$

    This trin ratio, which is below 1.0, would be taken as a bullish signal.

7. <u>Breadth</u>:

Advances	Declines	Net Advances
2,352	950	1,402

    Breadth is positive. This is a bullish signal (although no one would actually use a one-day measure as in this example).

8. This exercise is left to the student.

9. The confidence index increases from $(8\%/9\%) = 0.889$ to $(9\%/10\%) = 0.900$. This indicates slightly higher confidence. But the real reason for the increase in the index is the expectation of higher inflation, not higher confidence about the economy.

10. At the beginning of the period, the price of Computers, Inc. divided by the industry index was 0.39; by the end of the period, the ratio had increased to 0.50. As the ratio increased over the period, it appears that Computers, Inc. outperformed other firms in its industry. The overall trend, therefore, indicates relative strength, although some fluctuation existed during the period, with the ratio falling to a low point of 0.33 on day 19.

11. Five day moving averages:

Days 1 – 5: (19.63 + 20 + 20.5 + 22 + 21.13) / 5 = 20.65
Days 2 – 6 = 21.13
Days 3 – 7 = 21.50
Days 4 – 8 = 21.90
Days 5 – 9 = 22.13
Days 6 – 10 = 22.68
Days 7 – 11 = 23.18
Days 8 – 12 = 23.45 ← Sell signal (day 12 price < moving average)
Days 9 – 13 = 23.38
Days 10 – 14 = 23.15
Days 11 – 15 = 22.50
Days 12 – 16 = 21.65
Days 13 – 17 = 20.95
Days 14 – 18 = 20.28
Days 15 – 19 = 19.38
Days 16 – 20 = 19.05
Days 17 – 21 = 18.93 ← Buy signal (day 21 price > moving average)
Days 18 – 22 = 19.28
Days 19 – 23 = 19.93
Days 20 – 24 = 21.05
Days 21 – 25 = 22.05
Days 22 – 26 = 23.18
Days 23 – 27 = 24.13
Days 24 – 28 = 25.13
Days 25 – 29 = 26.00
Days 26 – 30 = 26.80
Days 27 – 31 = 27.45
Days 28 – 32 = 27.80
Days 29 – 33 = 27.90 ← Sell signal (day 33 price < moving average)
Days 30 – 34 = 28.20
Days 31 – 35 = 28.45
Days 32 – 36 = 28.65
Days 33 – 37 = 29.05
Days 34 – 38 = 29.25
Days 35 – 39 = 29.00
Days 36 – 40 = 28.75

12. This pattern shows a lack of breadth. Even though the index is up, more stocks
declined than advanced, which indicates a "lack of broad-based support" for the
rise in the index.

13.

Day	Advances	Declines	Net Advances	Cumulative Breadth
1	906	704	202	202
2	653	986	-333	-131
3	721	789	- 68	-199
4	503	968	-465	-664
5	497	1,095	-598	-1,262
6	970	702	268	-994
7	1,002	609	393	-601
8	903	722	181	-420
9	850	748	102	-318
10	766	766	0	-318

The signal is bearish as cumulative breadth is negative; however, the negative number is declining in magnitude, indicative of improvement. Perhaps the worst of the bear market has passed.

14. $$\text{Trin} = \frac{\text{Volume declining/Number declining}}{\text{Volume advancing/Number advancing}} = \frac{240 \text{ million} / 704}{330 \text{ million} / 906} = 0.936$$

This is a slightly bullish indicator, with average volume in advancing issues a bit greater than average volume in declining issues.

15. $$\text{Confidence Index} = \frac{\text{Yield on top-rated corporate bonds}}{\text{Yield on intermediate-grade corporate bonds}}$$

This year: Confidence Index = (8%/10.5%) = 0.762

Last year: Confidence Index = (8.5%/10%) = 0.850

Thus, the confidence index is decreasing.

16. [Note: In order to create the 26-week moving average for the S&P 500, we first converted the weekly returns to weekly index values, using a base of 100 for the week prior to the first week of the data set. The graph on the next page shows the resulting S&P 500 values and the 26-week moving average, beginning with the 26th week of the data set.]

a. The graph on the next page summarizes the data for the 26-week moving average. The graph also shows the values of the S&P 500 index.

S&P500 Index - 26-Week Moving Average

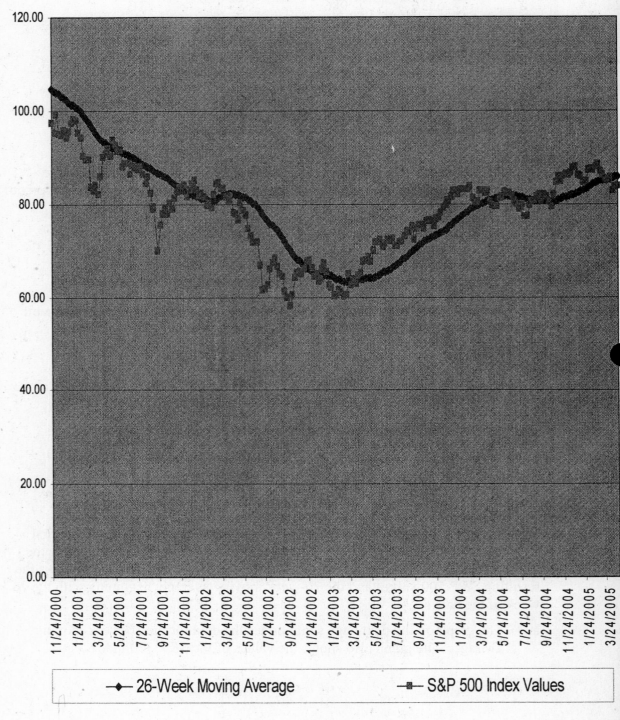

b. The S&P 500 crosses through its moving average from below fourteen times, as indicated in the table below. The index increases seven times in weeks following a cross-through and decreases seven times.

Date of cross-through	Direction of S&P 500 in subsequent week
05/18/01	Decrease
06/08/01	Decrease
12/07/01	Decrease
12/21/01	Increase
03/01/02	Increase
11/22/02	Increase
01/03/03	Increase
03/21/03	Decrease
04/17/03	Increase
06/10/04	Decrease
09/03/04	Increase
10/01/04	Decrease
10/29/04	Increase
04/08/05	Decrease

c. The S&P 500 crosses through its moving average from above fourteen times, as indicated in the table below. The index increases nine times in weeks following a cross-through and decreases five times.

Date of cross-through	Direction of S&P 500 in subsequent week
06/01/01	Increase
06/15/01	Increase
12/14/01	Increase
02/08/02	Increase
04/05/02	Decrease
12/13/02	Increase
01/24/03	Decrease
03/28/03	Increase
04/30/04	Decrease
07/02/04	Decrease
09/24/04	Increase
10/15/04	Decrease
03/24/05	Increase
04/15/05	Increase

d.   When the index crosses through its moving average from below, as in part (b) above, this is regarded as a bullish signal. However, in our sample, the index is as likely to increase as it is to decrease following such a signal. When the index crosses through its moving average from above, as in part (c), this is regarded as a bearish signal. In our sample, contrary to the bearish signal, the index is actually more likely to increase than it is to decrease following such a signal.

17.   [Note: In order to create the relative strength measure, we first converted the weekly returns for the Fidelity Banking Fund and for the S&P 500 to weekly index values, using a base of 100 for the week prior to the first week of the data set. The graph on the next page shows the resulting Fidelity Banking Fund values and the S&P 500 values, along with the Relative Strength measure (multiplied by 100). The graph on the following page shows the percentage change in the Relative Strength measure over 5-week intervals.]

a.   The graphs on the next two pages summarize the relative strength data for the Fidelity Banking Fund.

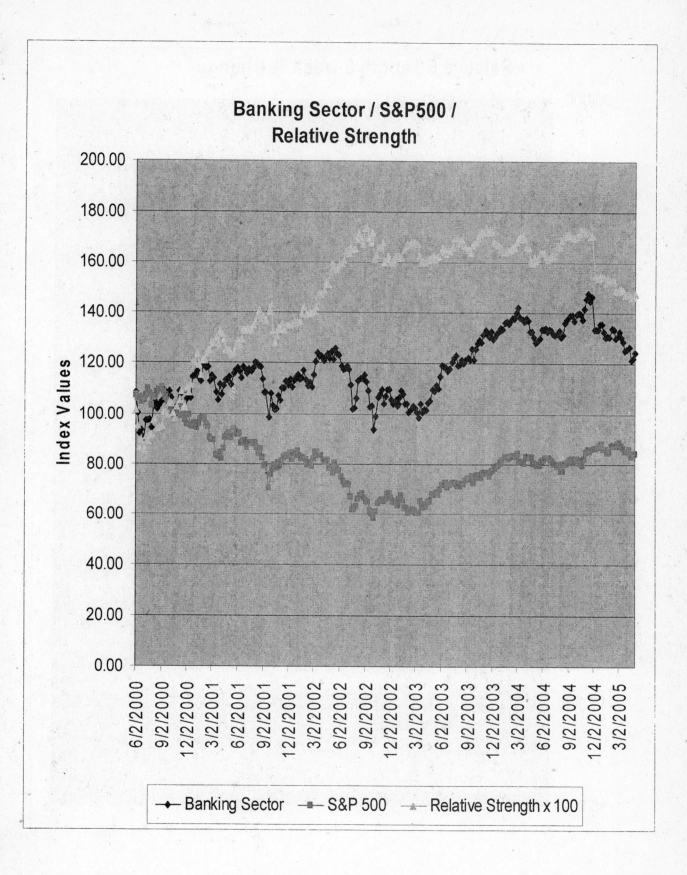

Banking Sector / S&P500 / Relative Strength

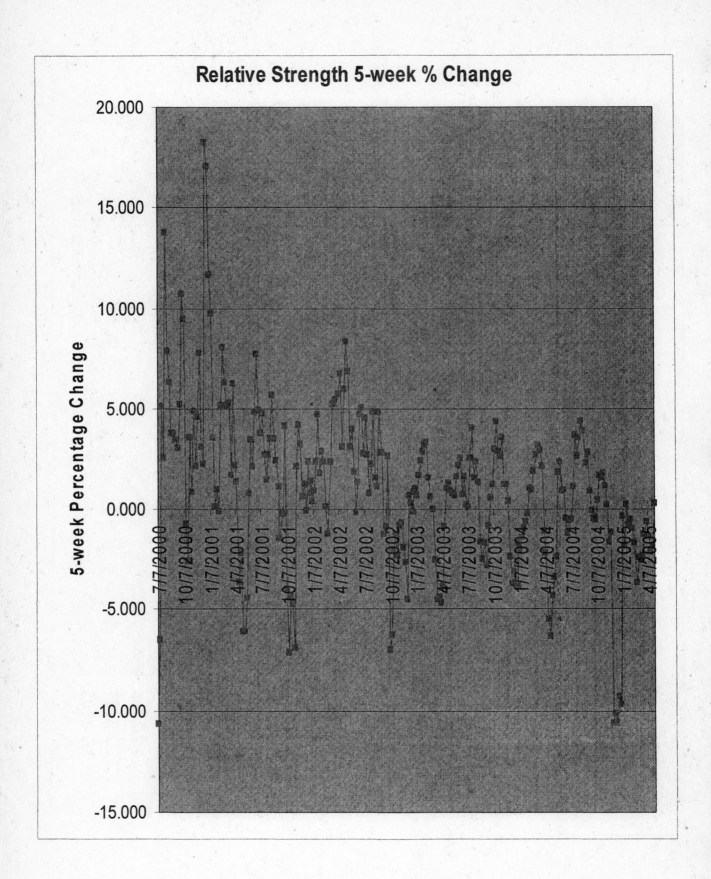

Relative Strength 5-week % Change

b. Over five-week intervals, relative strength increased by more than 5% twenty-nine times, as indicated in the table below. The Fidelity Banking Fund underperformed the S&P 500 index eighteen times and outperformed the S&P 500 index eleven times in weeks following an increase of more than 5%.

Date of Increase	Performance of Banking Fund in subsequent week
07/21/00	Outperformed
08/04/00	Outperformed
08/11/00	Underperformed
08/18/00	Outperformed
09/22/00	Outperformed
09/29/00	Underperformed
10/06/00	Underperformed
12/01/00	Underperformed
12/22/00	Underperformed
12/29/00	Outperformed
01/05/01	Underperformed
01/12/01	Underperformed
02/16/01	Underperformed
02/23/01	Outperformed
03/02/01	Underperformed
03/09/01	Outperformed
03/16/01	Underperformed
03/30/01	Underperformed
06/22/01	Underperformed
08/17/01	Underperformed
03/15/02	Outperformed
03/22/02	Underperformed
03/28/02	Outperformed
04/05/02	Outperformed
04/12/02	Underperformed
04/26/02	Outperformed
05/03/02	Underperformed
05/10/02	Underperformed
06/28/02	Underperformed

c. Over five-week intervals, relative strength decreases by more than 5% fifteen times, as indicated in the table below. The Fidelity Banking Fund underperformed the S&P 500 index six times and outperformed the S&P 500 index nine times in weeks following a decrease of more than 5%.

Date of Decrease	Performance of Banking Fund in subsequent week
07/07/00	Underperformed
07/14/00	Outperformed
05/04/01	Underperformed
05/11/01	Outperformed
10/12/01	Outperformed
11/02/01	Outperformed
10/04/02	Outperformed
10/11/02	Outperformed
04/16/04	Underperformed
04/23/04	Outperformed
12/03/04	Outperformed
12/10/04	Underperformed
12/17/04	Outperformed
12/23/04	Underperformed
12/31/04	Underperformed

d. An increase in relative strength, as in part (b) above, is regarded as a bullish signal. However, in our sample, the Fidelity Banking Fund is more likely to under perform the S&P 500 index than it is to outperform the index following such a signal. A decrease in relative strength, as in part (c), is regarded as a bearish signal. In our sample, contrary to the bearish signal, the Fidelity Banking Fund is actually more likely to outperform the index increase than it is to under perform following such a signal.

CHAPTER 13: EMPIRICAL EVIDENCE ON SECURITY RETURNS

Note: For end-of-chapter problems in Chapter 13, the focus is on the estimation *procedure*. To keep the exercise feasible, the sample was limited to returns on nine stocks plus a market index and a second factor over a period of 12 years. The data were generated to conform to a two-factor CAPM so that actual rates of return equal CAPM expectations plus random noise, and the true intercept of the SCL is zero for all stocks. The exercise will provide a feel for the pitfalls of verifying social-science models. However, due to the small size of the sample, results are not always consistent with the findings of other studies are reported in the chapter.

1.   Using the regression feature of Excel with the data presented in the text, the first-pass (SCL) estimation results are:

Stock:	A	B	C	D	E	F	G	H	I
R Square	0.06	0.06	0.06	0.37	0.17	0.59	0.06	0.67	0.70
Observations	12	12	12	12	12	12	12	12	12
Alpha	9.00	-0.63	-0.64	-5.05	0.73	-4.53	5.94	-2.41	5.92
Beta	-0.47	0.59	0.42	1.38	0.90	1.78	0.66	1.91	2.08
t-Alpha	0.73	-0.04	-0.06	-0.41	0.05	-0.45	0.33	-0.27	0.64
t-Beta	-0.81	0.78	0.78	2.42	1.42	3.83	0.78	4.51	4.81

2.   The hypotheses for the second-pass regression for the SML are:
- The intercept is zero; and,
- The slope is equal to the average return on the index portfolio.

3.   The second-pass data from first-pass (SCL) estimates are:

	Average Excess Return	Beta
A	5.18	-0.47
B	4.19	0.59
C	2.75	0.42
D	6.15	1.38
E	8.05	0.90
F	9.90	1.78
G	11.32	0.66
H	13.11	1.91
I	22.83	2.08
M	8.12	

The second-pass regression yields:

Regression Statistics	
Multiple R	0.7074
R Square	0.5004
Adjusted R Square	0.4291
Standard Error	4.6234
Observations	9

	Coefficients	Standard Error	t Statistic for β=0	t Statistic for β=8.12
Intercept	3.92	2.54	1.54	
Slope	5.21	1.97	2.65	-1.48

4. As we saw in the chapter, the intercept is too high (3.92% per year instead of 0) and the slope is too flat (5.21% instead of a predicted value equal to the sample-average risk premium: $r_M - r_f = 8.12\%$). The intercept is not significantly greater than zero (the t-statistic is less than 2) and the slope is not significantly different from its theoretical value (the t-statistic for this hypothesis is −1.48). This lack of statistical significance is probably due to the small size of the sample.

5. Arranging the securities in three portfolios based on betas from the SCL estimates, the first pass input data are:

Year	ABC	DEG	FHI
1	15.05	25.86	56.69
2	-16.76	-29.74	-50.85
3	19.67	-5.68	8.98
4	-15.83	-2.58	35.41
5	47.18	37.70	-3.25
6	-2.26	53.86	75.44
7	-18.67	15.32	12.50
8	-6.35	36.33	32.12
9	7.85	14.08	50.42
10	21.41	12.66	52.14
11	-2.53	-50.71	-66.12
12	-0.30	-4.99	-20.10
Average	4.04	8.51	15.28
Std. Dev.	19.30	29.47	43.96

The first-pass (SCL) estimates are:

	ABC	DEG	FHI
R Square	0.04	0.48	0.82
Observations	12	12	12
Alpha	2.58	0.54	-0.34
Beta	0.18	0.98	1.92
t-Alpha	0.42	0.08	-0.06
t-Beta	0.62	3.02	6.83

Grouping into portfolios has improved the SCL estimates as is evident from the higher R-square for Portfolio DEG and Portfolio FHI. This means that the beta (slope) is measured with greater precision, reducing the error-in-measurement problem at the expense of leaving fewer observations for the second pass.

The inputs for the second pass regression are:

	Average Excess Return	Beta
ABC	4.04	0.18
DEH	8.51	0.98
FGI	15.28	1.92
M	8.12	

The second-pass estimates are:

Regression Statistics	
Multiple R	0.9975
R Square	0.9949
Adjusted R Square	0.9899
Standard Error	0.5693
Observations	3

	Coefficients	Standard Error	t Statistic for $\beta=0$	t Statistic for $\beta=8.12$
Intercept	2.62	0.58	4.55	
Slope	6.47	0.46	14.03	-3.58

Despite the decease in the intercept and the increase in slope, the intercept is now significantly positive, and the slope is significantly less than the hypothesized value by more than three times the standard error.

6. Roll's critique suggests that the problem begins with the market index, which is not the theoretical portfolio against which the second pass regression should hold. Hence, even if the relationship is valid with respect to the true (unknown) index, we may not find it. As a result, the second pass relationship may be meaningless.

7.

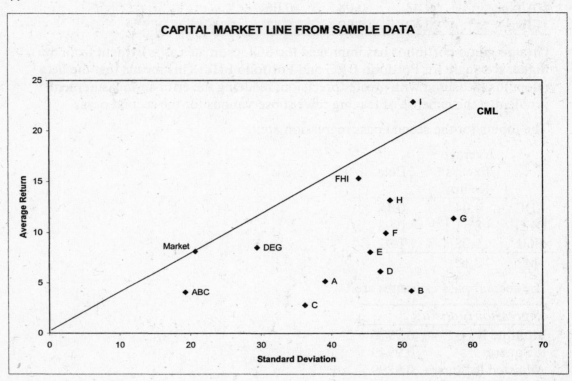

Except for Stock I, which realized an extremely positive surprise, the CML shows that the index dominates all other securities, and the three portfolios dominate all individual stocks. The power of diversification is evident despite the very small sample size.

8. The first-pass (SCL) regression results are summarized below:

	A	B	C	D	E	F	G	H	I
R-Square	0.07	0.36	0.11	0.44	0.24	0.84	0.12	0.68	0.71
Observations	12	12	12	12	12	12	12	12	12
Intercept	9.19	-1.89	-1.00	-4.48	0.17	-3.47	5.32	-2.64	5.66
Beta M	-0.47	0.58	0.41	1.39	0.89	1.79	0.65	1.91	2.08
Beta F	-0.35	2.33	0.67	-1.05	1.03	-1.95	1.15	0.43	0.48
t- Intercept	0.71	-0.13	-0.08	-0.37	0.01	-0.52	0.29	-0.28	0.59
t-Beta M	-0.77	0.87	0.75	2.46	1.40	5.80	0.75	4.35	4.65
t-Beta F	-0.34	2.06	0.71	-1.08	0.94	-3.69	0.77	0.57	0.63

9. The hypotheses for the second-pass regression for the two-factor SML are:
- The intercept is zero;
- The market-index slope coefficient equals the market-index average return; and,
- The factor slope coefficient equals the average return on the factor.
  (Note that the first two hypotheses are the same as those for the single factor model.)

10. The inputs for the second pass regression are:

	Average Excess Return	Beta M	Beta F
A	5.18	-0.47	-0.35
B	4.19	0.58	2.33
C	2.75	0.41	0.67
D	6.15	1.39	-1.05
E	8.05	0.89	1.03
F	9.90	1.79	-1.95
G	11.32	0.65	1.15
H	13.11	1.91	0.43
I	22.83	2.08	0.48
M	8.12		
F	0.60		

The second-pass regression yields:

Regression Statistics	
Multiple R	0.7234
R Square	0.5233
Adjusted R Square	0.3644
Standard Error	4.8786
Observations	9

	Coefficients	Standard Error	t Statistic for $\beta=0$	t Statistic for $\beta=8.12$	t Statistic for $\beta=0.6$
Intercept	3.35	2.88	1.16		
Beta M	5.53	2.16	2.56	-1.20	
Beta F	0.80	1.42	0.56		0.14

These results are slightly better than those for the single factor test; that is, the intercept is smaller and the slope on M is slightly greater. We cannot expect a great improvement since the factor we added does not appear to carry a large risk premium (average excess return is less than 1%), and its effect on mean returns is therefore small. The data do not reject the second factor because the slope is close to the average excess return and the difference is less than one standard error. However, with this sample size, the power of this test is extremely low.

11. When we use the actual factor, we implicitly assume that investors can perfectly replicate it, that is, they can invest in a portfolio that is perfectly correlated with the factor. When this is not possible, one cannot expect the CAPM equation (the second pass regression) to hold. Investors can use a replicating portfolio (a proxy for the factor) that maximizes the correlation with the factor. The CAPM equation is then expected to hold with respect to the proxy portfolio.

Using the bordered covariance matrix of the nine stocks and the Excel Solver we produce a proxy portfolio for factor F, denoted PF. To preserve the scale, we include constraints that require the nine weights to be in the range of [-1,1] and that the mean equal the factor mean of 0.60%. The resultant weights for the proxy and period returns are:

Proxy Portfolio for Factor F (PF)

	Weights on Universe Stocks	Year	PF Holding Period Returns
A	-0.14	1	-33.51
B	1.00	2	62.78
C	0.95	3	9.87
D	-0.35	4	-153.56
E	0.16	5	200.76
F	-1.00	6	-36.62
G	0.13	7	-74.34
H	0.19	8	-10.84
I	0.06	9	28.11
		10	59.51
		11	-59.15
		12	14.22
		Average	0.60

This proxy (PF) has an R-square with the actual factor of 0.80.

We next perform the first pass regressions for the two factor model using PF instead of P:

	A	B	C	D	E	F	G	H	I
R-square	0.08	0.55	0.20	0.43	0.33	0.88	0.16	0.71	0.72
Observations	12	12	12	12	12	12	12	12	12
Intercept	9.28	-2.53	-1.35	-4.45	-0.23	-3.20	4.99	-2.92	5.54
Beta M	-0.50	0.80	0.49	1.32	1.00	1.64	0.76	1.97	2.12
Beta PF	-0.06	0.42	0.16	-0.13	0.21	-0.29	0.21	0.11	0.08
t- Intercept	0.72	-0.21	-0.12	-0.36	-0.02	-0.55	0.27	-0.33	0.58
t-Beta M	-0.83	1.43	0.94	2.29	1.66	6.00	0.90	4.67	4.77
t-Beta PF	-0.44	3.16	1.25	-0.97	1.47	-4.52	1.03	1.13	0.78

Note that the betas of the nine stocks on M and the proxy (PF) are different from those in the first pass when we use the actual proxy.

The first-pass regression for the two-factor model with the proxy yields:

	Average Excess Return	Beta M	Beta PF
A	5.18	-0.50	-0.06
B	4.19	0.80	0.42
C	2.75	0.49	0.16
D	6.15	1.32	-0.13
E	8.05	1.00	0.21
F	9.90	1.64	-0.29
G	11.32	0.76	0.21
H	13.11	1.97	0.11
I	22.83	2.12	0.08
M	8.12		
PF	0.6		

The second-pass regression yields:

Regression Statistics	
Multiple R	0.71
R Square	0.51
Adjusted R Square	0.35
Standard Error	4.95
Observations	9

	Coefficients	Standard Error	t Statistic for $\beta=0$	t Statistic for $\beta=8.12$	t Statistic for $\beta=0.6$
Intercept	3.50	2.99	1.17		
Beta M	5.39	2.18	2.48	-1.25	
Beta PF	0.26	8.36	0.03		-0.04

We can see that the results are similar to, but slightly inferior to, those with the actual factor, since the intercept is larger and the slope coefficient smaller. Note also that we use here an in-sample test rather than tests with future returns, which is more forgiving than an out-of-sample test.

12. (i) Betas are estimated with respect to market indexes that are proxies for the true market portfolio, which is inherently unobservable.
(ii) Empirical tests of the CAPM show that average returns are not related to beta in the manner predicted by the theory. The empirical SML is flatter than the theoretical one.
(iii) Multi-factor models of security returns show that beta, which is a one-dimensional measure of risk, may not capture the true risk of the stock of portfolio.

13. a. The basic procedure in portfolio evaluation is to compare the returns on a managed portfolio to the return expected on an unmanaged portfolio having the same risk, using the SML. That is, expected return is calculated from:

$$E(r_P) = r_f + \beta_P [E(r_M) - r_f]$$

where r_f is the risk-free rate, $E(r_M)$ is the expected return for the *unmanaged* portfolio (or the market portfolio), and β_P is the beta coefficient (or systematic risk) of the managed portfolio. The performance benchmark then is the unmanaged portfolio. The typical proxy for this unmanaged portfolio is an aggregate stock market index such as the S&P 500.

b. The benchmark error might occur when the unmanaged portfolio used in the evaluation process is not "optimized." That is, market indices, such as the S&P 500, chosen as benchmarks are not on the manager's *ex ante* mean/variance efficient frontier.

c. Your graph should show an efficient frontier obtained from actual returns, and a different one that represents (unobserved) ex-ante expectations. The CML and SML generated from actual returns do not conform to the CAPM predictions, while the hypothesized lines do conform to the CAPM.

d. The answer to this question depends on one's prior beliefs. Given a consistent track record, an agnostic observer might conclude that the data support the claim of superiority. Other observers might start with a strong prior that, since so many managers are attempting to beat a passive portfolio, a small number are bound to produce seemingly convincing track records.

e. The question is really whether the CAPM is at all testable. The problem is that even a slight inefficiency in the benchmark portfolio may completely invalidate any test of the expected return-beta relationship. It appears from Roll's argument that the best guide to the question of the validity of the CAPM is the difficulty of beating a passive strategy.

14. The effect of an incorrectly specified market proxy is that the beta of Black's portfolio is likely to be underestimated (i.e., too low) relative to the beta calculated based on the "true" market portfolio. This is because the Dow Jones Industrial Average (DJIA), and other market proxies, are likely to have less diversification and therefore a higher variance of returns than the "true" market portfolio as specified by the capital asset pricing model. Consequently, beta computed using an overstated variance will be underestimated. This result is clear from the following formula:

$$\beta_{Portfolio} = \frac{Cov(r_{Portfolio}, r_{Market\ Proxy})}{\sigma^2_{Market\ Proxy}}$$

An incorrectly specified market proxy is likely to produce a slope for the security market line (i.e., the market risk premium) that is underestimated relative to the "true" market portfolio. This results from the fact that the "true" market portfolio is likely to be more efficient (plotting on a higher return point for the same risk) than the DJIA and similarly misspecified market proxies. Consequently, the proxy-based SML would offer less expected return per unit of risk.

CHAPTER 14: BOND PRICES AND YIELDS

1. a. Effective annual rate for 3-month T-bill:

$$\left(\frac{100,000}{97,645}\right)^4 - 1 = 1.02412^4 - 1 = 0.100 = 10.0\%$$

   b. Effective annual interest rate for coupon bond paying 5% semiannually:

$$(1.05)^2 - 1 = 0.1025 \text{ or } 10.25\%$$

   Therefore the coupon bond has the higher effective annual interest rate.

2. The effective annual yield on the semiannual coupon bonds is 8.16%. If the annual coupon bonds are to sell at par they must offer the same yield, which requires an annual coupon rate of 8.16%.

3. The bond callable at 105 should sell at a lower price because the call provision is more valuable to the firm. Therefore, its yield to maturity should be higher.

4. The bond price will be lower. As time passes, the bond price, which is now above par value, will approach par.

5. Yield to maturity: Using a financial calculator, enter the following:

   n = 3; PV = –953.10; FV = 1000; PMT = 80; COMP i

   This results in: YTM = 9.88%

   Realized compound yield: First, find the future value (FV) of reinvested coupons and principal:

   $$FV = (\$80 \times 1.10 \times 1.12) + (\$80 \times 1.12) + \$1,080 = \$1,268.16$$

   Then find the rate ($y_{realized}$) that makes the FV of the purchase price equal to $1,268.16:

   $$\$953.10 \times (1 + y_{realized})^3 = \$1,268.16 \Rightarrow y_{realized} = 9.99\% \text{ or approximately } 10\%$$

6. a. A sinking fund provision requires the early redemption of a bond issue. The provision may be for a specific number of bonds or a percentage of the bond issue over a specified time period. The sinking fund can retire all or a portion of an issue over the life of the issue.

    b. (i) Compared to a bond without a sinking fund, the sinking fund reduces the average life of the overall issue because some of the bonds are retired prior to the stated maturity.

    (ii) The company will make the same total principal payments over the life of the issue, although the timing of these payments will be affected. The total interest payments associated with the issue will be reduced given the early redemption of principal.

    c. From the investor's point of view, the key reason for demanding a sinking fund is to reduce credit risk. Default risk is reduced by the orderly retirement of the issue.

7. a. (i) Current yield = Coupon/Price = $70/$960 = 0.0729 = 7.29%

    (ii) YTM = 3.993% semiannually or 7.986% annual bond equivalent yield. On a financial calculator, enter: n = 10; PV = –960; FV = 1000; PMT = 35 Compute the interest rate.

    (iii) Realized compound yield is 4.166% (semiannually), or 8.332% annual bond equivalent yield. To obtain this value, first find the future value (FV) of reinvested coupons and principal. There will be six payments of $35 each, reinvested semiannually at 3% per period. On a financial calculator, enter: PV = 0; PMT = 35; n = 6; i = 3%. Compute: FV = 226.39

    Three years from now, the bond will be selling at the par value of $1,000 because the yield to maturity is forecast to equal the coupon rate. Therefore, total proceeds in three years will be: $226.39 + $1,000 = $1,226.39

    Then find the rate ($y_{realized}$) that makes the FV of the purchase price equal to $1,226.39:

    $$\$960 \times (1 + y_{realized})^6 = \$1,226.39 \Rightarrow y_{realized} = 4.166\% \text{ (semiannual)}$$

    b. Shortcomings of each measure:

    (i) Current yield does not account for capital gains or losses on bonds bought at prices other than par value. It also does not account for reinvestment income on coupon payments.

    (ii) Yield to maturity assumes the bond is held until maturity and that all coupon income can be reinvested at a rate equal to the yield to maturity.

    (iii) Realized compound yield is affected by the forecast of reinvestment rates, holding period, and yield of the bond at the end of the investor's holding period.

8. a.

	Zero coupon	8% coupon	10% coupon
Current prices	$463.19	$1,000.00	$1,134.20

b.

	Zero coupon	8% coupon	10% coupon
Price 1 year from now	$500.25	$1,000.00	$1,124.94
Price increase	$ 37.06	$ 0.00	– $ 9.26
Coupon income	$ 0.00	$ 80.00	$100.00
Pre-tax income	$ 37.06	$ 80.00	$ 90.74
Pre-tax rate of return	8.00%	8.00%	8.00%
Taxes*	$ 11.12	$ 24.00	$ 28.15
After-tax income	$ 25.94	$ 56.00	$ 62.59
After-tax rate of return	5.60%	5.60%	5.52%

c.

	Zero coupon	8% coupon	10% coupon
Price 1 year from now	$543.93	$1,065.15	$1,195.46
Price increase	$ 80.74	$ 65.15	$ 61.26
Coupon income	$ 0.00	$ 80.00	$100.00
Pre-tax income	$ 80.74	$145.15	$161.26
Pre-tax rate of return	17.43%	14.52%	14.22%
Taxes**	$ 19.86	$ 37.03	$ 42.25
After-tax income	$ 60.88	$108.12	$119.01
After-tax rate of return	13.14%	10.81%	10.49%

* In computing taxes, we assume that the 10% coupon bond was issued at par and that the decrease in price when the bond is sold at year end is treated as a capital loss and therefore is not treated as an offset to ordinary income.

** In computing taxes for the zero coupon bond, $37.06 is taxed as ordinary income (see part (b)) and the remainder of the price increase is taxed as a capital gain.

9. a. On a financial calculator, enter the following:

$$n = 40; FV = 1000; PV = –950; PMT = 40$$

You will find that the yield to maturity on a semi-annual basis is 4.26%. This implies a bond equivalent yield to maturity equal to: $4.26\% \times 2 = 8.52\%$

Effective annual yield to maturity = $(1.0426)^2 – 1 = 0.0870 = 8.70\%$

b. Since the bond is selling at par, the yield to maturity on a semi-annual basis is the same as the semi-annual coupon rate, i.e., 4%. The bond equivalent yield to maturity is 8%.

Effective annual yield to maturity = $(1.04)^2 – 1 = 0.0816 = 8.16\%$

c. Keeping other inputs unchanged but setting PV = –1050, we find a bond equivalent yield to maturity of 7.52%, or 3.76% on a semi-annual basis.

Effective annual yield to maturity = $(1.0376)^2 – 1 = 0.0766 = 7.66\%$

10. Since the bond payments are now made annually instead of semi-annually, the bond equivalent yield to maturity is the same as the effective annual yield to maturity. Using a financial calculator, enter: n = 20; FV = 1000; PV = –price, PMT = 80. The resulting yields for the three bonds are:

Bond Price	Bond equivalent yield = Effective annual yield
$950	8.53%
$1,000	8.00%
$1,050	7.51%

The yields computed in this case are lower than the yields calculated with semi-annual payments. All else equal, bonds with annual payments are less attractive to investors because more time elapses before payments are received. If the bond price is the same with annual payments, then the bond's yield to maturity is lower.

11.

Price	Maturity (years)	Bond equivalent YTM
$400.00	20.00	4.688%
$500.00	20.00	3.526%
$500.00	10.00	7.177%
$385.54	10.00	10.000%
$463.19	10.00	8.000%
$400.00	11.91	8.000%

12. a. The bond pays $50 every 6 months. The current price is:

$$[\$50 \times \text{Annuity factor } (4\%, 6)] + [\$1,000 \times \text{PV factor } (4\%, 6)] = \$1,052.42$$

Assuming the market interest rate remains 4% per half year, price six months from now is:

$$[\$50 \times \text{Annuity factor } (4\%, 5)] + [\$1,000 \times \text{PV factor } (4\%, 5)] = \$1,044.52$$

b. Rate of return $= \dfrac{\$50 + (\$1,044.52 - \$1,052.42)}{\$1,052.42} = \dfrac{\$50 - \$7.90}{\$1,052.42}$

$= 0.04 = 4.0\%$ per six months

13. a. Initial price $P_0 = \$705.46$ [n = 20; PMT = 50; FV = 1000; i = 8]

Next year's price $P_1 = \$793.29$ [n = 19; PMT = 50; FV = 1000; i = 7]

$$HPR = \dfrac{\$50 + (\$793.29 - \$705.46)}{\$705.46} = 0.1954 = 19.54\%$$

b. Using OID tax rules, the cost basis and imputed interest under the constant yield method are obtained by discounting bond payments at the *original* 8% yield, and simply reducing maturity by one year at a time:

Constant yield prices (compare these to actual prices to compute capital gains):
$P_0 = \$705.46$
$P_1 = \$711.89 \Rightarrow$ implicit interest over first year = \$6.43
$P_2 = \$718.84 \Rightarrow$ implicit interest over second year = \$6.95

Tax on explicit interest plus implicit interest in first year =

$$0.40 \times (\$50 + \$6.43) = \$22.57$$

Capital gain in first year = Actual price at 7% YTM – constant yield price =

$$\$793.29 - \$711.89 = \$81.40$$

Tax on capital gain = $0.30 \times \$81.40 = \$24.42$

Total taxes = \$22.57 + \$24.42 = \$46.99

c. After tax HPR = $\dfrac{\$50 + (\$793.29 - \$705.46) - \$46.99}{\$705.46} = 0.1288 = 12.88\%$

d. Value of bond after two years = \$798.82 [using n = 18; i = 7%]

Reinvested income from the two coupon interest payments =

$$\$50 \times 1.03 + \$50 = \$101.50$$

Total funds after two years = \$798.82 + \$101.50 = \$900.32

Therefore, the investment of \$705.46 grows to \$900.32 in two years:

$$\$705.46 \, (1 + r)^2 = \$900.32 \Rightarrow r = 0.1297 = 12.97\%$$

e.
Coupon interest received in first year:	\$50.00
Less: tax on coupon interest @ 40%:	– 20.00
Less: tax on imputed interest (0.40 × \$6.43):	– 2.57
Net cash flow in first year:	\$27.43

The year-1 cash flow can be invested at an after-tax rate of:

$$3\% \times (1 - 0.40) = 1.8\%$$

By year 2, this investment will grow to: \$27.43 × 1.018 = \$27.92

In two years, sell the bond for: $798.82   [n = 18; i = 7%]

Less: tax on *imputed* interest in second year: −2.78   [0.40 × $6.95]

Add: after-tax coupon interest received
in second year: +30.00   [$50 × (1 − 0.40)]

Less: Capital gains tax on
(sales price − constant yield value):   −23.99   [0.30 × (798.82 − 718.84)]

Add: CF from first year's coupon (reinvested):   +27.92   [from above]

Total $829.97

$$\$705.46 \, (1 + r)^2 = \$829.97 \Rightarrow r = 0.0847 = 8.47\%$$

14. The *reported* bond price is: 100 2/32 percent of par = $1,000.625
However, 15 days have passed since the last semiannual coupon was paid, so:

$$\text{accrued interest} = \$35 \times (15/182) = \$2.885$$

The invoice price is the reported price plus accrued interest: $1,003.51

15. If the yield to maturity is greater than the current yield, then the bond offers the prospect of price appreciation as it approaches its maturity date. Therefore, the bond must be selling below par value.

16. The coupon rate is less than 9%. If coupon divided by price equals 9%, and price is less than par, then price divided by par is less than 9%.

17.

Time	Inflation in year just ended	Par value	Coupon payment	Principal repayment
0		$1,000.00		
1	2%	$1,020.00	$40.80	$ 0.00
2	3%	$1,050.60	$42.02	$ 0.00
3	1%	$1,061.11	$42.44	$1,061.11

The *nominal* rate of return and *real* rate of return on the bond in each year are computed as follows:

$$\text{Nominal rate of return} = \frac{\text{interest} + \text{price appreciation}}{\text{initial price}}$$

$$\text{Real rate of return} = \frac{1 + \text{nominal return}}{1 + \text{inflation}} - 1$$

	Second year	Third year
Nominal return	$\dfrac{\$42.02 + \$30.60}{\$1,020} = 0.071196$	$\dfrac{\$42.44 + \$10.51}{\$1,050.60} = 0.050400$
Real return	$\dfrac{1.071196}{1.03} - 1 = 0.040 = 4.0\%$	$\dfrac{1.050400}{1.01} - 1 = 0.040 = 4.0\%$

The real rate of return in each year is precisely the 4% real yield on the bond.

18. The price schedule is as follows:

Year	Remaining Maturity (T)	Constant yield value $\$1,000/(1.08)^T$	Imputed interest (Increase in constant yield value)
0 (now)	20 years	$214.55	
1	19	$231.71	$17.16
2	18	$250.25	$18.54
19	1	$925.93	
20	0	$1,000.00	$74.07

19. The bond is issued at a price of $800. Therefore, its yield to maturity is: 6.8245% Therefore, using the constant yield method, we find that the price in one year (when maturity falls to 9 years) will be (at an unchanged yield) $814.60, representing an increase of $14.60. Total taxable income is: $40.00 + $14.60 = $54.60

20. a. The bond sells for $1,124.72 based on the 3.5% yield to *maturity*.
[n = 60; i = 3.5; FV = 1000; PMT = 40]

   Therefore, yield to *call* is 3.368% semiannually, 6.736% semi-annually.
[n = 10 semiannual periods; PV = –1124.72; FV = 1100; PMT = 40]

   b. If the call price were $1,050, we would set FV = 1,050 and redo part (a) to find that yield to call is 2.976% semiannually, 5.952% annually. With a lower call price, the yield to call is lower.

   c. Yield to call is 3.031% semiannually, 6.602% annually.
[n = 4; PV = –1124.72; FV = 1100; PMT = 40]

21. The stated yield to maturity, based on promised payments, equals 16.075%.
[n = 10; PV = –900; FV = 1000; PMT = 140]

Based on *expected* coupon payments of $70 annually, the expected yield to maturity is 8.526%.

22. The bond is selling at par value. Its yield to maturity equals the coupon rate, 10%. If the first-year coupon is reinvested at an interest rate of r percent, then total proceeds at the end of the second year will be: $[\$100 \times (1 + r)] + \$1,100$

Therefore, realized compound yield to maturity is a function of r, as shown in the following table:

r	Total proceeds	Realized YTM $= \sqrt{\text{Proceeds}/1000}\ - 1$
8%	$1,208	$\sqrt{1208/1000}\ - 1 = 0.0991 = 9.91\%$
10%	$1,210	$\sqrt{1210/1000}\ - 1 = 0.1000 = 10.00\%$
12%	$1,212	$\sqrt{1212/1000}\ - 1 = 0.1009 = 10.09\%$

23. Zero coupon bonds provide no coupons to be reinvested. Therefore, the investor's proceeds from the bond are independent of the rate at which coupons could be reinvested (if they were paid). There is no reinvestment rate uncertainty with zeros.

24. April 15 is midway through the semiannual coupon period. Therefore, the invoice price will be higher than the stated ask price by an amount equal to one-half of the semiannual coupon. The ask price is 101.125 percent of par, so the invoice price is:

$$\$1,011.25 + (\tfrac{1}{2} \times \$50) = \$1,036.25$$

25. Factors that might make the ABC debt more attractive to investors, therefore justifying a lower coupon rate and yield to maturity, are:

i. The ABC debt is a larger issue and therefore may sell with greater liquidity.

ii. An option to extend the term from 10 years to 20 years is favorable if interest rates ten years from now are lower than today's interest rates. In contrast, if interest rates increase, the investor can present the bond for payment and reinvest the money for a higher return.

iii. In the event of trouble, the ABC debt is a more senior claim. It has more underlying security in the form of a first claim against real property.

iv. The call feature on the XYZ bonds makes the ABC bonds relatively more attractive since ABC bonds cannot be called from the investor.

v. The XYZ bond has a sinking fund requiring XYZ to retire part of the issue each year. Since most sinking funds give the firm the option to retire this amount at the lower of par or market value, the sinking fund can be detrimental for bondholders.

26. a. The floating rate note pays a coupon that adjusts to market levels. Therefore, it will not experience dramatic price changes as market yields fluctuate. The fixed rate note will therefore have a greater price range.

b. Floating rate notes may not sell at par for any of several reasons:

The yield spread between one-year Treasury bills and other money market instruments of comparable maturity could be wider (or narrower) than when the bond was issued.

The credit standing of the firm may have eroded (or improved) relative to Treasury securities, which have no credit risk. Therefore, the 2% premium would become insufficient to sustain the issue at par.

The coupon increases are implemented with a lag, i.e., once every year. During a period of changing interest rates, even this brief lag will be reflected in the price of the security.

c. The risk of call is low. Because the bond will almost surely not sell for much above par value (given its adjustable coupon rate), it is unlikely that the bond will ever be called.

d. The fixed-rate note currently sells at only 88% of the call price, so that yield to maturity is greater than the coupon rate. Call risk is currently low, since yields would need to fall substantially for the firm to use its option to call the bond.

e. The 9% coupon notes currently have a remaining maturity of fifteen years and sell at a yield to maturity of 9.9%. This is the coupon rate that would be needed for a newly-issued fifteen-year maturity bond to sell at par.

f. Because the floating rate note pays a *variable stream* of interest payments to maturity, the effective maturity for comparative purposes with other debt securities is closer to the next coupon reset date than the final maturity date. Therefore, yield-to-maturity is an indeterminable calculation for a floating rate note, with "yield-to-recoupon date" a more meaningful measure of return.

27. a. The maturity of each bond is ten years, and we assume that coupons are paid semiannually. Since both bonds are selling at par value, the current yield for each bond is equal to its coupon rate.

If the yield declines by 1% to 5% (2.5% semiannual yield), the Sentinal bond will increase in value to \$107.79 [n=20; i = 2.5%; FV = 100; PMT = 3].

The price of the Colina bond will increase, but only to the call price of 102. The present value of *scheduled* payments is greater than 102, but the call price puts a ceiling on the actual bond price.

b. If rates are expected to fall, the Sentinal bond is more attractive: since it is not subject to call, its potential capital gains are greater.

If rates are expected to rise, Colina is a relatively better investment. Its higher coupon (which presumably is compensation to investors for the call feature of the bond) will provide a higher rate of return than the Sentinal bond.

c. An increase in the volatility of rates will increase the value of the firm's option to call back the Colina bond. If rates go down, the firm can call the bond, which puts a cap on possible capital gains. So, greater volatility makes the option to call back the bond more valuable to the issuer. This makes the bond less attractive to the investor.

28. a. The yield to maturity on the par bond equals its coupon rate, 8.75%. All else equal, the 4% coupon bond would be more attractive because its coupon rate is far below current market yields, and its price is far below the call price. Therefore, if yields fall, capital gains on the bond will not be limited by the call price. In contrast, the 8¾% coupon bond can increase in value to at most $1,050, offering a maximum possible gain of only 0.5%. The disadvantage of the 8¾% coupon bond, in terms of vulnerability to being called, shows up in its higher *promised* yield to maturity.

b. If an investor expects yields to fall substantially, the 4% bond offers a greater expected return.

c. Implicit call protection is offered in the sense that any likely fall in yields would not be nearly enough to make the firm consider calling the bond. In this sense, the call feature is almost irrelevant.

29. Market conversion value = value if converted into stock = 20.83 × $28 = $583.24

Conversion premium = Bond price – market conversion value

= $775.00 – $583.24 = $191.76

30. a. The call feature requires the firm to offer a higher coupon (or higher promised yield to maturity) on the bond in order to compensate the investor for the firm's option to call back the bond at a specified price if interest rate falls sufficiently. Investors are willing to grant this valuable option to the issuer, but only for a price that reflects the possibility that the bond will be called. That price is the higher promised yield at which they are willing to buy the bond.

b. The call feature reduces the expected life of the bond. If interest rates fall substantially so that the likelihood of a call increases, investors will treat the bond as if it will "mature" and be paid off at the call date, not at the stated maturity date. On the other hand if rates rise, the bond must be paid off at the maturity date, not later. This asymmetry means that the expected life of the bond is less than the stated maturity.

c. The advantage of a callable bond is the higher coupon (and higher promised yield to maturity) when the bond is issued. If the bond is never called, then an investor earns a higher realized compound yield on a callable bond issued at par than a non-callable bond issued at par on the same date. The disadvantage of the callable bond is the risk of call. If rates fall and the bond is called, then the investor receives the call price and then has to reinvest the proceeds at interest rates that are lower than the yield to maturity at which the bond originally was issued. In this event, the firm's savings in interest payments is the investor's loss.

31. a. (iii)

b. (iii) The yield to maturity on the callable bond must compensate the investor for the risk of call.

Choice (i) is wrong because, although the owner of a callable bond receives a premium plus the principal in the event of a call, the interest rate at which he can reinvest will be low. The low interest rate that makes it profitable for the issuer to call the bond also makes it a bad deal for the bond's holder.

Choice (ii) is wrong because a bond is more apt to be called when interest rates are low. Only if rates are low will there be an interest saving for the issuer.

c. (iii)

d. (ii)

e. (iii)

CHAPTER 15: THE TERM STRUCTURE OF INTEREST RATES

1. Expectations hypothesis: The yields on long-term bonds are geometric averages of present and expected future short rates. An upward sloping curve is explained by expected future short rates being higher than the current short rate. A downward-sloping yield curve implies expected future short rates are lower than the current short rate. Thus bonds of different maturities have different yields if expectations of future short rates are different from the current short rate.

    Liquidity preference hypothesis: Yields on long-term bonds are greater than the expected return from rolling-over short-term bonds in order to compensate investors in long-term bonds for bearing interest rate risk. Thus bonds of different maturities can have different yields even if expected future short rates are all equal to the current short rate. An upward sloping yield curve can be consistent even with expectations of falling short rates if liquidity premiums are high enough. If, however, the yield curve is downward sloping and liquidity premiums are assumed to be positive, then we can conclude that future short rates are expected to be lower than the current short rate.

2. d.

3. In general, the forward rate can be viewed as the sum of the market's expectation of the future short rate plus a potential risk or 'liquidity' premium. According to the expectations theory of the term structure of interest rates, the liquidity premium is zero so that the forward rate is equal to the market's expectation of the future short rate. Therefore, the market's expectation of future short rates (i.e., forward rates) can be derived from the yield curve, and there is no risk premium for longer maturities.

    The liquidity preference theory, on the other hand, specifies that the liquidity premium is positive so that the forward rate is less than the market's expectation of the future short rate. This could result in an upward sloping term structure even if the market does not anticipate an increase in interest rates. The liquidity preference theory is based on the assumption that the financial markets are dominated by short-term investors who demand a premium in order to be induced to invest in long maturity securities.

4. True. Under the expectations hypothesis, there are no risk premia built into bond prices. The only reason for long-term yields to exceed short-term yields is an expectation of higher short-term rates in the future.

5. Uncertain. Expectations of lower inflation will usually lead to lower nominal interest rates. Nevertheless, if the liquidity premium is sufficiently great, long-term yields may exceed short-term yields *despite* expectations of falling short rates.

6.

Maturity	Price	YTM	Forward Rate
1	$943.40	6.00%	
2	$898.47	5.50%	$(1.055^2/1.06) - 1 = 5.0\%$
3	$847.62	5.67%	$(1.0567^3/1.055^2) - 1 = 6.0\%$
4	$792.16	6.00%	$(1.06^4/1.0567^3) - 1 = 7.0\%$

7. The expected price path of the 4-year zero coupon bond is shown below. (Note that we discount the face value by the appropriate sequence of forward rates implied by this year's yield curve.)

Beginning of Year	Expected Price	Expected Rate of Return
1	$792.16	($839.69/$792.16) − 1 = 6.00%
2	$\dfrac{\$1,000}{1.05 \times 1.06 \times 1.07} = \$839.69$	($881.68/$839.69) − 1 = 5.00%
3	$\dfrac{\$1,000}{1.06 \times 1.07} = \$881.68$	($934.58/$881.68) − 1 = 6.00%
4	$\dfrac{\$1,000}{1.07} = \$934.58$	($1,000.00/$934.58) − 1 = 7.00%

8. a. $(1+y_4)^4 = (1+y_3)^3(1+f_4)$

   $(1.055)^4 = (1.05)^3(1+f_4)$

   $1.2388 = 1.1576(1+f_4) \Rightarrow f_4 = 0.0701 = 7.01\%$

  b.   The conditions would be those that underlie the expectations theory of the term structure: risk neutral market participants who are willing to substitute among maturities solely on the basis of yield differentials. This behavior would rule out liquidity or term premia relating to risk.

  c.   Under the expectations hypothesis, lower implied forward rates would indicate lower expected future spot rates for the corresponding period. Since the lower expected future rates embodied in the term structure are nominal rates, either lower expected future real rates or lower expected future inflation rates would be consistent with the specified change in the observed (implied) forward rate.

9. The given rates are annual rates, but each period is a half-year. Therefore, the per period spot rates are 2.5% on one-year bonds and 2% on six-month bonds. The semiannual forward rate is obtained by solving for f in the following equation:

$$1+f = \frac{1.025^2}{1.02} = 1.030$$

This means that the forward rate is 0.030 = 3.0% semiannually, or 6.0% annually.

10. The present value of each bond's payments can be derived by discounting each cash flow by the appropriate rate from the spot interest rate (i.e., the pure yield) curve:

Bond A: $PV = \dfrac{\$10}{1.05} + \dfrac{\$10}{1.08^2} + \dfrac{\$110}{1.11^3} = \$98.53$

Bond B: $PV = \dfrac{\$6}{1.05} + \dfrac{\$6}{1.08^2} + \dfrac{\$106}{1.11^3} = \$88.36$

Bond A sells for $0.13 (i.e., 0.13% of par value) less than the present value of its stripped payments. Bond B sells for $0.02 less than the present value of its stripped payments. Bond A is more attractively priced.

11. a. We obtain forward rates from the following table:

Maturity	YTM	Forward Rate	Price (for parts c, d)
1 year	10%		$1,000/1.10 = $909.09
2 years	11%	$(1.11^2/1.10) - 1 = 12.01\%$	$1,000/1.11^2 = $811.62
3 years	12%	$(1.12^3/1.11^2) - 1 = 14.03\%$	$1,000/1.12^3 = $711.78

b. We obtain next year's prices and yields by discounting each zero's face value at the forward rates for next year that we derived in part (a):

Maturity	Price	YTM
1 year	$1,000/1.1201 = $892.78	12.01%
2 years	$1,000/(1.1201 \times 1.1403) = $782.93	13.02%

Note that this year's upward sloping yield curve implies, according to the expectations hypothesis, a shift upward in next year's curve.

c. Next year, the 2-year zero will be a 1-year zero, and will therefore sell at a price of: $1,000/1.1201 = $892.78

Similarly, the current 3-year zero will be a 2-year zero and will sell for: $782.93

Expected total rate of return:

2-year bond: $\dfrac{\$892.78}{\$811.62} - 1 = 1.1000 - 1 = 10.00\%$

3-year bond: $\dfrac{\$782.93}{\$711.78} - 1 = 1.1000 - 1 = 10.00\%$

d. The current price of the bond should equal the value of each payment times the present value of $1 to be received at the "maturity" of that payment. The present value schedule can be taken directly from the prices of zero-coupon bonds calculated above.

Current price = ($120 × 0.90909) + ($120 × 0.81162) + ($1,120 × 0.71178)

= $109.0908 + $97.3944 + $797.1936 = $1,003.68

Similarly, the expected prices of zeros one year from now can be used to calculate the expected bond value at that time:

Expected price 1 year from now = ($120 × 0.89278) + ($1,120 × 0.78293)

= $107.1336 + $876.8816 = $984.02

Total expected rate of return =

$$\frac{\$120 + (\$984.02 - \$1,003.68)}{\$1,003.68} = 0.1000 = 10.00\%$$

12. a. A 3-year zero coupon bond with face value $100 will sell today at a yield of 6% and a price of:

$100/1.06^3 = $83.96

Next year, the bond will have a two-year maturity, and therefore a yield of 6% (from next year's forecasted yield curve). The price will be $89.00, resulting in a holding period return of 6%.

b. The forward rates based on today's yield curve are as follows:

Year	Forward Rate
2	$(1.05^2/1.04) - 1 = 6.01\%$
3	$(1.06^3/1.05^2) - 1 = 8.03\%$

Using the forward rates, the forecast for the yield curve *next* year is:

Maturity	YTM
1	6.01%
2	$(1.0601 \times 1.0803)^{1/2} - 1 = 7.02\%$

The market forecast is for a higher YTM on 2–year bonds than your forecast. Thus, the market predicts a lower price and higher rate of return.

13.   a. $P = \dfrac{\$9}{1.07} + \dfrac{\$109}{1.08^2} = \$101.86$

      b.   The yield to maturity is the solution for y in the following equation:

$$\frac{\$9}{1+y} + \frac{\$109}{(1+y)^2} = \$101.86$$

[Using a financial calculator, enter n = 2; FV = 100; PMT = 9; PV = –101.86; Compute i] YTM = 7.958%

      c.   The forward rate for next year, derived from the zero-coupon yield curve, is the solution for f_2 in the following equation:

$$1+f_2 = \frac{(1.08)^2}{1.07} = 1.0901 \Rightarrow f_2 = 0.0901 = 9.01\%.$$

Therefore, using an expected rate for next year of $r_2 = 9.01\%$, we find that the forecast bond price is:

$$P = \frac{\$109}{1.0901} = \$99.99$$

      d.   If the liquidity premium is 1% then the forecast interest rate is:

$E(r_2) = f_2 - \text{liquidity premium} = 9.01\% - 1.00\% = 8.01\%$

The forecast of the bond price is:

$$\frac{\$109}{1.0801} = \$100.92$$

14. a. Based on the pure expectations theory, VanHusen's conclusion is incorrect. According to this theory, the expected return over any time horizon would be the same, regardless of the maturity strategy employed.

    b. According to the liquidity preference theory, the shape of the yield curve implies that short-term interest rates are expected to rise in the future. This theory asserts that forward rates reflect expectations about future interest rates plus a liquidity premium that increases with maturity. Given the shape of the yield curve and the liquidity premium data provided, the yield curve would still be positively sloped (at least through maturity of eight years) after subtracting the respective liquidity premiums:

    $$2.90\% - 0.55\% = 2.35\%$$
    $$3.50\% - 0.55\% = 2.95\%$$
    $$3.80\% - 0.65\% = 3.15\%$$
    $$4.00\% - 0.75\% = 3.25\%$$
    $$4.15\% - 0.90\% = 3.25\%$$
    $$4.30\% - 1.10\% = 3.20\%$$
    $$4.45\% - 1.20\% = 3.25\%$$
    $$4.60\% - 1.50\% = 3.10\%$$
    $$4.70\% - 1.60\% = 3.10\%$$

15. The coupon bonds can be viewed as portfolios of stripped zeros: each coupon can stand alone as an independent zero-coupon bond. Therefore, yields on coupon bonds reflect yields on payments with dates corresponding to each coupon. When the yield curve is upward sloping, coupon bonds have lower yields than zeros with the same maturity because the yields to maturity on coupon bonds reflect the yields on the earlier interim coupon payments.

16. a. The current bond price is:

    $(\$85 \times 0.94340) + (\$85 \times 0.87352) + (\$1,085 \times 0.81637) = \$1,040.20$

    This price implies a yield to maturity of 6.97%, as shown by the following:

    $[\$85 \times \text{Annuity factor } (6.97\%, 3)] + [\$1,000 \times \text{PV factor } (6.97\%, 3)] = \$1,040.17$

    b. If one year from now $y = 8\%$, then the bond price will be:

    $[\$85 \times \text{Annuity factor } (8\%, 2)] + [\$1,000 \times \text{PV factor } (8\%, 2)] = \$1,008.92$

    The holding period rate of return is:

    $[\$85 + (\$1,008.92 - \$1,040.20)]/\$1,040.20 = 0.0516 = 5.16\%$

17.

Year	Forward Rate	PV of $1 received at period end
1	5%	$1/1.05 = $0.9524
2	7%	$1/(1.05×1.07) = $0.8901
3	8%	$1/(1.05×1.07×1.08) = $0.8241

a. Price = ($60 × 0.9524) + ($60 × 0.8901) + ($1,060 × 0.8241) = $984.10

b. To find the yield to maturity, solve for y in the following equation:

$984.10 = [$60 × Annuity factor (y, 3)] + [$1,000 × PV factor (y, 3)]

This can be solved using a financial calculator to show that y = 6.60%

c.

Period	Payment received at end of period:	Will grow by a factor of:	To a future value of:
1	$60.00	1.07 × 1.08	$69.34
2	$60.00	1.08	$64.80
3	$1,060.00	1.00	$1,060.00
			$1,194.14

$$\$984.10 \times (1 + y_{realized})^3 = \$1,194.14$$

$$1 + y_{realized} = \left(\frac{\$1,194.14}{\$984.10}\right)^{1/3} = 1.0666 \Rightarrow y_{realized} = 6.66\%$$

d. Next year, the price of the bond will be:

[$60 × Annuity factor (7%, 2)] + [$1,000 × PV factor (7%,2)] = $981.92

Therefore, there will be a capital loss equal to: $984.10 − $981.92 = $2.18

The holding period return is: $\dfrac{\$60 + (-\$2.18)}{\$984.10} = 0.0588 = 5.88\%$

18. The following table shows the expected short-term interest rate based on the projections of Federal Reserve rate cuts, the term premium (which increases at a rate of 0.10% per12 months), the forward rate (which is the sum of the expected rate and term premium), and the YTM, which is the geometric average of the forward rates.

Time	Expected short rate	Term premium	Forward rate (annual)	Forward rate (semi-annual)	YTM (semi-annual)
0	5.00%	0.00%	5.00%	2.500%	2.500%
6 months	4.50	0.05	4.55	2.275	2.387
12 months	4.00	0.10	4.10	2.050	2.275
18 months	4.00	0.15	4.15	2.075	2.225
24 months	5.00	0.20	5.20	2.600	2.300
30 months	5.00	0.25	5.25	2.625	2.354

This analysis is predicated on the liquidity preference theory of the term structure, which asserts that the forward rate in any period is the sum of the expected short rate plus the liquidity premium.

19. a. The return on the one-year zero-coupon bond will be 6.1%.
The price of the 4-year zero today is:

$$\$1,000/1.064^4 = \$780.25$$

Next year, if the yield curve is unchanged, today's 4-year zero coupon bond will have a 3-year maturity, a YTM of 6.3%, and therefore the price will be:

$$\$1,000/1.063^3 = \$832.53$$

The resulting one-year rate of return will be 6.70%.
Therefore, in this case, the longer-term bond is expected to provide the higher return because its YTM is expected to decline during the holding period.

   b. If you believe in the expectations hypothesis, you would not expect that the yield curve next year will be the same as today's curve. The upward slope in today's curve would be evidence that expected short rates are rising and that the yield curve will shift upward, reducing the holding period return on the four-year bond. Under the expectations hypothesis, all bonds have equal expected holding period returns. Therefore, you would predict that the HPR for the 4-year bond would be 6.1%, the same as for the 1-year bond.

20. a. <u>Five-year Spot Rate:</u>

$$\$1,000 = \frac{\$70}{(1+y_1)^1} + \frac{\$70}{(1+y_2)^2} + \frac{\$70}{(1+y_3)^3} + \frac{\$70}{(1+y_4)^4} + \frac{\$1,070}{(1+y_5)^5}$$

$$\$1,000 = \frac{\$70}{(1.05)} + \frac{\$70}{(1.0521)^2} + \frac{\$70}{(1.0605)^3} + \frac{\$70}{(1.0716)^4} + \frac{\$1,070}{(1+y_5)^5}$$

$$\$1,000 = \$66.67 + \$63.24 + \$58.69 + \$53.08 + \frac{\$1,070}{(1+y_5)^5}$$

$$\$758.32 = \frac{\$1,070}{(1+y_5)^5}$$

$$(1+y_5)^5 = \frac{\$1,070}{\$758.32} \Rightarrow y_5 = \sqrt[5]{1.411} - 1 = 7.13\%$$

<u>Five-year Forward Rate:</u>

$$\frac{(1.0713)^5}{(1.0716)^4} - 1 = 1.0701 - 1 = 7.01\%$$

b. The yield to maturity is the single discount rate that equates the present value of a series of cash flows to a current price. It is the internal rate of return.

The spot rate for a given period is the yield to maturity on a zero-coupon bond that matures at the end of the period. A spot rate is the discount rate for each period. Spot rates are used to discount each cash flow of a coupon bond in order to calculate a current price. Spot rates are the rates appropriate for discounting future cash flows of different maturities.

A forward rate is the implicit rate that links any two spot rates. Forward rates are directly related to spot rates, and therefore to yield to maturity. Some would argue (as in the expectations hypothesis) that forward rates are the market expectations of future interest rates. A forward rate represents a break-even rate that links two spot rates. It is important to note that forward rates link spot rates, not yields to maturity.

Yield to maturity is not unique for any particular maturity. In other words, two bonds with the same maturity but different coupon rates may have different yields to maturity. In contrast, spot rates and forward rates for each date are unique.

c.   The 4-year spot rate is 7.16%. Therefore, 7.16% is the theoretical yield to maturity for the zero-coupon U.S. Treasury note. The price of the zero-coupon note discounted at 7.16% is the present value of $1,000 to be received in 4 years. Using annual compounding:

$$PV = \frac{\$1,000}{(1.0716)^4} = \$758.35$$

21.   The price of the coupon bond, based on its yield to maturity, is:

[$120 × Annuity factor (5.8%, 2)] + [$1,000 × PV factor (5.8%, 2)] = $1,113.99

If the coupons were stripped and sold separately as zeros, then, based on the yield to maturity of zeros with maturities of one and two years, respectively, the coupon payments could be sold separately for:

$$\frac{\$120}{1.05} + \frac{\$1,120}{1.06^2} = \$1,111.08$$

The arbitrage strategy is to buy zeros with face values of $120 and $1,120 and respective maturities of one year and two years, and simultaneously sell the coupon bond. The profit equals $2.91 on each bond.

22.   a.   The one-year zero-coupon bond has a yield to maturity of 6%, as shown below:

$$\$94.34 = \frac{\$100}{1 + y_1} \Rightarrow y_1 = 0.06000 = 6.000\%$$

The yield on the two-year zero is 8.472%, as shown below:

$$\$84.99 = \frac{\$100}{(1 + y_2)^2} \Rightarrow y_2 = 0.08472 = 8.472\%$$

The price of the coupon bond is: $\dfrac{\$12}{1.06} + \dfrac{\$112}{(1.08472)^2} = \$106.51$

Therefore: yield to maturity for the coupon bond = 8.333%
[On a financial calculator, enter: n = 2; PV = –106.51; FV = 100; PMT = 12]

b. $f_2 = \dfrac{(1 + y_2)^2}{1 + y_1} - 1 = \dfrac{(1.08472)^2}{1.06} - 1 = 0.1100 = 11.00\%$

c.   Expected price $= \dfrac{\$112}{1.11} = \$100.90$

(Note that next year, the coupon bond will have one payment left.)

Expected holding period return =

$$\dfrac{\$12 + (\$100.90 - \$106.51)}{\$106.51} = 0.0600 = 6.00\%$$

This holding period return is the same as the return on the one-year zero.

d.   If there is a liquidity premium, then: $E(r_2) < f_2$

$$E(\text{Price}) = \dfrac{\$112}{1 + E(r_2)} > \$100.90$$

$E(\text{HPR}) > 6\%$

23. a.

Maturity (years)	Price	YTM	Forward rate
1	$925.93	8.00%	
2	$853.39	8.25%	8.50%
3	$782.92	8.50%	9.00%
4	$715.00	8.75%	9.50%
5	$650.00	9.00%	10.00%

b.   For each 3-year zero issued today, use the proceeds to buy:

$782.92/$715.00 = 1.095 four-year zeros

Your cash flows are thus as follows:

Time	Cash Flow	
0	$ 0	
3	-$1,000	The 3-year zero issued at time 0 matures; the issuer pays out $1,000 face value
4	+$1,095	The 4-year zeros purchased at time 0 mature; receive face value

This is a synthetic one-year loan originating at time 3. The rate on the synthetic loan is 0.095 = 9.5%, precisely the forward rate for year 3.

c.   For each 4-year zero issued today, use the proceeds to buy:

$715.00/\$650.00 = 1.100$ five-year zeros

Your cash flows are thus as follows:

Time	Cash Flow	
0	$ 0	
4	-$1,000	The 4-year zero issued at time 0 matures; the issuer pays out $1,000 face value
5	+$1,100	The 5-year zeros purchased at time 0 mature; receive face value

This is a synthetic one-year loan originating at time 4. The rate on the synthetic loan is $0.100 = 10.0\%$, precisely the forward rate for year 4.

24. a.   For each three-year zero you buy today, issue:

$782.92/\$650.00 = 1.2045$ five-year zeros

The time-0 cash flow equals zero.

b.   Your cash flows are thus as follows:

Time	Cash Flow	
0	$ 0	
3	+$1,000.00	The 3-year zero purchased at time 0 matures; receive $1,000 face value
5	-$1,204.50	The 5-year zeros issued at time 0 mature; issuer pays face value

This is a synthetic two-year loan originating at time 3.

c.   The effective two-year interest rate on the forward loan is:

$1,204.50/\$1,000 - 1 = 0.2045 = 20.45\%$

d.   The one-year forward rates for years 4 and 5 are 9.5% and 10%, respectively. Notice that:

$1.095 \times 1.10 = 1.2045 =$

$1 +$ (two-year forward rate on the 3-year ahead forward loan)

The 5-year YTM is 9.0%. The 3-year YTM is 8.5%. Therefore, another way to derive the 2-year forward rate for a loan starting at time 3 is:

$$f_3(2) = \frac{(1+y_5)^5}{(1+y_3)^3} - 1 = \frac{1.09^5}{1.085^3} - 1 = 0.2046 = 20.46\%$$

[Note: there is a slight discrepancy here due to rounding error in the YTM calculations above.]

25.   a.   The two-year implied annually compounded forward rate for a deferred loan beginning in 3 years is calculated as follows:

$$f_3(2) = \left[\frac{(1+y_5)^5}{(1+y_3)^3}\right]^{1/2} - 1 = \left[\frac{1.09^5}{1.11^3}\right]^{1/2} - 1 = 0.0607 = 6.07\%$$

b.   Assuming a par value of $1,000, the bond price is calculated as follows:

$$P = \frac{\$90}{(1+y_1)^1} + \frac{\$90}{(1+y_2)^2} + \frac{\$90}{(1+y_3)^3} + \frac{\$90}{(1+y_4)^4} + \frac{\$1,090}{(1+y_5)^5}$$

$$= \frac{\$90}{(1.13)^1} + \frac{\$90}{(1.12)^2} + \frac{\$90}{(1.11)^3} + \frac{\$90}{(1.10)^4} + \frac{\$1,090}{(1.09)^5} = \$987.10$$

CHAPTER 16: MANAGING BOND PORTFOLIOS

1. The percentage change in the bond's price is:

$$-\frac{\text{Duration}}{1+y} \times \Delta y = -\frac{7.194}{1.10} \times 0.005 = -0.0327 = -3.27\% \text{ or a 3.27\% decline}$$

2. a. <u>YTM = 6%</u>

(1) Time until Payment (years)	(2) Cash Flow	(3) PV of CF (Discount rate = 6%)	(4) Weight	(5) Column (1) × Column (4)
1	$60.00	$56.60	0.0566	0.0566
2	$60.00	$53.40	0.0534	0.1068
3	$1,060.00	$890.00	0.8900	2.6700
Column Sums		$1,000.00	1.0000	2.8334

Duration = 2.833 years

b. <u>YTM = 10%</u>

(1) Time until Payment (years)	(2) Cash Flow	(3) PV of CF (Discount rate = 10%)	(4) Weight	(5) Column (1) × Column (4)
1	$60.00	$54.55	0.0606	0.0606
2	$60.00	$49.59	0.0551	0.1102
3	$1,060.00	$796.39	0.8844	2.6532
Column Sums		$900.53	1.0000	2.8240

Duration = 2.824 years, which is less than the duration at the YTM of 6%.

3. For a semiannual 6% coupon bond selling at par, we use the following parameters: coupon = 3% per half-year period, y = 3%, T = 6 semiannual periods.

(1) Time until Payment (years)	(2) Cash Flow	(3) PV of CF (Discount rate = 3%)	(4) Weight	(5) Column (1) × Column (4)
1	$3.00	$2.913	0.02913	0.02913
2	$3.00	$2.828	0.02828	0.05656
3	$3.00	$2.745	0.02745	0.08236
4	$3.00	$2.665	0.02665	0.10662
5	$3.00	$2.588	0.02588	0.12939
6	$103.00	$86.261	0.86261	5.17565
Column Sums		$100.000	1.00000	5.57971

D = 5.5797 half-year periods = 2.7899 years

If the bond's yield is 10%, use a semiannual yield of 5%, and semiannual coupon of 3%:

(1) Time until Payment (years)	(2) Cash Flow	(3) PV of CF (Discount rate = 5%)	(4) Weight	(5) Column (1) × Column (4)
1	$3.00	$2.857	0.03180	0.03180
2	$3.00	$2.721	0.03029	0.06057
3	$3.00	$2.592	0.02884	0.08653
4	$3.00	$2.468	0.02747	0.10988
5	$3.00	$2.351	0.02616	0.13081
6	$103.00	$76.860	0.85544	5.13265
Column Sums		$89.849	1.00000	5.55223

D = 5.5522 half-year periods = 2.7761 years

4. a. Bond B has a higher yield to maturity than bond A since its coupon payments and maturity are equal to those of A, while its price is lower. (Perhaps the yield is higher because of differences in credit risk.) Therefore, the duration of Bond B must be shorter.

   b. Bond A has a lower yield and a lower coupon, both of which cause Bond A to have a longer duration than Bond B. Moreover, A cannot be called, so that its maturity is at least as long as that of B, which generally increases duration.

5. a.

(1) Time until Payment (years)	(2) Cash Flow	(3) PV of CF (Discount rate = 10%)	(4) Weight	(5) Column (1) × Column (4)
1	$10 million	$9.09 million	0.7857	0.7857
5	$4 million	$2.48 million	0.2143	1.0715
Column Sums		$11.57 million	1.0000	1.8572

D = 1.8572 years = required maturity of zero coupon bond.

b. The market value of the zero must be $11.57 million, the same as the market value of the obligations. Therefore, the face value must be:

$$\$11.57 \text{ million} \times (1.10)^{1.8572} = \$13.81 \text{ million}$$

6. a. The call feature provides a valuable option to the issuer, since it can buy back the bond at a specified call price even if the present value of the scheduled remaining payments is greater than the call price. The investor will demand, and the issuer will be willing to pay, a higher yield on the issue as compensation for this feature.

b. The call feature reduces both the duration (interest rate sensitivity) and the convexity of the bond. If interest rates fall, the increase in the price of the callable bond will not be as large as it would be if the bond were noncallable. Moreover, the usual curvature that characterizes price changes for a straight bond is reduced by a call feature. The price-yield curve (see Figure 16.6) flattens out as the interest rate falls and the option to call the bond becomes more attractive. In fact, at very low interest rates, the bond exhibits negative convexity.

7. In each case, choose the longer-duration bond in order to benefit from a rate decrease.

a. The Aaa-rated bond has the lower yield to maturity and therefore the longer duration.

b. The lower-coupon bond has the longer duration *and* greater de facto call protection.

c. The lower coupon bond has the longer duration.

8.   a. $10 \times 0.01 \times 800 = 80.00$

      b. $\frac{1}{2} \times 120 \times (0.015)^2 = 0.0135 = 1.35\%$

      c. $9/1.10 = 8.18$

      d.   (i)

      e.   (i)

      f.   (iii)

9.   The table below shows the holding period returns for each of the three bonds:

Maturity	1 year	2 years	3 years
YTM at beginning of year	7.00%	8.00%	9.00%
Beginning of year prices	$1,009.35	$1,000.00	$974.69
Prices at year end (at 9% YTM)	$1,000.00	$990.83	$982.41
Capital gain	−$9.35	−$9.17	$7.72
Coupon	$80.00	$80.00	$80.00
1-year total $ return	$70.65	$70.83	$87.72
1-year total rate of return	7.00%	7.08%	9.00%

You should buy the 3-year bond because it provides a 9% holding-period return over the next year, which is greater than the return on either of the other bonds.

10.   a. $\text{Modified duration} = \dfrac{\text{Macaulay duration}}{1 + \text{YTM}} = \dfrac{10}{1.08} = 9.26 \text{ years}$

      b.   For option-free coupon bonds, modified duration is a better measure of the bond's sensitivity to changes in interest rates. Maturity considers only the final cash flow, while modified duration includes other factors, such as the size and timing of coupon payments, and the level of interest rates (yield to maturity). Modified duration, unlike maturity, indicates the approximate percentage change in the bond price for a given change in yield to maturity.

      c.   i.   Modified duration increases as the coupon decreases.
            ii. Modified duration decreases as maturity decreases.

      d.   Convexity measures the curvature of the bond's price-yield curve. Such curvature means that the duration rule for bond price change (which is based only on the slope of the curve at the original yield) is only an approximation. Adding a term to account for the convexity of the bond increases the accuracy of the approximation. That convexity adjustment is the last term in the following equation:

$$\frac{\Delta P}{P} = (-D^* \times \Delta y) + \left[\frac{1}{2} \times \text{Convexity} \times (\Delta y)^2 \right]$$

11. a. PV of the obligation = $10,000 × Annuity factor (8%, 2) = $17,832.65

(1) Time until Payment (years)	(2) Cash Flow	(3) PV of CF (Discount rate = 8%)	(4) Weight	(5) Column (1) × Column (4)
1	$10,000.00	$9,259.259	0.51923	0.51923
2	$10,000.00	$8,573.388	0.48077	0.96154
Column Sums		$17,832.647	1.00000	1.48077

Duration = 1.4808 years

b. A zero-coupon bond maturing in 1.4808 years would immunize the obligation. Since the present value of the zero-coupon bond must be $17,832.65, the face value (i.e., the future redemption value) must be:

$$\$17,832.65 \times 1.08^{1.4808} = \$19,985.26$$

c. If the interest rate increases to 9%, the zero-coupon bond would decrease in value to:

$$\frac{\$19,985.26}{1.09^{1.4808}} = \$17,590.92$$

The present value of the tuition obligation would decrease to $17,591.11. The net position decreases in value by $0.19.

If the interest rate decreases to 7%, the zero-coupon bond would increase in value to:

$$\frac{\$19,985.26}{1.07^{1.4808}} = \$18,079.99$$

The present value of the tuition obligation would increase to $18,080.18. The net position decreases in value by $0.19.

The reason the net position changes at all is that, as the interest rate changes, so does the duration of the stream of tuition payments.

12. a. (i) Current yield = Coupon/Price = $70/$960 = 0.0729 = 7.29%

(ii) YTM = 3.993% semiannually or 7.986% annual bond equivalent yield. On a financial calculator, enter: n = 10; PV = –960; FV = 1000; PMT = 35 Compute the interest rate.

(iii) Horizon yield or realized compound yield is 4.166% (semiannually), or 8.332% annual bond equivalent yield. To obtain this value, first find the future value (FV) of reinvested coupons and principal. There will be six payments of $35 each, reinvested semiannually at 3% per period. On a financial calculator, enter:

PV = 0; PMT = $35; n = 6; i = 3%. Compute: FV = $226.39

Three years from now, the bond will be selling at the par value of $1,000 because the yield to maturity is forecast to equal the coupon rate. Therefore, total proceeds in three years will be $1,226.39.

Then find the rate ($y_{realized}$) that makes the FV of the purchase price equal to $1,226.39:

$$\$960 \times (1 + y_{realized})^6 = \$1,226.39 \Rightarrow y_{realized} = 4.166\% \text{ (semiannual)}$$

b.   Shortcomings of each measure:

(i) Current yield does not account for capital gains or losses on bonds bought at prices other than par value. It also does not account for reinvestment income on coupon payments.

(ii) Yield to maturity assumes the bond is held until maturity and that all coupon income can be reinvested at a rate equal to the yield to maturity.

(iii) Horizon yield or realized compound yield is affected by the forecast of reinvestment rates, holding period, and yield of the bond at the end of the investor's holding period.

Note: This criticism of horizon yield is a bit unfair: while YTM can be calculated without *explicit* assumptions regarding future YTM and reinvestment rates, you *implicitly* assume that these values equal the current YTM if you use YTM as a measure of expected return.

13.   a.   i. The effective duration of the 4.75% Treasury security is:

$$-\frac{\Delta P/P}{\Delta r} = \frac{(116.887 - 86.372)/100}{0.02} = 15.2575$$

ii. The duration of the portfolio is the weighted average of the durations of the individual bonds in the portfolio:

Portfolio Duration = $w_1 D_1 + w_2 D_2 + w_3 D_3 + \ldots + w_k D_k$

where
w_i = market value of bond *i*/market value of the portfolio
D_i = duration of bond *i*
k = number of bonds in the portfolio

The effective duration of the bond portfolio is calculated as follows:

[($48,667,680/$98,667,680) × 2.15] + [($50,000,000/$98,667,680) × 15.26] = 8.79

b. VanHusen's remarks would be correct if there were a small, parallel shift in yields. Duration is a first (linear) approximation only for small changes in yield. For larger changes in yield, the convexity measure is needed in order to approximate the change in price that is not explained by duration. Additionally, portfolio duration assumes that all yields change by the same number of basis points (parallel shift), so any non-parallel shift in yields would result in a difference in the price sensitivity of the portfolio compared to the price sensitivity of a single security having the same duration.

14. a. PV of obligation = $2 million/0.16 = $12.5 million

Duration of obligation = 1.16/0.16 = 7.25 years

Call w the weight on the 5-year maturity bond (which has duration of 4 years). Then:

$$(w \times 4) + [(1 - w) \times 11] = 7.25 \Rightarrow w = 0.5357$$

Therefore: $0.5357 \times \$12.5 = \$6.7$ million in the 5-year bond, and;

$0.4643 \times \$12.5 = \$5.8$ million in the 20-year bond.

b. The price of the 20-year bond is:

[$60 × Annuity factor (16%, 20)] + [$1,000 × PV factor (16%, 20)] = $407.12

Therefore, the bond sells for 0.4071 times its par value, and:

Market value = Par value × 0.4071

$5.8 million = Par value × 0.4071 ⇒ Par value = $14.25 million

Another way to see this is to note that each bond with par value $1,000 sells for $407.12. If total market value is $5.8 million, then you need to buy approximately 14,250 bonds, resulting in total par value of $14.25 million.

15. a. The duration of the perpetuity is: 1.05/0.05 = 21 years

Call w the weight of the zero-coupon bond. Then:

$$(w \times 5) + [(1 - w) \times 21] = 10 \Rightarrow w = 11/16 = 0.6875$$

Therefore, the portfolio weights would be as follows: 11/16 invested in the zero and 5/16 in the perpetuity.

b.   Next year, the zero-coupon bond will have a duration of 4 years and the perpetuity will still have a 21-year duration. To obtain the target duration of nine years, which is now the duration of the obligation, we again solve for w:

$$(w \times 4) + [(1 - w) \times 21] = 9 \Rightarrow w = 12/17 = 0.7059$$

So, the proportion of the portfolio invested in the zero increases to 12/17 and the proportion invested in the perpetuity falls to 5/17.

16. a.   The duration of the annuity *if* it were to start in 1 year would be:

(1) Time until Payment (years)	(2) Cash Flow	(3) PV of CF (Discount rate = 10%)	(4) Weight	(5) Column (1) × Column (4)
1	$10,000	$9,090.909	0.14795	0.14795
2	$10,000	$8,264.463	0.13450	0.26900
3	$10,000	$7,513.148	0.12227	0.36682
4	$10,000	$6,830.135	0.11116	0.44463
5	$10,000	$6,209.213	0.10105	0.50526
6	$10,000	$5,644.739	0.09187	0.55119
7	$10,000	$5,131.581	0.08351	0.58460
8	$10,000	$4,665.074	0.07592	0.60738
9	$10,000	$4,240.976	0.06902	0.62118
10	$10,000	$3,855.433	0.06275	0.62745
Column Sums		$61,445.671	1.00000	4.72546

D = 4.7255 years

Because the payment stream starts in five years, instead of one year, we add four years to the duration, so the duration is 8.7255 years.

b.   The present value of the deferred annuity is:

$$\frac{10{,}000 \times \text{Annuity factor }(10\%,10)}{1.10^4} = \$41{,}968$$

Call w the weight of the portfolio invested in the 5-year zero. Then:

$$(w \times 5) + [(1 - w) \times 20] = 8.7255 \Rightarrow w = 0.7516$$

The investment in the 5-year zero is equal to:

$$0.7516 \times \$41{,}968 = \$31{,}543$$

The investment in the 20-year zeros is equal to:

$$0.2484 \times \$41{,}968 = \$10{,}425$$

These are the present or *market* values of each investment. The face values are equal to the respective future values of the investments. The face value of the 5-year zeros is:

$$\$31{,}543 \times (1.10)^5 = \$50{,}800$$

Therefore, between 50 and 51 zero-coupon bonds, each of par value $1,000, would be purchased. Similarly, the face value of the 20-year zeros is:

$$\$10{,}425 \times (1.10)^{20} = \$70{,}134$$

17. a.   The Aa bond initially has a higher YTM (yield spread of 40 b.p. versus 31 b.p.), but it is expected to have a widening spread relative to Treasuries. This will reduce the rate of return. The Aaa spread is expected to be stable. Calculate comparative returns as follows:

Incremental return over Treasuries =

Incremental yield spread – (Change in spread × duration)

Aaa bond: 31 bp – (0 × 3.1 years) = 31 bp

Aa bond: 40 bp – (10 bp × 3.1 years) = 9 bp

Therefore, choose the Aaa bond.

b.   Other variables to be considered:

- Potential changes in issue-specific credit quality. If the credit quality of the bonds changes, spreads relative to Treasuries will also change.

- Changes in relative yield spreads for a given bond rating. If quality spreads in the general bond market change because of changes in required risk premiums, the yield spreads of the bonds will change even if there is no change in the assessment of the credit quality of these *particular* bonds.

- Maturity effect. As bonds near their maturity, the effect of credit quality on spreads can also change. This can affect bonds of different initial credit quality differently.

18. Using a financial calculator, we find that the actual price of the bond as a function of yield to maturity is:

Yield to maturity	Price
7%	$1,620.45
8%	$1,450.31
9%	$1,308.21

Using the Duration Rule, assuming yield to maturity falls to 7%:

$$\text{Predicted price change} = \left(-\frac{\text{Duration}}{1+y}\right) \times \Delta y \times P_0$$

$$= \left(-\frac{11.54}{1.08}\right) \times (-0.01) \times \$1,450.31 = \$154.97$$

Therefore: predicted new price = $1,450.31 + $154.97 = $1,605.28

The actual price at a 7% yield to maturity is $1,620.45. Therefore:

$$\% \text{ error} = \frac{\$1,605.28 - \$1,620.45}{\$1,620.45} = -0.0094 = -0.94\% \text{ (approximation is too low)}$$

Using the Duration Rule, assuming yield to maturity increases to 9%:

$$\text{Predicted price change} = \left(-\frac{\text{Duration}}{1+y}\right) \times \Delta y \times P_0$$

$$= \left(-\frac{11.54}{1.08}\right) \times 0.01 \times \$1,450.31 = -\$154.97$$

Therefore: predicted new price = $1,450.31 − $154.97 = $1,295.34

The actual price at a 9% yield to maturity is $1,308.21. Therefore:

$$\% \text{ error} = \frac{\$1,295.34 - \$1,308.21}{\$1,308.21} = -0.0098 = -0.98\% \text{ (approximation is too low)}$$

Using Duration-with-Convexity Rule, assuming yield to maturity falls to 7%

$$\text{Predicted price change} = \left\{\left[\left(-\frac{\text{Duration}}{1+y}\right) \times \Delta y\right] + \left[0.5 \times \text{Convexity} \times (\Delta y)^2\right]\right\} \times P_0$$

$$= \left\{\left[\left(-\frac{11.54}{1.08}\right) \times (-0.01)\right] + \left[0.5 \times 192.4 \times (-0.01)^2\right]\right\} \times \$1,450.31 = \$168.92$$

Therefore: predicted new price = $1,450.31 + $168.92 = $1,619.23

The actual price at a 7% yield to maturity is $1,620.45. Therefore:

$$\% \text{ error} = \frac{\$1,619.23 - \$1,620.45}{\$1,620.45} = -0.00075 = -0.075\% \text{ (approximation is too low)}$$

Using Duration-with-Convexity Rule, assuming yield to maturity rises to 9%:

$$\text{Predicted price change} = \left\{\left[\left(-\frac{\text{Duration}}{1+y}\right)\times \Delta y\right] + \left[0.5\times \text{Convexity}\times (\Delta y)^2\right]\right\}\times P_0$$

$$= \left\{\left[\left(-\frac{11.54}{1.08}\right)\times 0.01\right] + \left[0.5\times 192.4\times (0.01)^2\right]\right\}\times \$1,450.31 = -\$141.02$$

Therefore: predicted new price = $1,450.31 − $141.02 = $1,309.29

The actual price at a 9% yield to maturity is $1,308.21. Therefore:

$$\%\ \text{error} = \frac{\$1,309.29 - \$1,308.21}{\$1,308.21} = 0.00083 = 0.083\%\ \text{(approximation is too high)}$$

Conclusion: The duration-with-convexity rule provides more accurate approximations to the true change in price. In this example, the percentage error using convexity with duration is less than one-tenth the error using only duration to estimate the price change.

19. a. The price of the zero coupon bond ($1,000 face value) selling at a yield to maturity of 8% is $374.84 and the price of the coupon bond is $774.84.

At a YTM of 9% the actual price of the zero coupon bond is $333.28 and the actual price of the coupon bond is $691.79.

Zero coupon bond:

$$\text{Actual \% loss} = \frac{\$333.28 - \$374.84}{\$374.84} = -0.1109 = 11.09\%\ \text{loss}$$

The percentage loss predicted by the duration-with-convexity rule is:

$$\text{Predicted \% loss} = \left[(-11.81)\times 0.01\right] + \left[0.5\times 150.3\times 0.01^2\right] = -0.1106 = 11.06\%\ \text{loss}$$

Coupon bond:

$$\text{Actual \% loss} = \frac{\$691.79 - \$774.84}{\$774.84} = -0.1072 = 10.72\%\ \text{loss}$$

The percentage loss predicted by the duration-with-convexity rule is:

$$\text{Predicted \% loss} = \left[(-11.79)\times 0.01\right] + \left[0.5\times 231.2\times 0.01^2\right] = -0.1063 = 10.63\%\ \text{loss}$$

b. Now assume yield to maturity falls to 7%. The price of the zero increases to $422.04, and the price of the coupon bond increases to $875.91.

Zero coupon bond:

$$\text{Actual \% gain} = \frac{\$422.04 - \$374.84}{\$374.84} = 0.1259 = 12.59\% \text{ gain}$$

The percentage gain predicted by the duration-with-convexity rule is:

$$\text{Predicted \% gain} = [(-11.81) \times (-0.01)] + [0.5 \times 150.3 \times 0.01^2] = 0.1256 = 12.56\% \text{ gain}$$

Coupon bond

$$\text{Actual \% gain} = \frac{\$875.91 - \$774.84}{\$774.84} = 0.1304 = 13.04\% \text{ gain}$$

The percentage gain predicted by the duration-with-convexity rule is:

$$\text{Predicted \% gain} = [(-11.79) \times (-0.01)] + [0.5 \times 231.2 \times 0.01^2] = 0.1295 = 12.95\% \text{ gain}$$

c. The 6% coupon bond, which has higher convexity, outperforms the zero regardless of whether rates rise or fall. This can be seen to be a general property using the duration-with-convexity formula: the duration effects on the two bonds due to any change in rates are equal (since the respective durations are virtually equal), but the convexity effect, which is always positive, always favors the higher convexity bond. Thus, if the yields on the bonds change by equal amounts, as we assumed in this example, the higher convexity bond outperforms a lower convexity bond with the same duration and initial yield to maturity.

d. This situation cannot persist. No one would be willing to buy the lower convexity bond if it always underperforms the other bond. The price of the lower convexity bond will fall and its yield to maturity will rise. Thus, the lower convexity bond will sell at a higher initial yield to maturity. That higher yield is compensation for lower convexity. If rates change only slightly, the higher yield-lower convexity bond will perform better; if rates change by a substantial amount, the lower yield-higher convexity bond will perform better.

20. a. The following spreadsheet shows that the convexity of the bond is 64.933. The present value of each cash flow is obtained by discounting at 7%. (Since the bond has a 7% coupon and sells at par, its YTM is 7%.) Convexity equals: the sum of the last column (7,434.175) divided by:

$$[P \times (1 + y)^2] = 100 \times (1.07)^2 = 114.49$$

Time (t)	Cash flow (CF)	PV(CF)	$t^2 + t$	$(t^2 + t) \times PV(CF)$
1	7	6.542	2	13.084
2	7	6.114	6	36.684
3	7	5.714	12	68.569
4	7	5.340	20	106.805
5	7	4.991	30	149.727
6	7	4.664	42	195.905
7	7	4.359	56	244.118
8	7	4.074	72	293.333
9	7	3.808	90	342.678
10	107	54.393	110	5,983.271
Sum:		100.000		7,434.175
			Convexity:	64.933

The duration of the bond is:

(1) Time until Payment (years)	(2) Cash Flow	(3) PV of CF (Discount rate = 7%)	(4) Weight	(5) Column (1) × Column (4)
1	$7	$6.542	0.06542	0.06542
2	$7	$6.114	0.06114	0.12228
3	$7	$5.714	0.05714	0.17142
4	$7	$5.340	0.05340	0.21361
5	$7	$4.991	0.04991	0.24955
6	$7	$4.664	0.04664	0.27986
7	$7	$4.359	0.04359	0.30515
8	$7	$4.074	0.04074	0.32593
9	$7	$3.808	0.03808	0.34268
10	$107	$54.393	0.54393	5.43934
Column Sums	$100.000		1.00000	7.51523

D = 7.515 years

b. If the yield to maturity increases to 8%, the bond price will fall to 93.29% of par value, a percentage decrease of 6.71%.

c. The duration rule predicts a percentage price change of:

$$\left(-\frac{D}{1.07}\right) \times 0.01 = \left(-\frac{7.515}{1.07}\right) \times 0.01 = -0.0702 = -7.02\%$$

This overstates the actual percentage decrease in price by 0.31%.

The price predicted by the duration rule is 7.02% less than face value, or 92.98% of face value.

d. The duration-with-convexity rule predicts a percentage price change of:

$$\left[\left(-\frac{7.515}{1.07}\right) \times 0.01\right] + \left[0.5 \times 64.933 \times 0.01^2\right] = -0.0670 = -6.70\%$$

The percentage error is 0.01%, which is substantially less than the error using the duration rule.

The price predicted by the duration rule is 6.70% less than face value, or 93.30% of face value.

21. a. % price change = (−Effective duration) × Change in YTM (%)

CIC: $(-7.35) \times (-0.50\%) = 3.675\%$

PTR: $(-5.40) \times (-0.50\%) = 2.700\%$

b. Since we are asked to calculate horizon return over a period of only one coupon period, there is no reinvestment income.

$$\text{Horizon return} = \frac{\text{Coupon payment} + \text{Year-end price} - \text{Initial Price}}{\text{Initial price}}$$

CIC: $\dfrac{\$31.25 + \$1,055.50 - \$1,017.50}{\$1,017.50} = 0.06806 = 6.806\%$

PTR: $\dfrac{\$36.75 + \$1,041.50 - \$1,017.50}{\$1,017.50} = 0.05971 = 5.971\%$

c. Notice that CIC is non-callable but PTR is callable. Therefore, CIC has positive convexity, while PTR has negative convexity. Thus, the convexity correction to the duration approximation will be positive for CIC and negative for PTR.

22. The economic climate is one of impending interest rate increases. Hence, we will seek to shorten portfolio duration.

   a. Choose the short maturity (2009) bond.

   b. The Arizona bond likely has lower duration. The Arizona coupons are slightly lower, but the Arizona yield is higher.

   c. Choose the 12 3/8 % coupon bond. The maturities are approximately equal, but the 12 3/8 % coupon is much higher, resulting in a lower duration.

   d. The duration of the Shell bond is lower if the effect of the higher yield to maturity and earlier start of sinking fund redemption dominates its slightly lower coupon rate.

   e. The floating rate bond has a duration that approximates the adjustment period, which is only 6 months.

23. a. A manager who believes that the level of interest rates will change should engage in a rate anticipation swap, lengthening duration if rates are expected to fall, and shortening duration if rates are expected to rise.

   b. A change in yield spreads across sectors would call for an intermarket spread swap, in which the manager buys bonds in the sector for which yields are expected to fall relative to other bonds and sells bonds in the sector for which yields are expected to rise relative to other bonds.

   c. A belief that the yield spread on a particular instrument will change calls for a substitution swap in which that security is sold if its yield is expected to rise relative to the yield of other similar bonds, or is bought if its yield is expected to fall relative to the yield of other similar bonds.

24. While it is true that short-term rates are more volatile than long-term rates, the longer duration of the longer-term bonds makes their prices and their rates of return more volatile. The higher duration magnifies the sensitivity to interest-rate savings.

25. The minimum terminal value that the manager is willing to accept is determined by the requirement for a 3% annual return on the initial investment. Therefore, the floor is:

$$\$1 \text{ million} \times (1.03)^5 = \$1.16 \text{ million}$$

Three years after the initial investment, only two years remain until the horizon date, and the interest rate has risen to 8%. Therefore, at this time, in order to be assured that the target value can be attained, the manager needs a portfolio worth:

$$\$1.16 \text{ million}/(1.08)^2 = \$0.9945 \text{ million}$$

This is the trigger point.

26. The maturity of the 30-year bond will fall to 25 years, and its yield is forecast to be 8%. Therefore, the price forecast for the bond is: $893.25

[Using a financial calculator, enter the following: n = 25; i = 8; FV = 1000; PMT = 70]

At a 6% interest rate, the five coupon payments will accumulate to $394.60 after five years. Therefore, total proceeds will be: $394.60 + $893.25 = $1,287.85

Therefore, the 5-year return is: ($1,287.85/$867.42) − 1 = 0.4847

This is a 48.47% 5-year return, or 8.23% annually.

The maturity of the 20-year bond will fall to 15 years, and its yield is forecast to be 7.5%. Therefore, the price forecast for the bond is: $911.73

[Using a financial calculator, enter the following: n = 15; i = 7.5; FV = 1000; PMT = 65]

At a 6% interest rate, the five coupon payments will accumulate to $366.41 after five years. Therefore, total proceeds will be: $366.41 + $911.73 = $1,278.14

Therefore, the 5-year return is: ($1,278.14/$879.50) − 1 = 0.4533

This is a 45.33% 5-year return, or 7.76% annually. The 30-year bond offers the higher expected return.

27. a. The advantages of a bond indexing strategy are:
    - Historically, the majority of active managers underperform benchmark indexes in most periods; indexing reduces the possibility of underperformance at a given level of risk.
    - Indexed portfolios do not depend on advisor expectations and so have less risk of underperforming the market.
    - Management advisory fees for indexed portfolios are dramatically less than fees for actively managed portfolios. Fees charged by active managers generally range from 15 to 50 basis points, while fees for indexed portfolios range from 1 to 20 basis points (with the highest of those representing enhanced indexing). Other non-advisory fees (i.e., custodial fees) are also less for indexed portfolios.

- Plan sponsors have greater control over indexed portfolios because individual managers do not have as much freedom to vary from the parameters of the benchmark index. Some plan sponsors even decide to manage index portfolios with in-house investment staff.

- Indexing is essentially "buying the market." If markets are efficient, an indexing strategy should reduce unsystematic diversifiable risk, and should generate maximum return for a given level of risk.

The disadvantages of a bond indexing strategy are:

- Indexed portfolio returns may match the bond index, but do not necessarily reflect optimal performance. In some time periods, many active managers may outperform an indexing strategy at the same level of risk.

- The chosen bond index and portfolio returns may not meet the client objectives or the liability stream.

- Bond indexing may restrict the fund from participating in sectors or other opportunities that could increase returns.

b. The stratified sampling, or cellular, method divides the index into cells, with each cell representing a different characteristic of the index. Common cells used in the cellular method combine (but are not limited to) duration, coupon, maturity, market sectors, credit rating, and call and sinking fund features. The index manager then selects one or more bond issues to represent the entire cell. The total market weight of issues held for each cell is based on the target index's composition of that characteristic.

c. Tracking error is defined as the discrepancy between the performance of an indexed portfolio and the benchmark index. When the amount invested is relatively small and the number of cells to be replicated is large, a significant source of tracking error with the cellular method occurs because of the need to buy odd lots of issues in order to accurately represent the required cells. Odd lots generally must be purchased at higher prices than round lots. On the other hand, reducing the number of cells to limit the required number of odd lots would potentially increase tracking error because of the mismatch with the target.

28. a. For an option-free bond, the effective duration and modified duration are approximately the same. The duration of the bond is 7.1. Using the data provided, the duration is calculated as follows:

$$-\frac{\Delta P/P}{\Delta r} = \frac{(100.71 - 99.29)/100}{0.002} = 7.100$$

b. The total percentage price change for the bond is estimated as follows:

Percentage price change using duration = $-7.90 \times -0.02 \times 100 = 15.80\%$

Convexity adjustment = 1.66%

Total estimated percentage price change = $15.80\% + 1.66\% = 17.46\%$

c. The assistant's argument is incorrect. Because modified convexity does not recognize the fact that cash flows for bonds with an embedded option can change as yields change, modified convexity remains positive as yields move below the callable bond's stated coupon rate, just as it would for an option-free bond. Effective convexity, however, takes into account the fact that cash flows for a security with an embedded option can change as interest rates change. When yields move significantly below the stated coupon rate, the likelihood that the bond will be called by the issuer increases and the effective convexity turns negative.

29. $\Delta P/P = -D^* \, \Delta y$

For Strategy I:

5-year maturity: $\Delta P/P = -4.83 \times (-0.75\%) = 3.6225\%$

25-year maturity: $\Delta P/P = -23.81 \times 0.50\% = -11.9050\%$

Strategy I: $\Delta P/P = (0.5 \times 3.6225\%) + [0.5 \times (-11.9050\%)] = -4.1413\%$

For Strategy II:

15-year maturity: $\Delta P/P = -14.35 \times 0.25\% = -3.5875\%$

30. a. i. Strong economic recovery with rising inflation expectations. Interest rates and bond yields will most likely rise, and the prices of both bonds will fall. The probability that the callable bond will be called would decrease, and the callable bond will behave more like the non-callable bond. (Note that they have similar durations when priced to maturity). The slightly lower duration of the callable bond will result in somewhat better performance in the high interest rate scenario.

ii. Economic recession with reduced inflation expectations. Interest rates and bond yields will most likely fall. The callable bond is likely to be called. The relevant duration calculation for the callable bond is now modified duration to call. Price appreciation is limited as indicated by the lower duration. The non-callable bond, on the other hand, continues to have the same modified duration and hence has greater price appreciation.

b. Projected price change = (modified duration) × (change in YTM)

$$= (-6.80) \times (-0.75\%) = 5.1\%$$

Therefore, the price will increase to approximately $105.10 from its current level of $100.

c. For Bond A, the callable bond, bond life and therefore bond cash flows are uncertain. If one ignores the call feature and analyzes the bond on a "to maturity" basis, all calculations for yield and duration are distorted. Durations are too long and yields are too high. On the other hand, if one treats the premium bond selling above the call price on a "to call" basis, the duration is unrealistically short and yields too low. The most effective approach is to use an option valuation approach. The callable bond can be decomposed into two separate securities: a non-callable bond and an option:

Price of callable bond = Price of non-callable bond − price of option

Since the call option always has some positive value, the price of the callable bond is always less than the price of the non-callable security.

31.

a.

	Period	Time until Payment (Years)	Cash Flow	PV of CF Discount rate = 6% per period	Weight	Years × Weight
A. 8% coupon bond	1	0.5	$40	$37.736	0.0405	0.0203
	2	1.0	40	35.600	0.0383	0.0383
	3	1.5	40	33.585	0.0361	0.0541
	4	2.0	1,040	823.777	0.8851	1.7702
Sum:				$930.698	1.0000	1.8829
B. Zero-coupon	1	0.5	$0	$0.000	0.0000	0.0000
	2	1.0	0	0.000	0.0000	0.0000
	3	1.5	0	0.000	0.0000	0.0000
	4	2.0	1,000	792.094	1.0000	2.0000
Sum:				$792.094	1.0000	2.0000

For the coupon bond, the weight on the last payment in the table above is less than it is in Spreadsheet 16.1 because the discount rate is higher; the weights for the first three payments are larger than those in Spreadsheet 16.1. Consequently, the duration of the bond falls. The zero coupon bond, by contrast, has a fixed weight of 1.0 for the single payment at maturity.

b.

	Period	Time until Payment (Years)	Cash Flow	PV of CF Discount rate = 5% per period	Weight	Years × Weight
A. 8% coupon bond	1	0.5	$60	$57.143	0.0552	0.0276
	2	1.0	60	54.422	0.0526	0.0526
	3	1.5	60	51.830	0.0501	0.0751
	4	2.0	1,060	872.065	0.8422	1.6844
Sum:				$1,035.460	1.0000	1.8396

Since the coupon payments are larger in the above table, the weights on the earlier payments are higher than in Spreadsheet 16.1, so duration decreases.

32.

a.

	Time (t)	Cash Flow	PV(CF)	$t + t^2$	$(t + t^2) \times$ PV(CF)
Coupon = $80	1	$80	$72.727	2	145.455
YTM = 0.10	2	80	66.116	6	396.694
Maturity = 5	3	80	60.105	12	721.262
Price = $924.184	4	80	54.641	20	1,092.822
	5	1,080	670.595	30	20,117.851

Price: $924.184

Sum: 22,474.083

Convexity = Sum/[Price × $(1+y)^2$] = 20.097

b.

	Time (t)	Cash Flow	PV(CF)	$t^2 + t$	$(t^2 + t) \times$ PV(CF)
Coupon = $0	1	$0	$0.000	2	0.000
YTM = 0.10	2	0	0.000	6	0.000
Maturity = 5	3	0	0.000	12	0.000
Price = $924.184	4	0	0.000	20	0.000
	5	1,000	620.921	30	18,627.640

Price: $620.921

Sum: 18,627.640

Convexity = Sum/[Price × $(1+y)^2$] = 24.793

CHAPTER 17: MACROECONOMIC & INDUSTRY ANALYSIS

1. Expansionary (looser) monetary policy to lower interest rates would stimulate both investment and expenditures on consumer durables. Expansionary fiscal policy (i.e., lower taxes, increased government spending, increased welfare transfers) would stimulate aggregate demand directly.

2. a. Gold Mining. Gold traditionally is viewed as a hedge against inflation. Expansionary monetary policy may lead to increased inflation, and thus could enhance the value of gold mining stocks.

    b. Construction. Expansionary monetary policy will lead to lower interest rates which ought to stimulate housing demand. The construction industry should benefit.

3. a. Lowering reserve requirements would allow banks to lend out a higher fraction of deposits and thus increase the money supply.

    b. The Fed would buy Treasury securities, thereby increasing the money supply.

    c. The discount rate would be reduced, allowing banks to borrow additional funds at a lower rate.

4. a. Expansionary monetary policy is likely to increase the inflation rate, either because it may over stimulate the economy, or ultimately because the end result of more money in the economy is higher prices.

    b. Real output and employment should increase in response to the expansionary policy, at least in the short run.

    c. The real interest rate should fall, at least in the short-run, as the supply of funds to the economy has increased.

    d. The nominal interest rate could either increase or decrease. On the one hand, the real rate might fall [see part (c)], but the inflation premium might rise [see part (a)]. The nominal rate is the sum of these two components.

5. A depreciating dollar makes imported cars more expensive and American cars less expensive to foreign consumers. This should benefit the U.S. auto industry.

6.   Supply side economists believe that a reduction in income tax rates will make workers more willing to work at current or even slightly lower (gross-of-tax) wages. Such an effect ought to mitigate cost pressures on the inflation rate.

7.   a.   The robotics process entails higher fixed costs and lower variable (labor) costs. Therefore, this firm will perform better in a boom and worse in a recession. For example, costs will rise less rapidly than revenue when sales volume expands during a boom.

     b.   Because its profits are more sensitive to the business cycle, the robotics firm will have the higher beta.

8.   a.   Housing construction (cyclical but interest-rate sensitive): (iii) Healthy expansion

     b.   Health care (a non-cyclical industry): (i) Deep recession

     c.   Gold mining (counter-cyclical): (iv) Stagflation

     d.   Steel production (cyclical industry) (ii) Superheated economy

9.   a.   Oil well equipment: Relative decline (Environmental pressures, decline in easily-developed new oil fields)

     b.   Computer hardware: Consolidation

     c.   Computer software: Consolidation

     d.   Genetic engineering: Start-up

     e.   Railroads: Relative decline

10. a.   General Autos. Pharmaceuticals are less of a discretionary purchase than automobiles.

     b.   Friendly Airlines. Travel expenditure is more sensitive to the business cycle than movie consumption.

11. This exercise is left to the student

12. The index of consumer expectations is a useful leading economic indicator because, if consumers are optimistic about the future, they will be more willing to spend money, especially on consumer durables, which will increase aggregate demand and stimulate the economy.

13. Labor cost per unit is a useful lagging indicator because wages typically start rising only well into an economic expansion. At the beginning of an expansion, there is considerable slack in the economy and output can expand without employers bidding up the price of inputs or the wages of employees. By the time wages start increasing due to high demand for labor, the boom period has already progressed considerably.

14. a. The concept of an industrial life cycle refers to the tendency of most industries to go through various stages of growth. The rate of growth, the competitive environment, profit margins and pricing strategies tend to shift as an industry moves from one stage to the next, although it is generally difficult to identify precisely when one stage has ended and the next begun.

   The start-up stage is characterized by perceptions of a large potential market and by a high level of optimism for potential profits. However, this stage usually demonstrates a high rate of failure. In the second stage, often called stable growth or consolidation, growth is high and accelerating, the markets are broadening, unit costs are declining and quality is improving. In this stage, industry leaders begin to emerge. The third stage, usually called slowing growth or maturity, is characterized by decelerating growth caused by factors such as maturing markets and/or competitive inroads by other products. Finally, an industry reaches a stage of relative decline in which sales slow or even decline.

   Product pricing, profitability and industry competitive structure often vary by stage. Thus, for example, the first stage usually encompasses high product prices, high costs (R&D, marketing, etc.) and a (temporary) monopolistic industry structure. In stage two (stable growth), new entrants begin to appear and costs fall rapidly due to the learning curve. Prices generally do not fall as rapidly, however, allowing profit margins to increase. In stage three (slowing growth), growth begins to slow as the product or service begins to saturate the market, and margins are eroded by significant price reductions. In the final stage, industry cumulative production is so high that production costs have stopped declining, profit margins are thin (assuming competition exists), and the fate of the industry depends on replacement demand and the existence of substitute products/services.

   b. The passenger car business in the United States has probably entered the final stage in the industrial life cycle because normalized growth is quite low. The information processing business, on the other hand, is undoubtedly earlier in the cycle. Depending on whether or not growth is still accelerating, it is either in the second or third stage.

c. Cars: in the final stages of the life cycle, demand tends to be price sensitive. Thus, Universal can not raise prices without losing volume. Moreover, given the industry's maturity, cost structures are likely to be similar across all competitors, and any price cuts can be matched immediately. Thus, Universal's car business is boxed in: Product pricing is determined by the market, and the company is a "price-taker."

Idata: Idata should have much more pricing flexibility given its earlier stage in the industrial life cycle. Demand is growing faster than supply, and, depending on the presence and/or actions of an industry leader, Idata may set prices high to maximize current profits and generate cash for product development, or set prices low in an effort to gain market share.

15. a. A basic premise of the business cycle approach to investment timing is that stock prices anticipate fluctuations in the business cycle. For example, there is evidence that stock prices tend to move about six months ahead of the economy. In fact, stock prices are a leading indicator for the economy.

Over the course of a business cycle, this approach to investing would work roughly as follows. As the investor perceives that the top of a business cycle is approaching, stocks purchased should not be vulnerable to a recession. When the investor perceives that a downturn is at hand, stock holdings should be lightened with proceeds invested in fixed-income securities. Once the recession has matured to some extent, and interest rates fall, bond prices will rise. As the investor perceives that the recession is about to end, profits should be taken in the bonds and reinvested in stocks, particularly those in cyclical industries with a high beta.

Abnormal returns generally will only be earned if these asset allocation switches are timed better than those of other investors. Switches made after the turning points may not lead to excess returns.

b. Based on the business cycle approach to investment timing, the ideal time to invest in a cyclical stock such as a passenger car company would be just before the end of a recession. If the recovery is already underway, Adam's recommendation would be too late. The equities market generally anticipates the changes in the economic cycle. Therefore, since the "recovery is underway," the price of Universal Auto should already reflect the anticipated improvements in the economy.

16. The expiration of the patent means that General Weedkillers will soon face considerably greater competition from its competitors. We would expect prices and profit margins to fall, and total industry sales to increase somewhat as prices decline. The industry will probably enter the consolidation stage in which producers are forced to compete more extensively on the basis of price.

17. a. • The industry-wide ROE is leveling off, indicating that the industry may be approaching a later stage of the life cycle.

   • Average P/E ratios are declining, suggesting that investors are becoming less optimistic about growth prospects.

   • Dividend payout is increasing, suggesting that the firm sees less reason to reinvest earnings in the firm. There may be fewer growth opportunities in the industry.

   • Industry dividend yield is also increasing, even though market dividend yield is decreasing.

   b. • Industry growth rate is still forecast at 10% to 15%, higher than would be true of a mature industry.

   • Non-U.S. markets are still untapped, and some firms are now entering these markets.

   • Mail order sale segment is growing at 40% a year.

   • Niche markets are continuing to develop.

   • New manufacturers continue to enter the market.

18. a. Expected profit = Revenues – Fixed costs – Variable costs

   $$= \$120{,}000 - \$30{,}000 - [(1/3) \times \$120{,}000] = \$50{,}000$$

   b. $$DOL = 1 + \frac{fixed\ costs}{profits} = 1 + \frac{\$30{,}000}{\$50{,}000} = 1.60$$

   c. If sales are only $108,000, profits will fall to:

   $$\$108{,}000 - \$30{,}000 - [(1/3) \times \$108{,}000] = \$42{,}000$$

   This is a 16% decline from the forecasted value.

   d. The decrease in profits is 16%, which is equal to DOL times the 10% drop in sales.

   e. Profits must drop more than 100% for profits to turn negative. For profits to fall 100%, revenues must fall by:

   $$\frac{100\%}{DOL} = \frac{100\%}{1.60} = 62.5\%$$

   Therefore, revenues would be only 37.5% of the original forecast. At this level, revenues will be: $0.375 \times \$120{,}000 = \$45{,}000$

   f. If revenues are $45,000, profits will be:

   $$\$45{,}000 - \$30{,}000 - (1/3) \times \$45{,}000 = \$0$$

19. a. Relevant data from the table supporting the conclusion that the retail auto parts industry as a whole is in the maturity stage of the industry life cycle are:

- The population of 18-29 year olds, a major customer base for the industry, is gradually declining.
- The number of households with income less than $35,000, another important consumer base, is not expanding.
- The number of cars five to fifteen years old, an important end market, has experienced low annual growth (or actual declines in some years), so the number of units that potentially need parts is not growing.
- Automotive aftermarket industry retail sales have been growing slowly for several years.
- Consumer expenditures on automotive parts and accessories have grown slowly for several years.
- Average operating margins of all retail autoparts companies have steadily declined.

b. (i) Relevant data from the table supporting the conclusion that Wigwam Autoparts Heaven, Inc. (WAH) and its principal competitors are in the consolidation stage of their life cycle are:

- Sales growth of retail autoparts companies with 100 or more stores have been growing rapidly and at an increasing rate.
- Market share of retail autoparts stores with 100 or more stores has been increasing but is still less than 20 percent, leaving room for much more growth.
- Average operating margins for retail autoparts companies with 100 or more stores are high and rising.

(ii) Because of industry fragmentation (i.e., most of the market share is distributed among many companies with only a few stores), the retail autoparts industry apparently is undergoing marketing innovation and consolidation. The industry is moving toward the "category killer" format, in which a few major companies control large market shares through proliferation of outlets. The evidence suggests that a new "industry within an industry" is emerging in the form of the "category killer" large chain-store company. This industry subgroup is in its consolidation stage (i.e., rapid growth with high operating profit margins and emerging market leaders) despite the fact that the industry is in the maturity stage of its life cycle.

20. i.   *Substitutes – one year from now:* Currently the Carrycom, and other products in their industry segment, have automatic language conversion functionality and geographic region flexibility. This market segment is currently in a strong position.

          Substitutes – five years from now: White expects that other products in the broader consumer electronics industry, such as PDAs, PCs, and other consumer electronics, will eventually be able to incorporate both functionalities and so therefore diminish the strength of this force for Carrycom and other products in their market segment.

     ii.   *Threat of new (or potential) entrants – one year from now:* Wade has no threat of entrants into its market for the next three years because: (a) Wade has the exclusive ability to manufacture with ordinary copper, while other potential entrants do not have access to pari-copper, and; (b) Potential entrants do not have access to the exclusive production license for Carrycom technology.

          Threat of new (or potential) entrants – five years from now: Beyond the next three years, however, the threat is high. White expects competitors to market copper-based products, eliminating Carrycom's unique competitive advantage. In addition, the three-year exclusive production license expires.

    iii.   *Intensity of rivalry – one year from now:* Wade will experience only modest rivalry for three years as it has an exclusive production license for the next three years, which limits the availability of similar products. However, the broader electronics market may be integrating the automatic language conversion feature into its products after one year.

          Intensity of rivalry – five years from now: After the license expires in three years, White expects other competitors to produce a number of similar products which will limit their pricing power. This demonstrates a high intensity of rivalry.

21. a.   (iii)

     b.   (iii)

     c.   (iv)

     d.   (iii)

CHAPTER 18: EQUITY VALUATION MODELS

1. $P_0 = D_1/(k - g) = \$2.10/(0.11 - 0) = \$19.09$

2. I and II

3. a. $k = D_1/P_0 + g$

    $0.16 = \$2/\$50 + g \Rightarrow g = 0.12 = 12\%$

   b. $P_0 = D_1/(k - g) = \$2/(0.16 - 0.05) = \$18.18$

    The price falls in response to the more pessimistic dividend forecast. The forecast for *current* year earnings, however, is unchanged. Therefore, the P/E ratio falls. The lower P/E ratio is evidence of the diminished optimism concerning the firm's growth prospects.

4. a. $g = ROE \times b = 16\% \times 0.5 = 8\%$

    $D_1 = \$2(1 - b) = \$2(1 - 0.5) = \$1$

    $P_0 = D_1/(k - g) = \$1/(0.12 - 0.08) = \$25$

   b. $P_3 = P_0(1 + g)^3 = \$25(1.08)^3 = \$31.49$

5. a. This director is confused. In the context of the constant growth model [i.e., $P_0 = D_1/(k - g)$], it is true that price is higher when dividends are higher *holding everything else including dividend growth constant*. But everything else will not be constant. If the firm increases the dividend payout rate, the growth rate g will fall, and stock price will not necessarily rise. In fact, if $ROE > k$, price will fall.

   b. (i) An increase in dividend payout will reduce the sustainable growth rate as less funds are reinvested in the firm. The sustainable growth rate (i.e., $ROE \times$ plowback) will fall as plowback ratio falls.

    (ii) The increased dividend payout rate will reduce the growth rate of book value for the same reason -- less funds are reinvested in the firm.

6. a. $k = r_f + \beta[E(r_M) - r_f] = 6\% + 1.25(14\% - 6\%) = 16\%$

$g = 2/3 \times 9\% = 6\%$

$D_1 = E_0(1 + g)(1 - b) = \$3(1.06)(1/3) = \$1.06$

$$P_0 = \frac{D_1}{k - g} = \frac{\$1.06}{0.16 - 0.06} = \$10.60$$

b. Leading $P_0/E_1 = \$10.60/\$3.18 = 3.33$

Trailing $P_0/E_0 = \$10.60/\$3.00 = 3.53$

c. $PVGO = P_0 - \dfrac{E_1}{k} = \$10.60 - \dfrac{\$3.18}{0.16} = -\$9.275$

The low P/E ratios and negative PVGO are due to a poor ROE (9%) that is less than the market capitalization rate (16%).

d. Now, you revise b to 1/3, g to $1/3 \times 9\% = 3\%$, and D_1 to:

$E_0 \times 1.03 \times (2/3) = \$2.06$

Thus:

$V_0 = \$2.06/(0.16 - 0.03) = \$15.85$

V_0 increases because the firm pays out more earnings instead of reinvesting a poor ROE. This information is not yet known to the rest of the market.

7. Since beta = 1.0, then k = market return = 15%
Therefore:

$15\% = D_1/P_0 + g = 4\% + g \Rightarrow g = 11\%$

8. a. $P_0 = \dfrac{D_1}{k - g} = \dfrac{\$8}{0.10 - 0.05} = \$160$

b. The dividend payout ratio is 8/12 = 2/3, so the plowback ratio is b = 1/3. The implied value of ROE on future investments is found by solving:

$g = b \times ROE$ with $g = 5\%$ and $b = 1/3 \Rightarrow ROE = 15\%$

c. Assuming ROE = k, price is equal to:

$$P_0 = \frac{E_1}{k} = \frac{\$12}{0.10} = \$120$$

Therefore, the market is paying $40 per share ($160 – $120) for growth opportunities.

9. Using a two-stage dividend discount model, the current value of a share of Sundanci is calculated as follows.

$$V_0 = \frac{D_1}{(1+k)^1} + \frac{D_2}{(1+k)^2} + \frac{\dfrac{D_3}{(k-g)}}{(1+k)^2}$$

$$= \frac{\$0.3770}{1.14^1} + \frac{\$0.4976}{1.14^2} + \frac{\dfrac{\$0.5623}{(0.14-0.13)}}{1.14^2} = \$43.98$$

where:

$E_0 = \$0.952$

$D_0 = \$0.286$

$E_1 = E_0 (1.32)^1 = \$0.952 \times 1.32 = \$1.2566$

$D_1 = E_1 \times 0.30 = \$1.2566 \times 0.30 = \$0.3770$

$E_2 = E_0 (1.32)^2 = \$0.952 \times (1.32)^2 = \$1.6588$

$D_2 = E_2 \times 0.30 = \$1.6588 \times 0.30 = \$0.4976$

$E_3 = E_0 \times (1.32)^2 \times 1.13 = \$0.952 \times (1.32)^3 \times 1.13 = \$1.8744$

$D_3 = E_3 \times 0.30 = \$1.8743 \times 0.30 = \$0.5623$

10. a. Free cash flow to equity (FCFE) is defined as the cash flow remaining after meeting all financial obligations (including debt payment) and after covering capital expenditure and working capital needs. The FCFE is a measure of how much the firm can afford to pay out as dividends, but in a given year may be more or less than the amount actually paid out. Sundanci's FCFE for the year 2000 is computed as follows:

FCFE =

Earnings after tax + Depreciation expense − Capital expenditures − Increase in NWC

= $80 million + $23 million − $38 million − $41 million = $24 million

FCFE per share = FCFE/number of shares outstanding

= $24 million/84 million shares = $0.286

At the given dividend payout ratio, Sundanci's FCFE per share equals dividends per share.

b. The FCFE model requires forecasts of FCFE for the high growth years (2001 and 2002) plus a forecast for the first year of stable growth (2003) in order to allow for an estimate of the terminal value in 2002 based on perpetual growth. Because all of the components of FCFE are expected to grow at the same rate, the values can be obtained by projecting the FCFE at the common rate. (Alternatively, the components of FCFE can be projected and aggregated for each year.)

The following table shows the process for estimating Sundanci's current value on a per share basis.

Free Cash Flow to Equity
Base Assumptions
Shares outstanding: 84 million
Required return on equity (r): 14%

			Actual 2000	Projected 2001	Projected 2002	Projected 2003
Growth rate (g)				27%	27%	13%
	Total	Per share				
Earnings after tax	$80	$0.952	$1.2090	$1.5355	$1.7351
Plus: Depreciation expense	$23	$0.274	$0.3480	$0.4419	$0.4994
Less: Capital expenditures	$38	$0.452	$0.5740	$0.7290	$0.8238
Less: Increase in net working capital	$41	$0.488	$0.6198	$0.7871	$0.8894
Equals: FCFE	$24	$0.286	$0.3632	$0.4613	$0.5213
Terminal value				$52.1300*	
Total cash flows to equity			$0.3632	$52.5913**	
Discounted value			$0.3186***	$40.4673***	
Current value per share				$40.7859****	

*Projected 2002 Terminal value = (Projected 2003 FCFE)/(r – g)

**Projected 2002 Total cash flows to equity =

   Projected 2002 FCFE + Projected 2002 Terminal value

***Discounted values obtained using r = 14%

****Current value per share =

   Sum of Discounted Projected 2001 and 2002 Total cash flows to equity

c.   i. The DDM uses a strict definition of cash flows to equity, i.e. the expected dividends on the common stock. In fact, taken to its extreme, the DDM cannot be used to estimate the value of a stock that pays no dividends. The FCFE model expands the definition of cash flows to include the balance of residual cash flows after all financial obligations and investment needs have been met. Thus the FCFE model explicitly recognizes the firm's investment and financing policies as well as its dividend policy. In instances of a change of corporate control, and therefore the possibility of changing dividend policy, the FCFE model provides a better estimate of value. The DDM is biased toward finding low P/E ratio stocks with high dividend yields to be undervalued and conversely, high P/E ratio stocks with low dividend yields to be overvalued. It is considered a conservative model in that it tends to identify fewer undervalued firms as market prices rise relative to fundamentals. The DDM does not allow for the potential tax disadvantage of high dividends relative to the capital gains achievable from retention of earnings.

i. Both two-stage valuation models allow for two distinct phases of growth, an initial finite period where the growth rate is abnormal, followed by a stable growth period that is expected to last indefinitely. These two-stage models share the same limitations with respect to the growth assumptions. First, there is the difficulty of defining the duration of the extraordinary growth period. For example, a longer period of high growth will lead to a higher valuation, and there is the temptation to assume an unrealistically long period of extraordinary growth. Second, the assumption of a sudden shift form high growth to lower, stable growth is unrealistic. The transformation is more likely to occur gradually, over a period of time. Given that the assumed total horizon does not shift (i.e., is infinite), the timing of the shift form high to stable growth is a critical determinant of the valuation estimate. Third, because the value is quite sensitive to the steady-state growth assumption, over- or under-estimating this rate can lead to large errors in value. The two models share other limitations as well, notably difficulties in accurately forecasting required rates of return, in dealing with the distortions that result from substantial and/or volatile debt ratios, and in accurately valuing assets that do not generate any cash flows.

11.   a.   The formula for calculating a price earnings ratio (P/E) for a stable growth firm is the dividend payout ratio divided by the difference between the required rate of return and the growth rate of dividends. If the P/E is calculated based on trailing earnings (year 0), the payout ratio is increased by the growth rate. If the P/E is calculated based on next year's earnings (year 1), the numerator is the payout ratio.

P/E on trailing earnings:

P/E = [payout ratio × (1 + g)]/(r − g) = [0.30 × 1.13]/(0.14 − 0.13) = 33.9

P/E on next year's earnings:

P/E = payout ratio/(r − g) = 0.30/(0.14 − 0.13) = 30.0

b. The P/E ratio is a decreasing function of riskiness; as risk increases the P/E ratio decreases. Increases in the riskiness of Sundanci stock would be expected to lower the P/E ratio.
The P/E ratio is an increasing function of the growth rate of the firm; the higher the expected growth the higher the P/E ratio. Sundanci would command a higher P/E if analysts increase the expected growth rate.

The P/E ratio is a decreasing function of the market risk premium. An increased market risk premium would increase the required rate of return, lowering the price of a stock relative to its earnings. A higher market risk premium would be expected to lower Sundanci's P/E ratio.

12. a. The sustainable growth rate is equal to:

plowback ratio × return on equity = b × ROE

where

b = [Net Income − (Dividend per share × shares outstanding)]/Net Income

ROE = Net Income/Beginning of year equity

In 2000:

b = [208 − (0.80 × 100)]/208 = 0.6154

ROE = 208/1380 = 0.1507

Sustainable growth rate = 0.6154 × 0.1507 = 9.3%

In 2003:

b = [275 − (0.80 × 100)]/275 = 0.7091

ROE = 275/1836 = 0.1498

Sustainable growth rate = 0.7091 × 0.1498 = 10.6%

b. i. The increased retention ratio increased the sustainable growth rate.

Retention ratio = [Net Income − (Dividend per share × shares outstanding)]/Net Income

Retention ratio increased from 0.6154 in 2000 to 0.7091 in 2003.
This increase in the retention ratio directly increased the sustainable growth rate because the retention ratio is one of the two factors determining the sustainable growth rate.

ii. The decrease in leverage reduced the sustainable growth rate.

Financial leverage = (Total Assets/Beginning of year equity)

Financial leverage decreased from 2.34 (= 3230/1380) at the beginning of 2000 to 2.10 at the beginning of 2003 (= 3856/1836)
This decrease in leverage directly decreased ROE (and thus the sustainable growth rate) because financial leverage is one of the factors determining ROE (and ROE is one of the two factors determining the sustainable growth rate).

13. a. The formula for the Gordon model is:

$$V_0 = [D_0 \times (1 + g)]/(r - g)$$

where:

D_0 = dividend paid at time of valuation
g = annual growth rate of dividends
r = required rate of return for equity

In the above formula, P_0, the market price of the common stock, substitutes for V_0 and g becomes the dividend growth rate implied by the market:

$$P_0 = [D_0 \times (1 + g)]/(r - g)$$

Substituting, we have:

$$58.49 = [0.80 \times (1 + g)]/(0.08 - g) \Rightarrow g = 6.54\%$$

b. Use of the Gordon growth model would be inappropriate to value Dynamic's common stock, for the following reasons:

i. The Gordon growth model assumes a set of relationships about the growth rate for dividends, earnings, and stock values. Specifically, the model assumes that dividends, earnings, and stock values will grow at the same constant rate. In valuing Dynamic's common stock, the Gordon growth model is inappropriate because management's dividend policy has held dividends constant in dollar amount although earnings have grown, thus reducing the payout ratio. This policy is inconsistent with the Gordon model assumption that the payout ratio is constant.

ii. It could also be argued that use of the Gordon model, given Dynamic's current dividend policy, violates one of the general conditions for suitability of the model, namely that the company's dividend policy bears an understandable and consistent relationship with the company's profitability.

14. a. The industry's estimated P/E can be computed using the following model:

$$P_0/E_1 = \text{payout ratio}/(r - g)$$

However, since r and g are not explicitly given, they must be computed using the following formulas:

$$g_{ind} = ROE \times \text{retention rate} = 0.25 \times 0.40 = 0.10$$

$$r_{ind} = \text{government bond yield} + (\text{industry beta} \times \text{equity risk premium})$$

$$= 0.06 + (1.2 \times 0.05) = 0.12$$

Therefore:

$$P_0/E_1 = 0.60/(0.12 - 0.10) = 30.0$$

b.   i. Forecast growth in real GDP would cause P/E ratios to be generally higher for Country A. Higher expected growth in GDP implies higher earnings growth and a higher P/E.

ii. Government bond yield would cause P/E ratios to be generally higher for Country B. A lower government bond yield implies a lower risk-free rate and therefore a higher P/E.

iii. Equity risk premium would cause P/E ratios to be generally higher for Country B. A lower equity risk premium implies a lower required return and a higher P/E.

15.   a. $k = D_1/P_0 + g$

$D_1 = 0.5 \times \$2 = \$1$

$g = b \times ROE = 0.5 \times 0.20 = 0.10$

Therefore: $k = (\$1/\$10) + 0.10 = 0.20 = 20\%$

b.   Since k = ROE, the NPV of future investment opportunities is zero:

$$PVGO = P_0 - \frac{E_1}{k} = \$10 - \$10 = 0$$

c.   Since k = ROE, the stock price would be unaffected by cutting the dividend and investing the additional earnings.

16.   a. $g = ROE \times b = 20\% \times 0.5 = 10\%$

$$P_0 = \frac{D_1}{k-g} = \frac{D_0(1+g)}{k-g} = \frac{\$0.50 \times 1.10}{0.15 - 0.10} = \$11$$

b.

Time	EPS	Dividend	Comment
0	$1.0000	$0.5000	
1	$1.1000	$0.5500	g = 10%, plowback = 0.50
2	$1.2100	$0.7260	EPS has grown by 10% based on last year's earnings plowback and ROE; this year's earnings plowback ratio now falls to 0.40 and payout ratio = 0.60
3	$1.2826	$0.7696	EPS grows by (0.4) (15%) = 6% and payout ratio = 0.60

At time 2: $P_2 = \dfrac{D_3}{k-g} = \dfrac{\$0.7696}{0.15 - 0.06} = \$8.551$

At time 0: $V_0 = \dfrac{\$0.55}{1.15} + \dfrac{\$0.726 + \$8.551}{(1.15)^2} = \$7.493$

c. $P_0 = \$11$ and $P_1 = P_0(1 + g) = \$12.10$

(Because the market is unaware of the changed competitive situation, it believes the stock price should grow at 10% per year.)

$P_2 = \$8.551$ *after* the market becomes aware of the changed competitive situation.

$P_3 = \$8.551 \times 1.06 = \$9.064$ (The new growth rate is 6%.)

Year	Return
1	$\dfrac{(\$12.10 - \$11) + \$0.55}{\$11} = 0.150 = 15.0\%$
2	$\dfrac{(\$8.551 - \$12.10) + \$0.726}{\$12.10} = -0.233 = -23.3\%$
3	$\dfrac{(\$9.064 - \$8.551) + \$0.7696}{\$8.551} = 0.150 = 15.0\%$

Moral: In "normal periods" when there is no special information, the stock return $= k = 15\%$. When special information arrives, all the abnormal return accrues *in that period*, as one would expect in an efficient market.

17. a. $k = r_f + \beta[E(r_M) - r_f] = 8\% + 1.2(15\% - 8\%) = 16.4\%$

$g = b \times ROE = 0.6 \times 20\% = 12\%$

$$V_0 = \frac{D_0(1+g)}{k-g} = \frac{\$4 \times 1.12}{0.164 - 0.12} = \$101.82$$

b. $P_1 = V_1 = V_0(1 + g) = \$101.82 \times 1.12 = \$114.04$

$$E(r) = \frac{D_1 + P_1 - P_0}{P_0} = \frac{\$4.48 + \$114.04 - \$100}{\$100} = 0.1852 = 18.52\%$$

18. a. $k = r_f + \beta[E(r_M) - r_f] = 4.5\% + 1.15(14.5\% - 4.5\%) = 16\%$

b.

Year		Dividend
2007		$1.72
2008	$1.72 × 1.12 =	$1.93
2009	$1.72 × 1.12^2 =	$2.16
2010	$1.72 × 1.12^3 =	$2.42
2011	$1.72 × 1.12^3 × 1.09 =	$2.63

Present value of dividends paid in 2008 – 2010:

Year	PV of Dividend	
2008	$1.93/1.16^1 =	$1.66
2009	$2.16/1.16^2 =	$1.61
2010	$2.42/1.16^3 =	$1.55
	Total =	$4.82

$$\text{Price at year-end 2010} = \frac{D_{2011}}{k-g} = \frac{\$2.63}{0.16-0.09} = \$37.57$$

$$\text{PV in 2007 of this stock price} = \frac{\$37.57}{1.16^3} = \$24.07$$

Intrinsic value of stock = $4.82 + $24.07 = $28.89

c. The data in the problem indicate that Quick Brush is selling at a price substantially below its intrinsic value, while the calculations above demonstrate that SmileWhite is selling at a price somewhat above the estimate of its intrinsic value. Based on this analysis, Quick Brush offers the potential for considerable abnormal returns, while SmileWhite offers slightly below-market risk-adjusted returns.

d. Strengths of two-stage versus constant growth DDM:

- Two-stage model allows for separate valuation of two distinct periods in a company's future. This can accommodate life cycle effects. It also can avoid the difficulties posed by initial growth that is higher than the discount rate.

- Two-stage model allows for initial period of above-sustainable growth. It allows the analyst to make use of her expectations regarding when growth might shift from off-trend to a more sustainable level.

A weakness of all DDMs is that they are very sensitive to input values. Small changes in k or g can imply large changes in estimated intrinsic value. These inputs are difficult to measure.

19.

Time:	0	1	5	6
E_t	\$10.000	\$12.000	\$24.883	\$29.860
D_t	\$0.000	\$0.000	\$0.000	\$11.944
b	1.00	1.00	1.00	0.60
g	20.0%	20.0%	20.0%	9.0%

a. $$V_5 = \frac{D_6}{k-g} = \frac{\$11.944}{0.15-0.09} = \$199.07$$

$$V_0 = \frac{V_5}{(1+k)^5} = \frac{\$199.07}{1.15^5} = \$98.97$$

b. The price should rise by 15% per year until year 6: because there is no dividend, the entire return must be in capital gains.

c. The payout ratio would have no effect on intrinsic value because ROE = k.

20. a. The solution is shown in the Excel spreadsheet below:

Inputs			Year	Dividend	Div growth	Term value	Investor CF	
beta	1.35		2005	0.32			0.32	
mkt_prem	0.06		2006	0.41			0.41	
rf	0.05		2007	0.50			0.50	
k_equity	0.131		2008	0.60			0.60	
plowback	0.75		2009	0.72	0.20		0.72	
roe	0.14		2010	0.86	0.19		0.86	
term_gwth	0.105		2011	1.01	0.18		1.01	
			2012	1.18	0.17		1.18	
			2013	1.37	0.16		1.37	
			2014	1.58	0.15		1.58	
Value line			2015	1.80	0.14		1.80	
forecasts of			2016	2.03	0.13		2.03	
annual dividends			2017	2.28	0.12		2.28	
			2018	2.53	0.11		2.53	
			2019	2.78	0.10		2.78	
Transitional period			2020	3.07	0.10500	130.55	133.62	
with slowing dividend								
growth							24.82	= PV of CF
	Beginning of constant			E17 * (1+ F17)/(B5 - F17)				
	growth period						NPV(B5,H2:H17)	

b., c. Using the Excel spreadsheet, we find that the intrinsic values are \$25.76 and \$13.50, respectively.

21. The solutions derived from Spreadsheet 18.2 are as follows:

	Intrinsic value: FCFF	Intrinsic value: FCFE	Intrinsic value per share: FCFF	Intrinsic value per share: FCFE
a.	40,170	31,187	11.23	10.31
b.	47,087	36,507	13.52	12.07
c.	34,337	26,520	9.30	8.77

22. a. The value of a share of Rio National equity using the Gordon growth model and the capital asset pricing model is $22.40, as shown below.
Calculate the required rate of return using the capital asset pricing model:

$$k = r_f + \beta\,(k_M - r_f) = 4\% + 1.8(9\% - 4\%) = 13\%$$

Calculate the share value using the Gordon growth model:

$$P_0 = \frac{D_o \times (1+g)}{k-g} = \frac{\$0.20 \times (1+0.12)}{0.13-0.12} = \$22.40$$

b. The sustainable growth rate of Rio National is 9.97%, calculated as follows:

$$g = b \times ROE = \text{Earnings Retention Rate} \times ROE = (1 - \text{Payout Ratio}) \times ROE =$$

$$\left(1 - \frac{\text{Dividends}}{\text{Net Income}}\right) \times \frac{\text{Net Income}}{\text{Beginning Equity}} = \left(1 - \frac{\$3.20}{\$30.16}\right) \times \frac{\$30.16}{\$270.35} = 0.0997 = 9.97\%$$

23. a. To obtain free cash flow to equity (FCFE), the two adjustments that Shaar should make to cash flow from operations (CFO) are:

1. Subtract investment in fixed capital: CFO does not take into account the investing activities in long-term assets, particularly plant and equipment. The cash flows corresponding to those necessary expenditures are not available to equity holders and therefore should be subtracted from CFO to obtain FCFE.

2. Add net borrowing: CFO does not take into account the amount of capital supplied to the firm by lenders (e.g., bondholders). The new borrowings, net of debt repayment, are cash flows available to equity holders and should be added to CFO to obtain FCFE.

b.   *Note 1*: Rio National had $75 million in capital expenditures during the year.

Adjustment: negative $75 million

The cash flows required for those capital expenditures (−$75 million) are no longer available to the equity holders and should be subtracted from net income to obtain FCFE.

Note 2: A piece of equipment that was originally purchased for $10 million was sold for $7 million at year-end, when it had a net book value of $3 million. Equipment sales are unusual for Rio National.

Adjustment: positive $3 million

In calculating FCFE, only cash flow investments in fixed capital should be considered. The $7 million sale price of equipment is a cash inflow now available to equity holders and should be added to net income. However, the gain over book value that was realized when selling the equipment ($4 million) is already included in net income. Because the total sale is cash, not just the gain, the $3 million net book value must be added to net income. Therefore, the adjustment calculation is:

$7 million in cash received − $4 million of gain recorded in net income =

$3 million additional cash received added to net income to obtain FCFE.

Note 3: The decrease in long-term debt represents an unscheduled principal repayment; there was no new borrowing during the year.

Adjustment: negative $5 million

The unscheduled debt repayment cash flow (−$5 million) is an amount no longer available to equity holders and should be subtracted from net income to determine FCFE.

Note 4: On 1 January 2002, the company received cash from issuing 400,000 shares of common equity at a price of $25.00 per share.

No adjustment

Transactions between the firm and its shareholders do not affect FCFE. To calculate FCFE, therefore, no adjustment to net income is required with respect to the issuance of new shares.

Note 5: A new appraisal during the year increased the estimated market value of land held for investment by $2 million, which was not recognized in 2002 income.

No adjustment

The increased market value of the land did not generate any cash flow and was not reflected in net income. To calculate FCFE, therefore, no adjustment to net income is required.

c. Free cash flow to equity (FCFE) is calculated as follows:

$$FCFE = NI + NCC - FCINV - WCINV + \text{Net Borrowing}$$

where NCC = non-cash charges

FCINV = investment in fixed capital

WCINV = investment in working capital

	Million $	Explanation
NI =	$30.16	From Exhibit 18B
NCC =	+$67.17	$71.17 (depreciation and amortization from Exhibit 18B) − $4.00* (gain on sale from Note 2)
FCINV =	−$68.00	$75.00 (capital expenditures from Note 1) − $7.00* (cash on sale from Note 2)
WCINV =	−$24.00	−$3.00 (increase in accounts receivable from Exhibit 18A + −$20.00 (increase in inventory from Exhibit 18A) + −$1.00 (decrease in accounts payable from Exhibit 18A)
Net Borrowing =	+(−$5.00)	−$5.00 (decrease in long-term debt from Exhibit 18A)
FCFE =	$0.33	

*Supplemental Note 2 in Exhibit 18C affects both NCC and FCINV.

24. Rio National's equity is relatively undervalued compared to the industry on a P/E-to-growth (PEG) basis. Rio National's PEG ratio of 1.33 is below the industry PEG ratio of 1.66. The lower PEG ratio is attractive because it implies that the growth rate at Rio National is available at a relatively lower price than is the case for the industry. The PEG ratios for Rio National and the industry are calculated below:

Rio National

Current Price = $25.00

Normalized Earnings per Share = $1.71

Price-to-Earnings Ratio = $25/$1.71 = 14.62

Growth Rate (as a percentage) = 11

PEG Ratio = 14.62/11 = 1.33

Industry

Price-to-Earnings Ratio = 19.90

Growth Rate (as a percentage) = 12

PEG Ratio = 19.90/12 = 1.66

25.

Time:	0	1	2	3
D_t	$1.0000	$1.2500	$1.5625	$1.953125
g	25.0%	25.0%	25.0%	5.0%

a.   The dividend to be paid at the end of year 3 is the first installment of a dividend stream that will increase indefinitely at the constant growth rate of 5%. Therefore, we can use the constant growth model as of the end of year 2 in order to calculate intrinsic value by adding the present value of the first two dividends plus the present value of the price of the stock at the end of year 2.

The expected price 2 years from now is:

$P_2 = D_3/(k - g) = \$1.953125/(0.20 - 0.05) = \$13.02$

The PV of this expected price is: $\$13.02/1.20^2 = \$9.04$

The PV of expected dividends in years 1 and 2 is:

$$\frac{\$1.25}{1.20} + \frac{\$1.5625}{1.20^2} = \$2.13$$

Thus the current price should be: $\$9.04 + \$2.13 = \$11.17$

b.   Expected dividend yield $= D_1/P_0 = \$1.25/\$11.17 = 0.112 = 11.2\%$

c.   The expected price one year from now is the PV at that time of P_2 and D_2:

$P_1 = (D_2 + P_2)/1.20 = (\$1.5625 + \$13.02)/1.20 = \$12.15$

The implied capital gain is:

$(P_1 - P_0)/P_0 = (\$12.15 - \$11.17)/\$11.17 = 0.088 = 8.8\%$

The sum of the implied capital gains yield and the expected dividend yield is equal to the market capitalization rate. This is consistent with the DDM.

26.

Time:	0	1	4	5
E_t	$5.000	$6.000	$10.368	$12.4416
D_t	$0.000	$0.000	$0.000	$12.4416

Dividends = 0 for the next four years, so b = 1.0 (100% plowback ratio).

a. $P_4 = \dfrac{D_5}{k} = \dfrac{\$12.4416}{0.15} = \$82.944$

$V_0 = \dfrac{P_4}{(1+k)^4} = \dfrac{\$82.944}{1.15^4} = \$47.42$

b.   Price should increase at a rate of 15% over the next year, so that the HPR will equal k.

27. Before-tax cash flow from operations $2,100,000
    Depreciation   210,000
    Taxable Income   1,890,000
    Taxes (@ 35%)   661,500
    After-tax unleveraged income   1,228,500
    After-tax cash flow from operations
            (After-tax unleveraged income + depreciation)   1,438,500
    New investment (20% of cash flow from operations)   420,000
    Free cash flow
            (After-tax cash flow from operations – new investment) $1,018,500

The value of the firm (i.e., debt plus equity) is:

$$V_0 = \frac{C_1}{k-g} = \frac{\$1,018,500}{0.12 - 0.05} = \$14,550,000$$

Since the value of the debt is $4 million, the value of the equity is $10,550,000.

CHAPTER 19: FINANCIAL STATEMENT ANALYSIS

1. ROE = Net profits/Equity = Net profits/Sales × Sales/Assets × Assets/Equity

    = Net profit margin × Asset turnover × Leverage ratio

    = 5.5% × 2.0 × 2.2 = 24.2%

2. ROA = ROS × ATO

    The only way that Crusty Pie can have an ROS higher than the industry average and an ROA equal to the industry average is for its ATO to be lower than the industry average.

3. ABC's Asset turnover must be above the industry average.

4. ROE = (1 − Tax rate) × [ROA + (ROA − Interest rate)Debt/Equity]

    $ROE_A > ROE_B$

    Firms A and B have the same ROA. Assuming the same tax rate and assuming that ROA > interest rate, then Firm A must have either a lower interest rate or a higher debt ratio.

5. SmileWhite has higher quality of earnings for the following reasons:
    - SmileWhite amortizes its goodwill over a shorter period than does QuickBrush. SmileWhite therefore presents more conservative earnings because it has greater goodwill amortization expense.
    - SmileWhite depreciates its property, plant and equipment using an accelerated depreciation method. This results in recognition of depreciation expense sooner and also implies that its income is more conservatively stated.
    - SmileWhite's bad debt allowance is greater as a percent of receivables. SmileWhite is recognizing greater bad-debt expense than QuickBrush. If actual collection experience will be comparable, then SmileWhite has the more conservative recognition policy.

6. a.

$$\text{ROE} = \frac{\text{Net profits}}{\text{Equity}} = \frac{\text{Net profits}}{\text{Sales}} \times \frac{\text{Sales}}{\text{Assets}} \times \frac{\text{Assets}}{\text{Equity}}$$

$$= \text{Net profit margin} \times \text{Total asset turnover} \times \text{Assets/equity}$$

$$\frac{\text{Net profits}}{\text{Sales}} = \frac{510}{5,140} = 0.0992 = 9.92\%$$

$$\frac{\text{Sales}}{\text{Assets}} = \frac{5,140}{3,100} = 1.66$$

$$\frac{\text{Assets}}{\text{Equity}} = \frac{3,100}{2,200} = 1.41$$

b.
$$\text{ROE} = \frac{510}{5,140} \times \frac{5,140}{3,100} \times \frac{3,100}{2,200} = 9.92\% \times 1.66 \times 1.41 = 23.2\%$$

c.
$$g = \text{ROE} \times \text{plowback} = 23.2\% \times \frac{1.96 - 0.60}{1.96} = 16.1\%$$

7. a.

Palomba Pizza Stores
Statement of Cash Flows
For the year ended December 31, 1999

<u>Cash Flows from Operating Activities</u>

Cash Collections from Customers	$250,000	
Cash Payments to Suppliers	(85,000)	
Cash Payments for Salaries	(45,000)	
Cash Payments for Interest	<u>(10,000)</u>	
Net Cash Provided by Operating Activities		$110,000

<u>Cash Flows from Investing Activities</u>

Sale of Equipment	38,000	
Purchase of Equipment	(30,000)	
Purchase of Land	<u>(14,000)</u>	
Net Cash Used in Investing Activities		

<u>Cash Flows from Financing Activities</u>   (6,000)

Retirement of Common Stock	(25,000)	
Payment of Dividends	<u>(35,000)</u>	
Net Cash Used in Financing Activities		<u>(60,000)</u>
Net Increase in Cash		44,000
Cash at Beginning of Year		<u>50,000</u>
Cash at End of Year		$94,000

19-2

b. Cash flow from operations (CFO) focuses on measuring the cash flow generated by operations and not on measuring profitability. If used as a measure of performance, CFO is less subject to distortion than the net income figure. Analysts use CFO as a check on the quality of earnings. CFO then becomes a check on the reported net earnings figure, but is not a substitute for net earnings. Companies with high net income but low CFO may be using income recognition techniques that are suspect. The ability of a firm to generate cash from operations on a consistent basis is one indication of the financial health of the firm. For most firms, CFO is the "life blood" of the firm. Analysts search for trends in CFO to indicate future cash conditions and the potential for cash flow problems.

Cash flow from investing activities (CFI) is an indication of how the firm is investing its excess cash. The analyst must consider the ability of the firm to continue to grow and to expand activities, and CFI is a good indication of the attitude of management in this area. Analysis of this component of total cash flow indicates the type of capital expenditures being made by management to either expand or maintain productive activities. CFI is also an indicator of the firm's financial flexibility and its ability to generate sufficient cash to respond to unanticipated needs and opportunities. A decreasing CFI may be a sign of a slowdown in the firm's growth.

Cash flow from financing activities (CFF) indicates the feasibility of financing, the sources of financing, and the types of sources management supports. Continued debt financing may signal a future cash flow problem. The dependency of a firm on external sources of financing (either borrowing or equity financing) may present problems in the future, such as debt servicing and maintaining dividend policy. Analysts also use CFF as an indication of the quality of earnings. It offers insights into the financial habits of management and potential future policies.

8. a. CF from operating activities = $260 – $85 – $12 – $35 = $128

b. CF from investing activities = –$8 + $30 – $40 = –$18

c. CF from financing activities = –$32 – $37 = –$69

9. a. QuickBrush has had higher sales and earnings growth (per share) than SmileWhite. Margins are also higher. But this does not mean that QuickBrush is necessarily a better investment. SmileWhite has a higher ROE, which has been stable, while QuickBrush's ROE has been declining. We can see the source of the difference in ROE using DuPont analysis:

Component	Definition	QuickBrush	SmileWhite
Tax burden $(1 - t)$	Net profits/pretax profits	67.4%	66.0%
Interest burden	Pretax profits/EBIT	1.000	0.955
Profit margin	EBIT/Sales	8.5%	6.5%
Asset turnover	Sales/Assets	1.42	3.55
Leverage	Assets/Equity	1.47	1.48
ROE	Net profits/Equity	12.0%	21.4%

While tax burden, interest burden, and leverage are similar, profit margin and asset turnover differ. Although SmileWhite has a lower profit margin, it has a far higher asset turnover.

Sustainable growth = ROE × plowback ratio

	ROE	Plowback ratio	Sustainable growth rate	Ludlow's estimate of growth rate
QuickBrush	12.0%	1.00	12.0%	30%
SmileWhite	21.4%	0.34	7.3%	10%

Ludlow has overestimated the sustainable growth rate for both companies. QuickBrush has little ability to increase its sustainable growth – plowback already equals 100%. SmileWhite could increase its sustainable growth by increasing its plowback ratio.

b. QuickBrush's recent EPS growth has been achieved by increasing book value per share, not by achieving greater profits per dollar of equity. A firm can increase EPS even if ROE is declining as is true of QuickBrush. QuickBrush's book value per share has more than doubled in the last two years.

Book value per share can increase either by retaining earnings or by issuing new stock at a market price greater than book value. QuickBrush has been retaining all earnings, but the increase in the number of outstanding shares indicates that it has also issued a substantial amount of stock.

10. a. ROE = operating margin × interest burden × asset turnover × leverage × tax burden
ROE for Eastover (EO) and for Southampton (SHC) in 2002 are found as follows:

profit margin = $\dfrac{\text{EBIT}}{\text{Sales}}$ SHC: 145/1,793 =   8.1%
                             EO: 795/7,406 =   10.7%

interest burden = $\dfrac{\text{Pretax profits}}{\text{EBIT}}$ SHC: 137/145 =   0.95
                             EO: 600/795 =   0.75

asset turnover = $\dfrac{\text{Sales}}{\text{Assets}}$ SHC: 1,793/2,104 =   0.85
                             EO: 7,406/8,265 =   0.90

leverage = $\dfrac{\text{Assets}}{\text{Equity}}$ SHC: 2,140/1,167 =   1.80
                             EO: 8,265/3,864 =   2.14

tax burden = $\dfrac{\text{Net profits}}{\text{Pretax profits}}$ SHC: 91/137 =   0.66
                             EO: 394/600 =   0.66

ROE   SHC: 7.8%
         EO: 10.2%

b. The differences in the components of ROE for Eastover and Southampton are:

Profit margin   EO has a higher margin

Interest burden   EO has a higher interest burden because its pretax profits are a lower percentage of EBIT

Asset turnover   EO is more efficient at turning over its assets

Leverage   EO has higher financial leverage

Tax Burden   No major difference here between the two companies

ROE   EO has a higher ROE than SHC, but this is only in part due to higher margins and a better asset turnover -- greater financial leverage also plays a part.

c. The sustainable growth rate can be calculated as: ROE times plowback ratio. The sustainable growth rates for Eastover and Southampton are as follows:

	ROE	Plowback ratio*	Sustainable growth rate
Eastover	10.2%	0.36	3.7%
Southampton	7.8%	0.58	4.5%

*Plowback = (1 − payout ratio)

EO: Plowback = (1 − 0.64) = 0.36

SHC: Plowback = (1 − 0.42) = 0.58

The sustainable growth rates derived in this manner are not likely to be representative of future growth because 2002 was probably not a "normal" year. For Eastover, earnings had not yet recovered to 1999-2000 levels; earnings retention of only 0.36 seems low for a company in a capital intensive industry. Southampton's earnings fell by over 50 percent in 2002 and its earnings retention will probably be higher than 0.58 in the future. There is a danger, therefore, in basing a projection on one year's results, especially for companies in a cyclical industry such as forest products.

11. a. The formula for the constant growth discounted dividend model is:

$$P_0 = \frac{D_0(1+g)}{k-g}$$

For Eastover:

$$P_0 = \frac{\$1.20 \times 1.08}{0.11-0.08} = \$43.20$$

This compares with the current stock price of $28. On this basis, it appears that Eastover is undervalued.

b. The formula for the two-stage discounted dividend model is:

$$P_0 = \frac{D_1}{(1+k)^1} + \frac{D_2}{(1+k)^2} + \frac{D_3}{(1+k)^3} + \frac{P_3}{(1+k)^3}$$

For Eastover: $g_1 = 0.12$ and $g_2 = 0.08$

$D_0 = 1.20$

$D_1 = D_0(1.12)^1 = \$1.34$

$D_2 = D_0(1.12)^2 = \$1.51$

$D_3 = D_0(1.12)^3 = \$1.69$

$D_4 = D_0(1.12)^3(1.08) = \$1.82$

$$P_3 = \frac{D_4}{k-g_2} = \frac{\$1.82}{0.11-0.08} = \$60.67$$

$$P_0 = \frac{\$1.34}{(1.11)^1} + \frac{\$1.51}{(1.11)^2} + \frac{\$1.69}{(1.11)^3} + \frac{\$60.67}{(1.11)^3} = \$48.03$$

This approach makes Eastover appear even more undervalued than was the case using the constant growth approach.

c. Advantages of the constant growth model include: (1) logical, theoretical basis; (2) simple to compute; (3) inputs can be estimated.

Disadvantages include: (1) very sensitive to estimates of growth; (2) g and k difficult to estimate accurately; (3) only valid for g < k; (4) constant growth is an unrealistic assumption; (5) assumes growth will never slow down; (6) dividend payout must remain constant; (7) not applicable for firms not paying dividends.

Improvements offered by the two-stage model include:

(1) The two-stage model is more realistic. It accounts for low, high, or zero growth in the first stage, followed by constant long-term growth in the second stage. (2) The model can be used to determine stock value when the growth rate in the first stage exceeds the required rate of return.

12. a. In order to determine whether a stock is undervalued or overvalued, analysts often compute price-earnings ratios (P/Es) and price-book ratios (P/Bs); then, these ratios are compared to benchmarks for the market, such as the S&P 500 index. The formulas for these calculations are:

$$\text{Relative P/E} = \frac{\text{P/E of specific company}}{\text{P/E of S\&P 500}}$$

$$\text{Relative P/B} = \frac{\text{P/B of specific company}}{\text{P/B of S\&P 500}}$$

To evaluate EO and SHC using a relative P/E model, Mulroney can calculate the five-year average P/E for each stock, and divide that number by the 5-year average P/E for the S&P 500 (shown in the last column of Table 19E). This gives the historical average relative P/E. Mulroney can then compare the average historical relative P/E to the current relative P/E (i.e., the current P/E on each stock, using the estimate of this year's earnings per share in Table 19F, divided by the current P/E of the market).

For the price/book model, Mulroney should make similar calculations, i.e., divide the five-year average price-book ratio for a stock by the five year average price/book for the S&P 500, and compare the result to the current relative price/book (using current book value). The results are as follows:

P/E model	EO	SHC	S&P500
5-year average P/E	16.56	11.94	15.20
Relative 5-year P/E	1.09	0.79	
Current P/E	17.50	16.00	20.20
Current relative P/E	0.87	0.79	

Price/Book model	EO	SHC	S&P500
5-year average price/book	1.52	1.10	2.10
Relative 5-year price/book	0.72	0.52	
Current price/book	1.62	1.49	2.60
Current relative price/book	0.62	0.57	

From this analysis, it is evident that EO is trading at a discount to its historical 5-year relative P/E ratio, whereas Southampton is trading right at its historical 5-year relative P/E. With respect to price/book, Eastover is trading at a discount to its historical relative price/book ratio, whereas SHC is trading modestly above its 5-year relative price/book ratio. As noted in the preamble to the problem (see problem 10), Eastover's book value is understated due to the very low historical cost basis for its timberlands. The fact that Eastover is trading below its 5-year average relative price to book ratio, even though its book value is understated, makes Eastover seem especially attractive on a price/book basis.

b. Disadvantages of the relative P/E model include: (1) the relative P/E measures only relative, rather than absolute, value; (2) the accounting earnings estimate for the next year may not equal sustainable earnings; (3) accounting practices may not be standardized; (4) changing accounting standards may make historical comparisons difficult.

Disadvantages of relative P/B model include: (1) book value may be understated or overstated, particularly for a company like Eastover, which has valuable assets on its books carried at low historical cost; (2) book value may not be representative of earning power or future growth potential; (3) changing accounting standards make historical comparisons difficult.

13. The following table summarizes the valuation and ROE for Eastover and Southampton:

	Eastover	Southampton
Stock Price	$28.00	$48.00
Constant-growth model	$43.20	$29.00
2-stage growth model	$48.03	$35.50
Current P/E	17.50	16.00
Current relative P/E	0.87	0.79
5-year average P/E	16.56	11.94
Relative 5 year P/E	1.09	0.79
Current P/B	1.62	1.49
Current relative P/B	0.62	0.57
5-year average P/B	1.52	1.10
Relative 5 year P/B	0.72	0.52
Current ROE	10.2%	7.8%
Sustainable growth rate	3.7%	4.5%

Eastover seems to be undervalued according to each of the discounted dividend models. Eastover also appears to be cheap on both a relative P/E and a relative P/B basis. Southampton, on the other hand, looks overvalued according to each of the discounted dividend models and is slightly overvalued using the relative price/book model. On a relative P/E basis, SHC appears to be fairly valued. Southampton does have a slightly higher sustainable growth rate, but not appreciably so, and its ROE is less than Eastover's.

The current P/E for Eastover is based on relatively depressed current earnings, yet the stock is still attractive on this basis. In addition, the price/book ratio for Eastover is overstated due to the low historical cost basis used for the timberland assets. This makes Eastover seem all the more attractive on a price/book basis. Based on this analysis, Mulroney should select Eastover over Southampton.

14. a.   Net income can increase even while cash flow from operations decreases. This can occur if there is a buildup in net working capital -- for example, increases in accounts receivable or inventories, or reductions in accounts payable. Lower depreciation expense will also increase net income but can reduce cash flow through the impact on taxes owed.

    b.   Cash flow from operations might be a good indicator of a firm's quality of earnings because it shows whether the firm is actually generating the cash necessary to pay bills and dividends without resorting to new financing. Cash flow is less susceptible to arbitrary accounting rules than net income is.

15. $1,200

    Cash flow from operations = sales – cash expenses – increase in A/R

    Ignore depreciation because it is a non-cash item and its impact on taxes is already accounted for.

16. a   Both current assets and current liabilities will decrease by equal amounts. But this is a larger percentage decrease for current liabilities because the initial current ratio is above 1.0. So the current ratio increases. Total assets are lower, so turnover increases.

17. a   Cost of goods sold is understated so income is higher, and assets (inventory) are valued at most recent cost so they are valued higher.

18. a   Since goods still in inventory are valued at recent versus historical cost.

19. Considering the components of after-tax ROE, there are several possible explanations for a stable after-tax ROE despite declining operating income:

    1. Declining operating income could have been offset by an increase in non-operating income (i.e., from discontinued operations, extraordinary gains, gains from changes in accounting policies) because both are components of profit margin (net income/sales).

    2. Another offset to declining operating income could have been declining interest rates on any interest rate obligations, which would have decreased interest expense while allowing pre-tax margins to remain stable.

3. Leverage could have increased as a result of a decline in equity from: (a) writing down an equity investment, (b) stock repurchases, (c) losses; or, (d) selling new debt. The effect of the increased leverage could have offset a decline in operating income.

4. An increase in asset turnover could also offset a decline in operating income. Asset turnover could increase as a result of a sales growth rate that exceeds the asset growth rate, or from the sale or write-off of assets.

5. If the effective tax rate declined, the resulting increase in earnings after tax could offset a decline in operating income. The decline in effective tax rates could result from increased tax credits, the use of tax loss carry-forwards, or a decline in the statutory tax rate.

20.

		2005	2009
(1) Operating margin =	$\dfrac{\text{Operating income} - \text{Depreciation}}{\text{Sales}}$	$\dfrac{38-3}{542}=6.5\%$	$\dfrac{76-9}{979}=6.8\%$
(2) Asset turnover =	$\dfrac{\text{Sales}}{\text{Total Assets}}$	$\dfrac{542}{245}=2.21$	$\dfrac{979}{291}=3.36$
(3) Interest Burden =	$\dfrac{[\text{Op Inc} - \text{Dep}] - \text{Int Expense}}{\text{Operating Income} - \text{Depreciation}}$	$\dfrac{38-3-3}{38-3}=0.914$	1.0
(4) Financial Leverage =	$\dfrac{\text{Total Assets}}{\text{Shareholders Equity}}$	$\dfrac{245}{159}=1.54$	$\dfrac{291}{220}=1.32$
(5) Income tax rate =	$\dfrac{\text{Income taxes}}{\text{Pre-tax income}}$	$\dfrac{13}{32}=40.63\%$	$\dfrac{37}{67}=55.22\%$

Using the Du Pont formula:

ROE = $[1.0 - (5)] \times (3) \times (1) \times (2) \times (4)$

ROE(2005) = $0.5937 \times 0.914 \times 0.065 \times 2.21 \times 1.54 = 0.120 = 12.0\%$

ROE(2009) = $0.4478 \times 1.0 \times 0.068 \times 3.36 \times 1.32 = 0.135 = 13.5\%$

(Because of rounding error, these results differ slightly from those obtained by directly calculating ROE as net income/equity.)

b.   Asset turnover measures the ability of a company to minimize the level of assets (current or fixed) to support its level of sales. The asset turnover increased substantially over the period, thus contributing to an increase in the ROE.

Financial leverage measures the amount of financing other than equity, including short and long-term debt. Financial leverage declined over the period, thus adversely affecting the ROE. Since asset turnover rose substantially more than financial leverage declined, the net effect was an increase in ROE.

CHAPTER 20: OPTIONS MARKETS: INTRODUCTION

1.

		Cost	Payoff	Profit
a.	Call option, X = $80.00	$4.40	$5.00	$0.60
b.	Put option, X = $80.00	$0.75	$0.00	-$0.75
c.	Call option, X = $85.00	$1.35	$0.00	-$1.35
d.	Put option, X = $85.00	$2.90	$0.00	-$2.90
e.	Call option, X = $90.00	$0.25	$0.00	-$0.25
f.	Put option, X = $90.00	$6.80	$5.00	-$1.80

2. In terms of dollar returns, based on a $10,000 investment:

	Price of Stock 6 Months from Now			
Stock Price	$80	$100	$110	$120
All stocks (100 shares)	$8,000	$10,000	$11,000	$12,000
All options (1,000 options)	$0	$0	$10,000	$20,000
Bills + 100 options	$9,360	$9,360	$10,360	$11,360

In terms of rate of return, based on a $10,000 investment:

	Price of Stock 6 Months from Now			
Stock Price	$80	$100	$110	$120
All stocks (100 shares)	-20%	0%	10%	20%
All options (1,000 options)	-100%	-100%	0%	100%
Bills + 100 options	-6.4%	-6.4%	3.6%	13.6%

3. a. From put-call parity:
$$P = C - S_0 + [X/(1 + r_f)^T] = 10 - 100 + [100/(1.10)^{1/4}] = \$7.65$$

   b. Purchase a straddle, i.e., both a put and a call on the stock. The total cost of the straddle is: $10 + $7.65 = $17.65
   This is the amount by which the stock would have to move in either direction for the profit on the call or put to cover the investment cost (not including time value of money considerations). Accounting for time value, the stock price would have to move in either direction by: $17.65 \times 1.10^{1/4} = \$18.08$

4. a. From put-call parity:
$$C = P + S_0 - [X/(1 + r_f)^T] = 4 + 50 - [50/(1.10)^{1/4}] = \$5.18$$

   b. Sell a straddle, i.e., sell a call and a put to realize premium income of:
   $$\$5.18 + \$4 = \$9.18$$

   If the stock ends up at $50, both of the options will be worthless and your profit will be $9.18. This is your maximum possible profit since, at any other stock price, you will have to pay off on either the call or the put. The stock price can move by $9.18 in either direction before your profits become negative.

   c. Buy the call, sell (write) the put, lend: $50/(1.10)^{1/4}$

   The payoff is as follows:

Position	Immediate CF	CF in 3 months	
		$S_T \leq X$	$S_T > X$
Call (long)	$C = 5.18$	0	$S_T - 50$
Put (short)	$-P = 4.00$	$-(50 - S_T)$	0
Lending position	$\dfrac{50}{1.10^{1/4}} = 48.82$	50	50
Total	$C - P + \dfrac{50}{1.10^{1/4}} = 50.00$	S_T	S_T

   By the put-call parity theorem, the initial outlay equals the stock price:
   $$S_0 = \$50$$

   In either scenario, you end up with the same payoff as you would if you bought the stock itself.

5. a.

Outcome	$S_T \leq X$	$S_T > X$
Stock	$S_T + D$	$S_T + D$
Put	$X - S_T$	0
Total	$X + D$	$S_T + D$

b.

Outcome	$S_T \leq X$	$S_T > X$
Call	0	$S_T - X$
Zeros	$X + D$	$X + D$
Total	$X + D$	$S_T + D$

The total payoffs for the two strategies are equal regardless of whether S_T exceeds X.

c. The cost of establishing the stock-plus-put portfolio is: $S_0 + P$
The cost of establishing the call-plus-zero portfolio is: $C + PV(X + D)$
Therefore:

$$S_0 + P = C + PV(X + D)$$

This result is identical to equation 20.2.

6. a.

Position	$S_T < X_1$	$X_1 \leq S_T \leq X_2$	$X_2 < S_T \leq X_3$	$X_3 < S_T$
Long call (X_1)	0	$S_T - X_1$	$S_T - X_1$	$S_T - X_1$
Short 2 calls (X_2)	0	0	$-2(S_T - X_2)$	$-2(S_T - X_2)$
Long call (X_3)	0	0	0	$S_T - X_3$
Total	0	$S_T - X_1$	$2X_2 - X_1 - S_T$	$(X_2 - X_1) - (X_3 - X_2) = 0$

b.

Position	$S_T < X_1$	$X_1 \leq S_T \leq X_2$	$X_2 < S_T$
Buy call (X_2)	0	0	$S_T - X_2$
Buy put (X_1)	$X_1 - S_T$	0	0
Total	$X_1 - S_T$	0	$S_T - X_2$

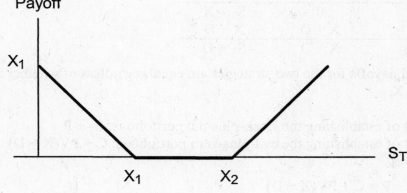

7.

Position	$S_T < X_1$	$X_1 \leq S_T \leq X_2$	$X_2 < S_T$
Buy call (X_2)	0	0	$S_T - X_2$
Sell call (X_1)	0	$-(S_T - X_1)$	$-(S_T - X_1)$
Total	0	$X_1 - S_T$	$X_1 - X_2$

8.   a.   By writing covered call options, Jones receives premium income of $30,000. If, in January, the price of the stock is less than or equal to $45, then Jones will have his stock plus the premium income. But the *most* he can have at that time is ($450,000 + $30,000) because the stock will be called away from him if the stock price exceeds $45. (We are ignoring here any interest earned over this short period of time on the premium income received from writing the option.) The payoff structure is:

Stock price	Portfolio value
less than $45	10,000 times stock price + $30,000
greater than $45	$450,000 + $30,000 = $480,000

This strategy offers some extra premium income but leaves Jones subject to substantial downside risk. At an extreme, if the stock price fell to zero, Jones would be left with only $30,000. This strategy also puts a cap on the final value at $480,000, but this is more than sufficient to purchase the house.

b.   By buying put options with a $35 strike price, Jones will be paying $30,000 in premiums in order to insure a minimum level for the final value of his position. That minimum value is: ($35 × 10,000) − $30,000 = $320,000 This strategy allows for upside gain, but exposes Jones to the possibility of a moderate loss equal to the cost of the puts. The payoff structure is:

Stock price	Portfolio value
less than $35	$350,000 − $30,000 = $320,000
greater than $35	10,000 times stock price − $30,000

c.   The net cost of the collar is zero. The value of the portfolio will be as follows:

Stock price	Portfolio value
less than $35	$350,000
between $35 and $45	10,000 times stock price
greater than $45	$450,000

If the stock price is less than or equal to $35, then the collar preserves the $350,000 principal. If the price exceeds $45, then Jones gains up to a cap of $450,000. In between $35 and $45, his proceeds equal 10,000 times the stock price.

The best strategy in this case would be (c) since it satisfies the two requirements of preserving the $350,000 in principal while offering a chance of getting $450,000. Strategy (a) should be ruled out since it leaves Jones exposed to the risk of substantial loss of principal.

Our ranking would be: (1) strategy c; (2) strategy b; (3) strategy a.

9. a.

Position	$S_T \leq 780$	$S_T > 780$
Buy stock	S_T	S_T
Buy put	$780 - S_T$	0
Total	780	S_T

Position	$S_T \leq 840$	$S_T > 840$
Buy call	0	$S_T - 840$
Buy T-bills	840	840
Total	840	S_T

b. The bills plus call strategy has a greater payoff for some values of S_T and never a lower payoff. Since its payoffs are always at least as attractive and sometimes greater, it must be more costly to purchase.

c. The initial cost of the stock plus put position is: $900 + $6 = $906
The initial cost of the bills plus call position is: $810 + $120 = $930

	$S_T = 700$	$S_T = 840$	$S_T = 900$	$S_T = 960$
Stock	700	840	900	960
+ Put	80	0	0	0
Payoff	780	840	900	960
Profit	−126	−66	−6	54
Bill	840	840	840	840
+ Call	0	0	60	120
Payoff	840	840	900	960
Profit	−90	−90	−30	+30

Profit

d. The stock and put strategy is riskier. This strategy performs worse when the market is down and better when the market is up. Therefore, its beta is higher.

e. Parity is not violated because these options have different exercise prices. Parity applies only to puts and calls with the same exercise price and expiration date.

10. a. Donie should choose the long strangle strategy. A long strangle option strategy consists of buying a put and a call with the same expiration date and the same underlying asset, but different exercise prices. In a strangle strategy, the call has an exercise price above the stock price and the put has an exercise price below the stock price. An investor who buys (goes long) a strangle expects that the price of the underlying asset (TRT Materials in this case) will either move substantially below the exercise price on the put or above the exercise price on the call. With respect to TRT, the long strangle investor buys both the put option and the call option for a total cost of $9.00, and will experience a profit if the stock price moves more than $9.00 above the call exercise price or more than $9.00 below the put exercise price. This strategy would enable Donie's client to profit from a large move in the stock price, either up or down, in reaction to the expected court decision.

b.   i. The maximum possible loss per share is $9.00, which is the total cost of the two options ($5.00 + $4.00).

ii. The maximum possible gain is unlimited if the stock price moves outside the breakeven range of prices.

iii. The breakeven prices are $46.00 and $69.00. The put will just cover costs if the stock price finishes $9.00 below the put exercise price (i.e., $55 − $9 = $46), and the call will just cover costs if the stock price finishes $9.00 above the call exercise price (i.e., $60 + $9 = $69).

11.   a. & b. The Excel spreadsheet for both parts (a) and (b) is shown on the next page, and the profit diagrams are on the following page.

12.   The farmer has the option to sell the crop to the government for a guaranteed minimum price if the market price is too low. If the support price is denoted P_S and the market price P_m then the farmer has a put option to sell the crop (the asset) at an exercise price of P_S even if the price of the underlying asset (P_m) is less than P_S.

13.   The bondholders have, in effect, made a loan which requires repayment of B dollars, where B is the face value of bonds. If, however, the value of the firm (V) is less than B, the loan is satisfied by the bondholders taking over the firm. In this way, the bondholders are forced to "pay" B (in the sense that the loan is cancelled) in return for an asset worth only V. It is as though the bondholders wrote a put on an asset worth V with exercise price B. Alternatively, one might view the bondholders as giving the right to the equity holders to reclaim the firm by paying off the B dollar debt. The bondholders have issued a call to the equity holders.

14.   The manager gets a bonus if the stock price exceeds a certain value and gets nothing otherwise. This is the same as the payoff to a call option.

Spreadsheet for Problem 11:

Stock Prices						
Beginning Market Price	116.5					
Ending Market Price	130					X 130 Straddle
					Ending	Profit
Buying Options:					Stock Price	-37.20
Call Options Strike	**Price**	**Payoff**	**Profit**	**Return %**	50	42.80
110	22.80	20.00	-2.80	-12.28%	60	32.80
120	16.80	10.00	-6.80	-40.48%	70	22.80
130	13.60	0.00	-13.60	-100.00%	80	12.80
140	10.30	0.00	-10.30	-100.00%	90	2.80
					100	-7.20
Put Options Strike	**Price**	**Payoff**	**Profit**	**Return %**	110	-17.20
110	12.60	0.00	-12.60	-100.00%	120	-27.20
120	17.20	0.00	-17.20	-100.00%	130	-37.20
130	23.60	0.00	-23.60	-100.00%	140	-27.20
140	30.50	10.00	-20.50	-67.21%	150	-17.20
					160	-7.20
Straddle	**Price**	**Payoff**	**Profit**	**Return %**	170	2.80
110	35.40	20.00	-15.40	-43.50%	180	12.80
120	34.00	10.00	-24.00	-70.59%	190	22.80
130	37.20	0.00	-37.20	-100.00%	200	32.80
140	40.80	10.00	-30.80	-75.49%	210	42.80
Selling Options:						Bullish
Call Options Strike	**Price**	**Payoff**	**Profit**	**Return %**	Ending	Spread
110	22.80	-20	2.80	12.28%	Stock Price	6.80
120	16.80	-10	6.80	40.48%	50	-3.2
130	13.60	0	13.60	100.00%	60	-3.2
140	10.30	0	10.30	100.00%	70	-3.2
					80	-3.2
Put Options Strike	**Price**	**Payoff**	**Profit**	**Return %**	90	-3.2
110	12.60	0	12.60	100.00%	100	-3.2
120	17.20	0	17.20	100.00%	110	-3.2
130	23.60	0	23.60	100.00%	120	-3.2
140	30.50	10	40.50	132.79%	130	6.8
					140	6.8
Money Spread	**Price**	**Payoff**	**Profit**		150	6.8
Bullish Spread					160	6.8
Purchase 120 Call	16.80	10.00	-6.80		170	6.8
Sell 130 Call	13.60	0	13.60		180	6.8
Combined Profit		10.00	6.80		190	6.8
					200	6.8
					210	6.8

Profit diagram for problem 11:

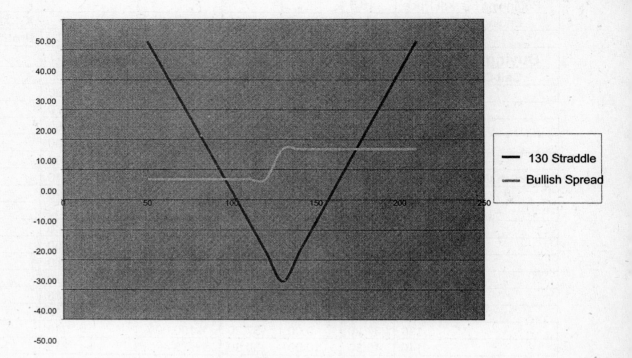

15. i.   Equity index-linked note: Unlike traditional debt securities that pay a scheduled rate of coupon interest on a periodic basis and the par amount of principal at maturity, the equity index-linked note typically pays little or no coupon interest; at maturity, however, a unit holder receives the original issue price plus a supplemental redemption amount, the value of which depends on where the equity index settled relative to a predetermined initial level.

    ii.   Commodity-linked bear bond: Unlike traditional debt securities that pay a scheduled rate of coupon interest on a periodic basis and the par amount of principal at maturity, the commodity-linked bear bond allows an investor to participate in a decline in a commodity's price. In exchange for a lower than market coupon, buyers of a bear tranche receive a redemption value that exceeds the purchase price if the commodity price has declined by the maturity date.

16. a.

Position	$S_T < 80$	$80 \leq S_T \leq 85$	$S_T > 85$
Write call, X = $85	0	0	$-(S_T - 85)$
Write put, X = $80	$-(80 - S_T)$	0	0
Total	$S_T - 80$	0	$85 - S_T$

Payoff

b.   Proceeds from writing options:

Call: $0.95
Put: $0.55
Total: $1.50

If IBM sells at $83 on the option maturity date, both options expire out of the money, and profit = $1.50. If IBM sells at $90 on the option maturity date, the call written results in a cash outflow of $5 at maturity, and an overall profit of: $1.50 – $5 = –$3.50

c.   You break even when either the put or the call results in a cash outflow of $1.50. For the put, this requires that:

$$\$1.50 = \$80.00 - S_T \Rightarrow S_T = \$78.50$$

For the call, this requires that:

$$\$1.50 = S_T - \$90 \Rightarrow S_T = \$91.50$$

d.   The investor is betting that IBM stock price will have low volatility. This position is similar to a straddle.

17. The put with the higher exercise price must cost more. Therefore, the net outlay to establish the portfolio is positive.

Position	$S_T < 90$	$90 \leq S_T \leq 95$	$S_T > 95$
Write put, X = $90	$-(90 - S_T)$	0	0
Buy put, X = $95	$95 - S_T$	$95 - S_T$	0
Total	5	$95 - S_T$	0

The payoff and profit diagram is:

18. Buy the X = 62 put (which should cost more but does not) and write the X = 60 put. Since the options have the same price, your net outlay is zero. Your proceeds at maturity may be positive, but cannot be negative.

Position	$S_T < 60$	$60 \leq S_T \leq 62$	$S_T > 62$
Buy put, X = $62	$62 - S_T$	$62 - S_T$	0
Write put, X = $60	$-(60 - S_T)$	0	0
Total	2	$62 - S_T$	0

Payoff = Profit (because net investment = 0)

19. According to put-call parity (assuming no dividends), the present value of a payment of $85 can be calculated using the options with April maturity and exercise price of $85.

$$PV(X) = S_0 + P - C$$

$$PV(\$85) = \$83.20 + \$2.45 - \$0.95 = \$84.70$$

20. The following payoff table shows that the portfolio is riskless with time-T value equal to $10:

Position	$S_T \leq 10$	$S_T > 10$
Buy stock	S_T	S_T
Write call, X = $10	0	$-(S_T - 10)$
Buy put, X = $10	$10 - S_T$	0
Total	10	10

Therefore, the risk-free rate is: ($10/$9.50) − 1 = 0.0526 = 5.26%

21. From put-call parity:

$$C - P = S_0 - X/(1 + r_f)^T$$

If the options are at the money, then $S_0 = X$ and:

$$C - P = X - X/(1 + r_f)^T$$

The right-hand side of the equation is positive, and we conclude that C > P.

22. a., b.

Position	$S_T < 100$	$100 \leq S_T \leq 110$	$S_T > 110$
Buy put, X = $110	$110 - S_T$	$110 - S_T$	0
Write put, X = $100	$-(100 - S_T)$	0	0
Total	10	$110 - S_T$	0

The net outlay to establish this position is positive. The put you buy has a higher exercise price than the put you write, and therefore must cost more than the put that you write. Therefore, net profits will be less than the payoff at time T.

c. The value of this portfolio generally decreases with the stock price. Therefore, its beta is negative.

23 a. Joe's strategy

Position	Cost	Payoff	
		$S_T \leq 400$	$S_T > 400$
Stock index	400	S_T	S_T
Put option, X = $400	20	$400 - S_T$	0
Total	420	400	S_T
Profit = payoff – $420		–20	$S_T - 420$

Sally's strategy

Position	Cost	Payoff	
		$S_T \leq 390$	$S_T > 390$
Stock index	400	S_T	S_T
Put option, X = $390	15	$390 - S_T$	0
Total	415	390	S_T
Profit = payoff – $415		–25	$S_T - 415$

b. Sally does better when the stock price is high, but worse when the stock price is low. The break-even point occurs at $S_T = \$395$, when both positions provide losses of $20.

c. Sally's strategy has greater systematic risk. Profits are more sensitive to the value of the stock index.

24. a., b. (See graph below)

This strategy is a bear spread. Initial proceeds = $9 – $3 = $6

The payoff is either negative or zero:

Position	$S_T < 50$	$50 \leq S_T \leq 60$	$S_T > 60$
Buy call, X = $60	0	0	$S_T - 60$
Write call, X = $50	0	$-(S_T - 50)$	$-(S_T - 50)$
Total	0	$-(S_T - 50)$	-10

c. Breakeven occurs when the payoff offsets the initial proceeds of $6, which occurs at stock price $S_T = \$56$. The investor must be bearish: the position does worse when the stock price increases.

25. Buy a share of stock, write a call with X = $50, write a call with X = $60, and buy a call with X = $110.

Position	$S_T < 50$	$50 \leq S_T \leq 60$	$60 < S_T \leq 110$	$S_T > 110$
Buy stock	S_T	S_T	S_T	S_T
Write call, X = $50	0	$-(S_T - 50)$	$-(S_T - 50)$	$-(S_T - 50)$
Write call, X = $60	0	0	$-(S_T - 60)$	$-(S_T - 60)$
Buy call, X = $110	0	0	0	$S_T - 110$
Total	S_T	50	$110 - S_T$	0

The investor is making a volatility bet. Profits will be highest when volatility is low and the stock price S_T is between $50 and $60.

26. i. Conversion value of a convertible bond is the value of the security if it is converted immediately. That is:

Conversion value =

market price of the common stock × conversion ratio =

$40 × 22 = $880

ii. Market conversion price is the price that an investor effectively pays for the common stock if the convertible bond is purchased:

Market conversion price =

market price of the convertible bond/conversion ratio =

$1,050/22 = $47.73

27. a. i. The current market conversion price is computed as follows:

Market conversion price =

market price of the convertible bond/conversion ratio =

$980/25 = $39.20

ii. The expected one-year return for the Ytel convertible bond is:

Expected return = [(end of year price + coupon)/current price] – 1

= [($1,125 + $40)/$980] – 1 = 0.1888 = 18.88%

iii. The expected one-year return for the Ytel common equity is:

Expected return = [(end of year price + dividend)/current price] – 1

= ($45/$35) – 1 = 0.2857 = 28.57%

b. The two components of a convertible bond's value are:

- the straight bond value, which is the convertible bond's value as a bond, and;
- the option value, which is the value associated with the potential conversion into equity.

(i.) In response to the increase in Ytel's common equity price, the straight bond value should stay the same and the option value should increase.

The increase in equity price does not affect the straight bond value component of the Ytel convertible. The increase in equity price increases the option value component significantly, because the call option becomes deep "in the money" when the $51 per share equity price is compared to the convertible's conversion price of: $1,000/25 = $40 per share.

(ii.) In response to the increase in interest rates, the straight bond value should decrease and the option value should increase.

The increase in interest rates decreases the straight bond value component (bond values decline as interest rates increase) of the convertible bond and increases the value of the equity call option component (call option values increase as interest rates increase). This increase may be small or even unnoticeable when compared to the change in the option value resulting from the increase in the equity price.

28. a. (ii)   [Profit = $40 – $25 + $2.50 – $4.00]
    b. (i)

CHAPTER 21: OPTION VALUATION

1. The value of a put option also increases with the volatility of the stock. We see this from the put-call parity theorem as follows:

$$P = C - S_0 + PV(X) + PV(Dividends)$$

Given a value for S and a risk-free interest rate, then, if C increases because of an increase in volatility, P must also increase in order to maintain the equality of the parity relationship.

2. a. Put A must be written on the stock with the lower price. Otherwise, given the lower volatility of Stock A, Put A would sell for less than Put B.

   b. Put B must be written on the stock with the lower price. This would explain its higher price.

   c. Call B must have the lower time to maturity. Despite the higher price of Stock B, Call B is cheaper than Call A. This can be explained by a lower time to maturity.

   d. Call B must be written on the stock with higher volatility. This would explain its higher price.

   e. Call A must be written on the stock with higher volatility. This would explain its higher price.

3.

Exercise Price	Hedge Ratio
115	5/30 = 0.167
100	20/30 = 0.667
75	30/30 = 1.000
50	30/30 = 1.000
25	30/30 = 1.000
10	30/30 = 1.000

As the option becomes more in the money, the hedge ratio increases to a maximum of 1.0.

4.

S	d_1	$N(d_1)$
45	-0.0268	0.4893
50	0.5000	0.6915
55	0.9766	0.8356

5. a. $uS_0 = 130 \Rightarrow P_u = 0$

$dS_0 = 80 \Rightarrow P_d = 30$

The hedge ratio is: $H = \dfrac{P_u - P_d}{uS_0 - dS_0} = \dfrac{0 - 30}{130 - 80} = -\dfrac{3}{5}$

b.

Riskless Portfolio	S = 80	S = 130
Buy 3 shares	240	390
Buy 5 puts	150	0
Total	390	390

Present value = $390/1.10 = $354.545

c. The portfolio cost is: $3S + 5P = 300 + 5P$

The value of the portfolio is: $354.545

Therefore: P = $54.545/5 = $10.91

6. The hedge ratio for the call is: $H = \dfrac{C_u - C_d}{uS_0 - dS_0} = \dfrac{20 - 0}{130 - 80} = \dfrac{2}{5}$

Riskless Portfolio	S = 80	S = 130
Buy 2 shares	160	260
Write 5 calls	0	-100
Total	160	160

Present value = $160/1.10 = $145.455

The portfolio cost is: $2S - 5C = $200 - 5C$

The value of the portfolio is: $145.455

Therefore: C = $54.545/5 = $10.91

Does $P = C + PV(X) - S$?

10.91 = 10.91 + 110/1.10 - 100 = 10.91

7. $d_1 = 0.3182 \Rightarrow N(d_1) = 0.6248$

   $d_2 = -0.0354 \Rightarrow N(d_2) = 0.4859$

   $Xe^{-rT} = 47.56$

   $C = \$8.13$

8. $P = \$5.69$

   This value is derived from our Black-Scholes spreadsheet, but note that we could have derived the value from put-call parity:

   $P = C + PV(X) - S_0 = \$8.13 + \$47.56 - \$50 = \$5.69$

9. a.   C falls to $5.5541

   b.   C falls to $4.7911

   c.   C falls to $6.0778

   d.   C rises to $11.5066

   e.   C rises to $8.7187

10. According to the Black-Scholes model, the call option should be priced at:

   $[\$55 \times N(d_1)] - [50 \times N(d_2)] = (\$55 \times 0.6) - (\$50 \times 0.5) = \$8$

   Since the option actually sells for more than $8, implied volatility is greater than 0.30.

11. A straddle is a call and a put. The Black-Scholes value would be:

   $C + P = S_0 N(d_1) - Xe^{-rT} N(d_2) + Xe^{-rT} [1 - N(d_2)] - S_0 [1 - N(d_1)]$

   $\quad = S_0 [2N(d_1) - 1] + Xe^{-rT} [1 - 2N(d_2)]$

   On the Excel spreadsheet (Spreadsheet 21.1), the valuation formula would be:

   B5*(2*E4 − 1) + B6*EXP(−B4*B3)*(1 − 2*E5)

12. A $1 increase in a call option's exercise price would lead to a decrease in the option's value of less than $1. The change in the call price would equal $1 only if: (i) there were a 100% probability that the call would be exercised, and (ii) the interest rate were zero.

13. Holding firm-specific risk constant, higher beta implies higher total stock volatility. Therefore, the value of the put option increases as beta increases.

14. Holding beta constant, the stock with a lot of firm-specific risk has higher total volatility. The option on the stock with higher firm-specific risk is worth more.

15. A call option with a high exercise price has a lower hedge ratio. This call option is less in the money. Both d_1 and $N(d_1)$ are lower when X is higher.

16. The rate of return of a call option on a long-term Treasury bond should be more sensitive to changes in interest rates than is the rate of return of the underlying bond. The option elasticity exceeds 1.0. In other words, the option is effectively a levered investment and the rate of return on the option is more sensitive to interest rate swings.

17. Implied volatility has increased. If not, the call price would have fallen as a result of the decrease in stock price.

18. Implied volatility has increased. If not, the put price would have fallen as a result of the decreased time to maturity.

19. The hedge ratio approaches one. As S increases, the probability of exercise approaches 1.0. $N(d_1)$ approaches 1.0.

20. The hedge ratio approaches –1.0. As S decreases, the probability of exercise approaches 1. $[N(d_1) - 1]$ approaches –1 as $N(d_1)$ approaches 0.

21. A straddle is a call and a put. The hedge ratio of the straddle is the sum of the hedge ratios of the individual options: $0.4 + (-0.6) = -0.2$

22. a. The spreadsheet appears as follows:

INPUTS		OUTPUTS	
Standard deviation (annual)	0.3213	d1	0.0089
Maturity (in years)	0.5	d2	-0.2183
Risk-free rate (annual)	0.05	N(d1)	0.5036
Stock Price	100	N(d2)	0.4136
Exercise price	105	B/S call value	8.0000
Dividend yield (annual)	0	B/S put value	10.4076

The standard deviation is: 0.3213

b.   The spreadsheet below shows the standard deviation has increased to: 0.3568

INPUTS		OUTPUTS	
Standard deviation (annual)	0.3568	d1	0.0318
Maturity (in years)	0.5	d2	-0.2204
Risk-free rate (annual)	0.05	N(d1)	0.5127
Stock Price	100	N(d2)	0.4128
Exercise price	105	B/S call value	9.0000
Dividend yield (annual)	0	B/S put value	11.4075

Implied volatility has increased because the value of an option increases with greater volatility.

c.   Implied volatility increases to 0.4087 when maturity decreases to four months. The shorter maturity decreases the value of the option; therefore, in order for the option price to remain unchanged at $8, implied volatility must increase.

INPUTS		OUTPUTS	
Standard deviation (annual)	0.4087	d1	-0.0182
Maturity (in years)	0.33333	d2	-0.2541
Risk-free rate (annual)	0.05	N(d1)	0.4928
Stock Price	100	N(d2)	0.3997
Exercise price	105	B/S call value	8.0001
Dividend yield (annual)	0	B/S put value	11.2646

d.   Implied volatility decreases to 0.2406 when exercise price decreases to $100. The decrease in exercise price increases the value of the call, so that, in order to the option price to remain at $8, implied volatility decreases.

INPUTS		OUTPUTS	
Standard deviation (annual)	0.2406	d1	0.2320
Maturity (in years)	0.5	d2	0.0619
Risk-free rate (annual)	0.05	N(d1)	0.5917
Stock Price	100	N(d2)	0.5247
Exercise price	100	B/S call value	8.0010
Dividend yield (annual)	0	B/S put value	5.5320

e.   The decrease in stock price decreases the value of the call. In order for the option price to remain at $8, implied volatility increases.

INPUTS		OUTPUTS	
Standard deviation (annual)	0.3566	d1	-0.0484
Maturity (in years)	0.5	d2	-0.3006
Risk-free rate (annual)	0.05	N(d1)	0.4807
Stock Price	98	N(d2)	0.3819
Exercise price	105	B/S call value	8.0000
Dividend yield (annual)	0	B/S put value	12.4075

23. a. The delta of the collar is calculated as follows:

Position	Delta
Buy stock	1.0
Buy put, X = $45	$N(d_1) - 1 = -0.40$
Write call, X = $55	$-N(d_1) = -0.35$
Total	0.25

If the stock price increases by $1, then the value of the collar increases by $0.25. The stock will be worth $1 more, the loss on the purchased put will be $0.40, and the call written represents a *liability* that increases by $0.35.

b. If S becomes very large, then the delta of the collar approaches zero. Both $N(d_1)$ terms approach 1. Intuitively, for very large stock prices, the value of the portfolio is simply the (present value of the) exercise price of the call, and is unaffected by small changes in the stock price.

As S approaches zero, the delta also approaches zero: both $N(d_1)$ terms approach 0. For very small stock prices, the value of the portfolio is simply the (present value of the) exercise price of the put, and is unaffected by small changes in the stock price.

24. Statement a: The hedge ratio (determining the number of futures contracts to sell) ought to be adjusted by the beta of the equity portfolio, which is 1.20. The correct hedge ratio would be:

$$\frac{\$100 \text{ million}}{\$100 \times 500} \times \beta = 2{,}000 \times \beta = 2{,}000 \times 1.2 = 2{,}400$$

Statement b: The portfolio will be hedged, and should therefore earn the risk-free rate, not zero, as the consultant claims. Given a futures price of 100 and an equity price of 100, the rate of return over the 3-month period is:

$(100 - 99)/99 = 1.01\% =$ approximately 4.1% annualized

25.

Put	X	Delta
A	10	-0.1
B	20	-0.5
C	30	-0.9

26. a. Choice A: Calls have higher elasticity than shares. For equal dollar investments, a call's capital gain potential is greater than that of the underlying stock.

b. Choice B: Calls have hedge ratios less than 1.0, so the shares have higher profit potential. For an equal number of shares controlled, the dollar exposure of the shares is greater than that of the calls, and the profit potential is therefore greater.

27. a. The value of the call option is expected to decrease if the volatility of the underlying stock price decreases. The less volatile the underlying stock price, the less the chance of extreme price movements and the lower the probability that the option expires in the money. This makes the participation feature on the upside less valuable.

The value of the call option is expected to increase if the time to expiration of the option increases. The longer the time to expiration, the greater the chance that the option will expire in the money resulting in an increase in the time premium component of the option's value.

b. i. When European options are out of the money, investors are essentially saying that they are willing to pay a premium for the right, but not the obligation, to buy or sell the underlying asset. The out-of-the-money option has no intrinsic value, but, since options require little capital (just the premium paid) to obtain a relatively large potential payoff, investors are willing to pay that premium even if the option may expire worthless. The Black-Scholes model does not reflect investors' demand for any premium above the time value of the option. Hence, if investors are willing to pay a premium for an out-of-the-money option above its time value, the Black-Scholes model does not value that excess premium.

ii. With American options, investors have the right, but not the obligation, to exercise the option prior to expiration, even if they exercise for non-economic reasons. This increased flexibility associated with American options has some value but is not considered in the Black-Scholes model because the model only values options to their expiration date (European options).

28. S = 100; current value of portfolio

X = 100; floor promised to clients (0% return)

σ = 0.25; volatility

r = 0.05; risk-free rate

T = 4 years; horizon of program

a. Using the Black-Scholes formula, we find that:

$d_1 = 0.65$, $N(d_1) = 0.7422$, $d_2 = 0.15$, $N(d_2) = 0.5596$

Put value = $10.27

Therefore, total funds to be managed equals $110.27 million: $100 million portfolio value plus the $10.27 million fee for the insurance program.

The put delta is: $N(d_1) - 1 = 0.7422 - 1 = -0.2578$

Therefore, sell off 25.78% of the equity portfolio, placing the remaining funds in T-bills. The amount of the portfolio in equity is therefore $74.22 million, while the amount in T-bills is: $110.27 million – $74.22 million = $36.05 million

b.	At the new portfolio value, the put delta becomes: −0.2779
This means that you must reduce the delta of the portfolio by:

$$0.2779 - 0.2578 = 0.0201$$

You should sell an additional 2.01% of the equity position and use the proceeds to buy T-bills. Since the stock price is now at only 97% of its original value, you need to sell:

$$\$97 \text{ million} \times 0.0201 = \$1.950 \text{ million of stock}$$

29.	a.	American options should cost more (have a higher premium). American options give the investor greater flexibility than European options since the investor can *choose* whether to exercise early. When the stock pays a dividend, the option to exercise a call early can be valuable. But regardless of the dividend, a European option (put or call) never sells for more than an otherwise-identical American option.

b.	$C = S_0 + P - PV(X) = \$43 + \$4 - \$45/1.055 = \$4.346$

Note: we assume that Abaco does not pay any dividends.

c.	• An increase in short-term interest rate $\Rightarrow$ PV(exercise price) is lower, and call value increases.

• An increase in stock price volatility $\Rightarrow$ the call value increases.

• A decrease in time to option expiration $\Rightarrow$ the call value decreases.

30.	a.	$uS_0 = 110 \Rightarrow P_u = 0$

$dS_0 = 90 \Rightarrow P_d = 10$

The hedge ratio is: $H = \dfrac{P_u - P_d}{uS_0 - dS_0} = \dfrac{0 - 10}{110 - 90} = -\dfrac{1}{2}$

A portfolio comprised of one share and two puts provides a guaranteed payoff of \$110, with present value: \$110/1.05 = \$104.76

Therefore:

$$S + 2P = \$104.76$$

$$\$100 + 2P = \$104.76 \Rightarrow P = \$2.38$$

b.	Cost of protective put portfolio = \$100 + \$2.38 = \$102.38

c. Our goal is a portfolio with the same exposure to the stock as the hypothetical protective put portfolio. Since the put's hedge ratio is –0.5, the portfolio consists of $(1 - 0.5) = 0.5$ shares of stock, which costs $50, and the remaining funds ($52.38) invested in T-bills, earning 5% interest.

Portfolio	S = 90	S = 110
Buy 0.5 shares	45	55
Invest in T-bills	55	55
Total	100	110

This payoff is identical to that of the protective put portfolio. Thus, the stock plus bills strategy replicates both the cost and payoff of the protective put.

31. The put values in the second period are:

$$P_{uu} = 0$$

$$P_{ud} = P_{du} = 110 - 104.50 = 5.50$$

$$P_{dd} = 110 - 90.25 = 19.75$$

To compute P_u, first compute the hedge ratio:

$$H = \frac{P_{uu} - P_{ud}}{uuS_0 - udS_0} = \frac{0 - 5.50}{121 - 104.50} = -\frac{1}{3}$$

Form a riskless portfolio by buying one share of stock and buying three puts.

The cost of the portfolio is: $S + 3P_u = \$110 + 3P_u$

The payoff for the riskless portfolio equals $121:

Riskless Portfolio	S = 104.50	S = 121
Buy 1 share	104.50	121.00
Buy 3 puts	16.50	0.00
Total	121.00	121.00

Therefore, find the value of the put by solving:

$$\$110 + 3P_u = \$121/1.05 \Rightarrow P_u = \$1.746$$

To compute P_d, compute the hedge ratio:

$$H = \frac{P_{du} - P_{dd}}{duS_0 - ddS_0} = \frac{5.50 - 19.75}{104.50 - 90.25} = -1.0$$

Form a riskless portfolio by buying one share and buying one put.

The cost of the portfolio is: $S + P_d = \$95 + P_d$

The payoff for the riskless portfolio equals $110:

Riskless Portfolio	S = 90.25	S = 104.50
Buy 1 share	90.25	104.50
Buy 1 put	19.75	5.50
Total	110.00	110.00

Therefore, find the value of the put by solving:

$$\$95 + P_d = \$110/1.05 \Rightarrow P_d = \$9.762$$

To compute P, compute the hedge ratio:

$$H = \frac{P_u - P_d}{uS_0 - dS_0} = \frac{1.746 - 9.762}{110 - 95} = -0.5344$$

Form a riskless portfolio by buying 0.5344 of a share and buying one put. The cost of the portfolio is: $0.5344S + P = \$53.44 + P$

The payoff for the riskless portfolio equals $60.53:

Riskless Portfolio	S = 95	S = 110
Buy 0.5344 share	50.768	58.784
Buy 1 put	9.762	1.746
Total	60.530	60.530

Therefore, find the value of the put by solving:

$$\$53.44 + P = \$60.53/1.05 \Rightarrow P = \$4.208$$

Finally, we verify this result using put-call parity. Recall from Example 21.1 that:

$$C = \$4.434$$

Put-call parity requires that:

$$P = C + PV(X) - S$$

$$\$4.208 = \$4.434 + (\$110/1.05^2) - \$100$$

Except for minor rounding error, put-call parity is satisfied.

32. a. The two possible values of the index in the first period are:

$$uS_0 = 1.20 \times 50 = 60$$
$$dS_0 = 0.80 \times 50 = 40$$

The possible values of the index in the second period are:

$$uuS_0 = (1.20)^2 \times 50 = 72$$
$$udS_0 = 1.20 \times 0.80 \times 50 = 48$$
$$duS_0 = 0.80 \times 1.20 \times 50 = 48$$
$$ddS_0 = (0.80)^2 \times 50 = 32$$

b. The call values in the second period are:

$$C_{uu} = 72 - 60 = 12$$
$$C_{ud} = C_{du} = C_{dd} = 0$$

Since $C_{ud} = C_{du} = 0$, then $C_d = 0$.

To compute C_u, first compute the hedge ratio:

$$H = \frac{C_{uu} - C_{ud}}{uuS_0 - udS_0} = \frac{12 - 0}{72 - 48} = \frac{1}{2}$$

Form a riskless portfolio by buying one share of stock and writing two calls. The cost of the portfolio is: $S - 2C_u = \$60 - 2C_u$

The payoff for the riskless portfolio equals $48:

Riskless Portfolio	S = 48	S = 72
Buy 1 share	48	72
Write 2 calls	0	-24
Total	48	48

Therefore, find the value of the call by solving:

$$\$60 - 2C_u = \$48/1.06 \Rightarrow C_u = \$7.358$$

To compute C, compute the hedge ratio:

$$H = \frac{C_u - C_d}{uS_0 - dS_0} = \frac{7.358 - 0}{60 - 40} = 0.3679$$

Form a riskless portfolio by buying 0.3679 of a share and writing one call. The cost of the portfolio is: $0.3679S - C = \$18.395 - C$

The payoff for the riskless portfolio equals $14.716:

Riskless Portfolio	S = 40	S = 60
Buy 0.3679 share	14.716	22.074
Write 1 call	0.000	−7.358
Total	14.716	14.716

Therefore, find the value of the call by solving:

$$\$18.395 - C = \$14.716/1.06 \Rightarrow C = \$4.512$$

c. The put values in the second period are:

$$P_{uu} = 0$$
$$P_{ud} = P_{du} = 60 - 48 = 12$$
$$P_{dd} = 60 - 32 = 28$$

To compute P_u, first compute the hedge ratio:

$$H = \frac{P_{uu} - P_{ud}}{uuS_0 - udS_0} = \frac{0-12}{72-48} = -\frac{1}{2}$$

Form a riskless portfolio by buying one share of stock and buying two puts. The cost of the portfolio is: $S + 2P_u = \$60 + 2P_u$

The payoff for the riskless portfolio equals $72:

Riskless Portfolio	S = 48	S = 72
Buy 1 share	48	72
Buy 2 puts	24	0
Total	72	72

Therefore, find the value of the put by solving:

$$\$60 + 2P_u = \$72/1.06 \Rightarrow P_u = \$3.962$$

To compute P_d, compute the hedge ratio:

$$H = \frac{P_{du} - P_{dd}}{duS_0 - ddS_0} = \frac{12-28}{48-32} = -1.0$$

Form a riskless portfolio by buying one share and buying one put. The cost of the portfolio is: $S + P_d = \$40 + P_d$

The payoff for the riskless portfolio equals $60:

Riskless Portfolio	$S = 32$	$S = 48$
Buy 1 share	32	48
Buy 1 put	28	12
Total	60	60

Therefore, find the value of the put by solving:

$$\$40 + P_d = \$60/1.06 \Rightarrow P_d = \$16.604$$

To compute P, compute the hedge ratio:

$$H = \frac{P_u - P_d}{uS_0 - dS_0} = \frac{3.962 - 16.604}{60 - 40} = -0.6321$$

Form a riskless portfolio by buying 0.6321 of a share and buying one put. The cost of the portfolio is: $0.6321S + P = \$31.605 + P$

The payoff for the riskless portfolio equals $41.888:

Riskless Portfolio	$S = 40$	$S = 60$
Buy 0.6321 share	25.284	37.926
Buy 1 put	16.604	3.962
Total	41.888	41.888

Therefore, find the value of the put by solving:

$$\$31.605 + P = \$41.888/1.06 \Rightarrow P = \$7.912$$

d. According to put-call-parity:

$$C = S_0 + P - PV(X) = \$50 + \$7.912 - \$60/(1.06^2) = \$4.512$$

This is the value of the call calculated in part (b) above.

33. If r = 0, then one should never exercise a put early. There is no "time value cost" to waiting to exercise, but there is a "volatility benefit" from waiting. To show this more rigorously, consider the following portfolio: lend $X and short one share of stock. The cost to establish the portfolio is $(X - S_0)$. The payoff at time T (with zero interest earnings on the loan) is $(X - S_T)$. In contrast, a put option has a payoff at time T of $(X - S_T)$ if that value is positive, and zero otherwise. The put's payoff is *at least* as large as the portfolio's, and therefore, the put must cost at least as much as the portfolio to purchase. Hence, $P \geq (X - S_0)$, and the put can be sold for more than the proceeds from immediate exercise. We conclude that it doesn't pay to exercise early.

34. a. Xe^{-rT}

    b. X

    c. 0

    d. 0

    e. It is optimal to exercise immediately a put on a stock whose price has fallen to zero. The value of the American put equals the exercise price. Any delay in exercise lowers value by the time value of money.

35. Step 1: Calculate the option values at expiration. The two possible stock prices and the corresponding call values are:

    $uS_0 = 120 \Rightarrow C_u = 20$

    $dS_0 = 80 \Rightarrow C_d = 0$

    Step 2: Calculate the hedge ratio.

    $$H = \frac{C_u - C_d}{uS_0 - dS_0} = \frac{20 - 0}{120 - 80} = \frac{1}{2}$$

    Therefore, form a riskless portfolio by buying one share of stock and writing two calls. The cost of the portfolio is: $S - 2C = 100 - 2C$

    Step 3: Show that the payoff for the riskless portfolio equals $80:

Riskless Portfolio	S = 80	S = 120
Buy 1 share	80	120
Write 2 calls	0	-40
Total	80	80

    Therefore, find the value of the call by solving:

    $\$100 - 2C = \$80/1.10 \Rightarrow C = \$13.636$

    Notice that we did not use the probabilities of a stock price increase or decrease. These are not needed to value the call option.

36. The two possible stock prices and the corresponding call values are:

$$uS_0 = 130 \Rightarrow C_u = 30$$

$$dS_0 = 70 \Rightarrow C_d = 0$$

The hedge ratio is: $H = \dfrac{C_u - C_d}{uS_0 - dS_0} = \dfrac{30 - 0}{130 - 70} = \dfrac{1}{2}$

Form a riskless portfolio by buying one share of stock and writing two calls. The cost of the portfolio is: $S - 2C = 100 - 2C$

The payoff for the riskless portfolio equals $70:

Riskless Portfolio	S = 70	S = 130
Buy 1 share	70	130
Write 2 calls	0	-60
Total	70	70

Therefore, find the value of the call by solving:

$$\$100 - 2C = \$70/1.10 \Rightarrow C = \$18.182$$

Here, the value of the call is greater than the value in the lower-volatility scenario.

37. The two possible stock prices and the corresponding put values are:

$$uS_0 = 120 \Rightarrow P_u = 0$$

$$dS_0 = 80 \Rightarrow P_d = 20$$

The hedge ratio is: $H = \dfrac{P_u - P_d}{uS_0 - dS_0} = \dfrac{0 - 20}{120 - 80} = -\dfrac{1}{2}$

Form a riskless portfolio by buying one share of stock and buying two puts. The cost of the portfolio is: $S + 2P = 100 + 2P$

The payoff for the riskless portfolio equals $120:

Riskless Portfolio	S = 80	S = 120
Buy 1 share	80	120
Buy 2 puts	40	0
Total	120	120

Therefore, find the value of the put by solving:

$$\$100 + 2P = \$120/1.10 \Rightarrow P = \$4.545$$

According to put-call parity: $P + S = C + PV(X)$

Our estimates of option value satisfy this relationship:

$$\$4.545 + \$100 = \$13.636 + \$100/1.10 = \$104.545$$

38. If we assume that the only possible exercise date is just prior to the ex-dividend date, then the relevant parameters for the Black-Scholes formula are:

$$S_0 = 60$$
$$r = 0.5\% \text{ per month}$$
$$X = 55$$
$$\sigma = 7\%$$
$$T = 2 \text{ months}$$

In this case: C = $6.04

If instead, one commits to foregoing early exercise, then we reduce the stock price by the present value of the dividends. Therefore, we use the following parameters:

$$S_0 = 60 - 2e^{-(0.005 \times 2)} = 58.02$$
$$r = 0.5\% \text{ per month}$$
$$X = 55$$
$$\sigma = 7\%$$
$$T = 3 \text{ months}$$

In this case, C = $5.05

The pseudo-American option value is the higher of these two values: $6.04

39. a. (i) Index increases to 701. The combined portfolio will suffer a loss. The written calls expire in the money; the protective put purchased expires worthless. Let's analyze the outcome on a per-share basis. The payout for each call option is $26, for a total cash outflow of $52. The stock is worth $701. The portfolio will thus be worth: $701 − $52 = $649
The net cost of the portfolio when the option positions are established is:
$668 + $8.05 (put) − [2 × $4.30] (calls written) = $667.45

(ii) Index remains at 668. Both options expire out of the money. The portfolio will thus be worth $668 (per share), compared to an initial cost 30 days earlier of $667.45. The portfolio experiences a very small gain of $0.55.

(iii) Index declines to 635. The calls expire worthless. The portfolio will be worth $665, the exercise price of the protective put. This represents a very small loss of $2.45 compared to the initial cost 30 days earlier of $667.45.

b. (i) Index increases to 701. The delta of the call approaches 1.0 as the stock goes deep into the money, while expiration of the call approaches and exercise becomes essentially certain. The put delta approaches zero.

(ii) Index remains at 668. Both options expire out of the money. Delta of each approaches zero as expiration approaches and it becomes certain that the options will not be exercised.

(iii) Index declines to 635. The call is out of the money as expiration approaches. Delta approaches zero. Conversely, the delta of the put approaches −1.0 as exercise becomes certain.

c. The call sells at an implied volatility (11.00%) that is less than recent historical volatility (12.00%); the put sells at an implied volatility (14.00%) that is greater than historical volatility. The call seems relatively cheap; the put seems expensive.

40. True. The call option has an elasticity greater than 1.0. Therefore, the call's percentage rate of return is greater than that of the underlying stock. Hence the GM call responds more than proportionately when the GM stock price changes in response to broad market movements. Therefore, the beta of the GM call is greater than the beta of GM stock.

41. True. The elasticity of a call option is higher the more out of the money is the option. (Even though the delta of the call is lower, the value of the call is also lower. The *proportional* response of the call price to the stock price increases. You can confirm this with numerical examples.) Therefore, the rate of return of the call with the higher exercise price responds more sensitively to changes in the market index, and therefore it has the higher beta.

42. As the stock price increases, conversion becomes increasingly more assured. The hedge ratio approaches 1.0. The price of the convertible bond will move one-for-one with changes in the price of the underlying stock.

43. Salomon believes that the market assessment of volatility is too high. Therefore, Salomon should sell options because the analysis suggests the options are overpriced with respect to true volatility. The delta of the call is 0.6, while that of the put is $0.6 - 1 = -0.4$. Therefore, Salomon should sell puts and calls in the ratio of 0.6 to 0.4. For example, if Salomon sells 2 calls and 3 puts, the position will be delta neutral:

$$\text{Delta} = (2 \times 0.6) + [3 \times (-0.4)] = 0$$

44. Using the true volatility (32%) and time to maturity $T = 0.25$ years, the hedge ratio for Exxon is $N(d_1) = 0.5567$. Because you believe the calls are under-priced (selling at an implied volatility that is too low), you will buy calls and short 0.5567 shares for each call you buy.

45. The calls are cheap (implied $\sigma = 0.30$) and the puts are expensive (implied $\sigma = 0.34$). Therefore, buy calls and sell puts. Using the "true" volatility of $\sigma = 0.32$, the call delta is 0.5567 and the put delta is: $0.5567 - 1.0 = -0.4433$. Therefore, for each call purchased, buy: $0.5567/0.4433 = 1.256$ puts

46. a. To calculate the hedge ratio, suppose that the market index increases by 1%. Then the stock portfolio would be expected to increase by:

$$1\% \times 1.5 = 1.5\% \text{ or } 0.015 \times \$1,250,000 = \$18,750$$

Given the option delta of 0.8, the option portfolio would increase by:

$$\$18,750 \times 0.8 = \$15,000$$

Salomon's liability from writing these options would increase by the same amount. The market index portfolio would increase in value by 1%. Therefore, Salomon Brothers should purchase $1,500,000 of the market index portfolio in order to hedge its position so that a 1% change in the index would result in a $15,000 change in the value of the portfolio.

b. The delta of a put option is:

$$0.8 - 1 = -0.2$$

Therefore, for every 1% the market increases, the index will rise by 10 points and the value of the put option contract will change by:

$$\text{delta} \times 10 \times \text{contract multiplier} = -0.2 \times 10 \times 100 = -\$200$$

Therefore, Salomon should write: $12,000/\$200 = 60$ put contracts

47. If the stock market index increases 1%, the 1 million shares of stock on which the options are written would be expected to increase by:

$$0.75\% \times \$5 \times 1 \text{ million} = \$37,500$$

The options would increase by:

$$\text{delta} \times \$37,500 = 0.8 \times \$37,500 = \$30,000$$

In order to hedge your market exposure, you must sell $3,000,000 of the market index portfolio so that a 1% change in the index would result in a $30,000 change in the value of the portfolio.

CHAPTER 22: FUTURES MARKETS

1. a. The closing futures price for the June contract was 1,307.50, which has a dollar value of:

    $$\$250 \times 1,307.50 = \$326,875$$

    Therefore, the required margin deposit is: $32,687.50

    b. The futures price increases by: $1,320.00 - 1,307.50 = 12.50$

    The credit to your margin account would be: $12.50 \times \$250 = \$3,125$

    This is a percent gain of: $\$3,125/\$32,687.50 = 0.0956 = 9.56\%$

    Note that the futures price itself increased by only 0.956%.

    c. Following the reasoning in part (b), any change in F is magnified by a ratio of (1 /margin requirement). This is the leverage effect. The return will be –10%.

2. There is little hedging or speculative demand for cement futures, since cement prices are fairly stable and predictable. The trading activity necessary to support the futures market would not materialize.

3. The ability to buy on margin is one advantage of futures. Another is the ease with which one can alter one's holdings of the asset. This is especially important if one is dealing in commodities, for which the futures market is far more liquid than the spot market.

4. Short selling results in an immediate cash inflow, whereas the short futures position does not:

Action	Initial CF	Final CF
Short Sale	$+P_0$	$-P_T$
Short Futures	0	$F_0 - P_T$

5. a. False. For any given level of the stock index, the futures price will be lower when the dividend yield is higher. This follows from spot-futures parity:

$$F_0 = S_0 (1 + r_f - d)^T$$

b. False. The parity relationship tells us that the futures price is determined by the stock price, the interest rate, and the dividend yield; it is not a function of beta.

c. True. The short futures position will profit when the market falls. This is a negative beta position.

6. a. $F_0 = S_0(1 + r_f) = \$150 \times 1.06 = \$159$

b. $F_0 = S_0(1 + r_f)^3 = \$150 \times 1.06^3 = \$178.65$

c. $F_0 = 150 \times 1.08^3 = \$188.96$

7. As S increases, so will F. You should buy the futures. A long position in futures is better than buying the stock since you get the advantage of buying on margin.

8. a. Take a short position in T-bond futures, to offset interest rate risk. If rates increase, the loss on the bond will be offset to some extent by gains on the futures.

b. Again, a short position in T-bond futures will offset the interest rate risk.

c. You want to protect your cash outlay when the bond is purchased. If bond prices increase, you will need extra cash to purchase the bond. Thus, you should take a long futures position that will generate a profit if prices increase.

9. $F_0 = S_0(1 + r_f - d) = 1,300(1 + 0.06 - 0.02) = 1,352$

10. The put-call parity relation states that:

$$P = C - S_0 + X/(1 + r_f)^T$$

If $X = F$, then: $P = C - S_0 + F/(1 + r_f)^T$

But spot-futures parity tells us that:

$$F = S_0(1 + r_f)^T$$

Substituting, we find that:

$$P = C - S_0 + [S_0(1 + r_f)^T]/(1 + r_f)^T = C - S_0 + S_0 \text{ which implies that } P = C.$$

11. According to the parity relation, the proper price for December futures is:

$$F_{Dec} = F_{June}(1 + r_f)^{1/2} = 546.30 \times 1.05^{1/2} = 559.79$$

The actual futures price for December is very slightly high relative to the June price. You should short the December contract and take a long position in the June contract. (However, transactions costs might eliminate any arbitrage profit.)

12. a. The strategy that would take advantage of the arbitrage opportunity is a "reverse cash and carry." A reverse cash and carry opportunity results when the following relationship does not hold true:

$$F_0 \geq S_0 (1 + C)$$

If the futures price is less than the spot price plus the cost of carrying the goods to the futures delivery date, then an arbitrage opportunity exists. A trader would be able to sell the asset short, use the proceeds to lend at the prevailing interest rate, and then buy the asset for future delivery. At the future delivery, the trader would then collect the proceeds of the loan with interest, accept delivery of the asset, and cover the short position in the commodity.

b.

| | Cash Flows | |
Action	Now	One year from now
Sell the spot commodity short	+$120.00	−$125.00
Buy the commodity futures expiring in 1 year	$0.00	$0.00
Contract to lend $120 at 8% for 1 year	−$120.00	+$129.60
Total cash flow	$0.00	+$4.60

13. a. $120 \times 1.06 = \$127.20$

b. The stock price falls to: $120 \times (1 - 0.03) = \$116.40$

The futures price falls to: $116.4 \times 1.06 = \$123.384$

The investor loses: $(127.20 - 123.384) \times 1,000 = \$3,816$

c. The percentage loss is: $\$3,816/\$12,000 = 0.318 = 31.8\%$

14. a. The initial futures price is $F_0 = 1000 \times (1 + 0.005 - 0.002)^{12} = \$1,036.60$

   In one month, the futures price will be:

   $$F_0 = 1020 \times (1 + 0.005 - 0.002)^{11} = \$1,054.17$$

   The increase in the futures price is 17.57, so the cash flow will be:

   $$17.57 \times \$250 = \$4,392.50$$

   b. The holding period return is: $\$4,392.50/\$15,000 = 0.2928 = 29.28\%$

15. a. The call option is distinguished by its asymmetric payoff. If the Swiss franc rises in value, then the company can buy francs for a given number of dollars to service its debt, and thereby put a cap on the dollar cost of its financing. If the franc falls, the company will benefit from the change in the exchange rate.

   The futures and forward contracts have symmetric payoffs. The dollar cost of the financing is locked in regardless of whether the franc appreciates or depreciates. The major difference from the firm's perspective between futures and forwards is in the mark-to-market feature of futures. The consequence of this is that the firm must be ready for the cash management issues surrounding cash inflows or outflows as the currency values and futures prices fluctuate.

   b. The call option gives the company the ability to benefit from depreciation in the franc, but at a cost equal to the option premium. Unless the firm has some special expertise in currency speculation, it seems that the futures or forward strategy, which locks in a dollar cost of financing without an option premium, may be the better strategy.

16. The treasurer would like to buy the bonds today, but cannot. As a proxy for this purchase, T-bond futures contracts can be purchased. If rates do in fact fall, the treasurer will have to buy back the bonds for the sinking fund at prices higher than the prices at which they could be purchased today. However, the gains on the futures contracts will offset this higher cost to some extent.

17. The important distinction between a futures contract and an options contract is that the futures contract is an obligation. When an investor purchases or sells a futures contract, the investor has an obligation to either accept or deliver, respectively, the underlying commodity on the expiration date. In contrast, the buyer of an option contract is not obligated to accept or deliver the underlying commodity but instead has the right, or choice, to accept delivery (for call holders) or make delivery (for put holders) of the underlying commodity anytime during the life of the contract.

Futures and options modify a portfolio's risk in different ways. Buying or selling a futures contract affects a portfolio's upside risk and downside risk by a similar magnitude. This is commonly referred to as symmetrical impact. On the other hand, the addition of a call or put option to a portfolio does not affect a portfolio's upside risk and downside risk to a similar magnitude. Unlike futures contracts, the impact of options on the risk profile of a portfolio is asymmetric.

18. The parity value of F is: $1,300 \times (1 + 0.04 - 0.01) = 1,339$

The actual futures price is 1,330, too low by 9.

Arbitrage Portfolio	CF now	CF in 1 year
Short index	1,300	$-S_T - (0.01 \times 1,300)$
Buy Futures	0	$S_T - 1,330$
Lend	−1,300	$1,300 \times 1.04$
Total	0	9

19. a. The investor should sell the forward contract to protect the value of the bond against rising interest rates during the holding period. Because the investor intends to take a long position in the underlying asset, the hedge requires a short position in the derivative instrument.

    b. The value of the forward contract on expiration date is equal to the spot price of the underlying asset on expiration date minus the forward price of the contract:

       $$\$978.40 - \$1,024.70 = -\$46.30$$

    The contract has a negative value. This is the value to the holder of a long position in the forward contract. In this example, the investor should be *short* the forward contract, so that the value to this investor would be +$46.30 since this is the cash flow the investor expects to receive.

c. The value of the combined portfolio at the end of the six-month holding period is:

$978.40 + $46.30 = $1,024.70

The change in the value of the combined portfolio during this six-month period is: $24.70

The value of the combined portfolio is the sum of the market value of the bond and the value of the *short* position in the forward contract. At the start of the six-month holding period, the bond is worth $1,000 and the forward contract has a value of zero (because this is not an off-market forward contract, no money changes hands at initiation). Six months later, the bond value is $978.40 and the value of the *short* position in the forward contract is $46.30, as calculated in part (b).

The fact that the combined value of the long position in the bond and the short position in the forward contract at the forward contract's maturity date is equal to the forward price on the forward contract at its initiation date is not a coincidence. By taking a long position in the underlying asset and a short position in the forward contract, the investor has created a fully hedged (and hence risk-free) position, and should earn the risk-free rate of return. The six-month risk-free rate of return is 5.00% (annualized), which produces a return of $24.70 over a six-month period:

$$(\$1,000 \times 1.05^{(1/2)}) - \$1,000 = \$24.70$$

These results support VanHusen's statement that selling a forward contract on the underlying bond protects the portfolio during a period of rising interest rates. The loss in the value of the underlying bond during the six month holding period is offset by the cash payment made at expiration date to holder of the short position in the forward contract; that is, a short position in the forward contract protects (hedges) the long position in the underlying asset.

20. a. Accurate. Futures contracts are marked to the market daily. Holding a short position on a bond futures contract during a period of rising interest rates (declining bond prices) generates positive cash inflow from the daily mark to market. If an investor in a futures contract has a long position when the price of the underlying asset increases, then the daily mark to market generates a positive cash inflow that can be reinvested. Forward contracts settle only at expiration date and do not generate any cash flow prior to expiration.

b. Inaccurate. According to the cost of carry model, the futures contract price is adjusted upward by the cost of carry for the underlying asset. Bonds (and other financial instruments), however, do not have any significant storage costs. Moreover, the cost of carry is reduced by any coupon payments paid to the bondholder during the life of the futures contract. Any "convenience yield" from holding the underlying bond also reduces the cost of carry. As a result, the cost of carry for a bond is likely to be negative.

21. a. The current yield for Treasury bonds (coupon divided by price) plays the role of the dividend yield.

    b. When the yield curve is upward sloping, the current yield exceeds the short rate. Hence, T-bond futures prices on more distant contracts are lower than those on near-term contracts.

22. a.

	Cash Flows		
Action	Now	T_1	T_2
Long futures with maturity T_1	0	$P_1 - F(T_1)$	0
Short futures with maturity T_2	0	0	$F(T_2) - P_2$
Buy asset at T_1, sell at T_2	0	$-P_1$	$+P_2$
At T_1, borrow $F(T_1)$	0	$F(T_1)$	$-F(T_1) \times (1 + r_f)^{(T_2 - T_1)}$
Total	0	0	$F(T_2) - F(T_1) \times (1 + r_f)^{(T_2 - T_1)}$

    b. Since the T_2 cash flow is riskless and the net investment was zero, then any profits represent an arbitrage opportunity.

    c. The zero-profit no-arbitrage restriction implies that

$$F(T_2) = F(T_1) \times (1 + r_f)^{(T_2 - T_1)}$$

23. a. Futures prices are determined from the spreadsheet as follows:

Spot Futures Parity and Time Spreads		
Spot price	1,100	
Income yield (%)	1.5	Futures prices versus maturity
Interest rate (%)	3.0	
Today's date	1/1/2008	Spot price	1,100.00
Maturity date 1	2/14/2008	Futures 1	1,101.96
Maturity date 2	5/21/2008	Futures 2	1,106.39
Maturity date 3	11/18/2008	Futures 3	1,114.52
Time to maturity 1	0.12		
Time to maturity 2	0.39		
Time to maturity 3	0.88		
		LEGEND:	
		Enter data	
		Value calculated	
		See comment	

b.   The spreadsheet demonstrates that the futures prices now decrease with increased time to maturity:

Spot Futures Parity and Time Spreads			
Spot price	1,100		
Income yield (%)	4.0	Futures prices versus maturity	
Interest rate (%)	3.0		
Today's date	1/1/2008	Spot price	1,100.00
Maturity date 1	2/14/2008	Futures 1	1,098.68
Maturity date 2	5/21/2008	Futures 2	1,095.71
Maturity date 3	11/18/2008	Futures 3	1,090.31
Time to maturity 1	0.12		
Time to maturity 2	0.39		
Time to maturity 3	0.88		
		LEGEND:	
		Enter data	
		Value calculated	
		See comment	

24. The futures price is the agreed-upon price for deferred delivery of the asset. If that price is fair, then the value of the agreement ought to be zero; that is, the contract will be a zero-NPV agreement for each trader.

25. Because long positions equal short positions, futures trading must entail a "canceling out" of bets on the asset. Moreover, no cash is exchanged at the inception of futures trading. Thus, there should be minimal impact on the spot market for the asset, and futures trading should not be expected to reduce capital available for other uses.

CHAPTER 23: FUTURES AND SWAPS: MARKETS AND APPLICATIONS

1. a. $S_0 \times (1 + r_M) - D = (1{,}425 \times 1.06) - 15 = 1{,}495.50$

   b. $S_0 \times (1 + r_f) - D = (1{,}425 \times 1.03) - 15 = 1{,}452.75$

   c. The futures price is too low. Buy futures, short the index, and invest the proceeds of the short sale in T-bills:

	CF Now	CF in 6 months
Buy futures	0	$S_T - 1{,}422$
Short index	1,425	$-S_T - 15$
Buy T-bills	−1,425	1,467.75
Total	0	30.75

2. a. The value of the underlying stock is:

   $$\$250 \times 1{,}350 = \$337{,}500$$

   $$25/\$337{,}500 = 0.000074 = 0.0074\% \text{ of the value of the stock}$$

   b. $\$40 \times 0.000074 = \$0.0030$ (less than half of one cent)

   c. $\$0.20/\$0.0030 = 67$

   The transaction cost in the stock market is 67 times the transaction cost in the futures market.

3. a. From parity: $F_0 = 1{,}200 \times (1 + 0.03) - 15 = 1{,}221$

   Actual F_0 is 1,218; so the futures price is 3 below the "proper" level.

   b. Buy the relatively cheap futures, sell the relatively expensive stock and lend the proceeds of the short sale:

	CF Now	CF in 6 months
Buy futures	0	$S_T - 1{,}218$
Sell shares	1,200	$-S_T - 15$
Lend $1,200	−1,200	1,236
Total	0	3

c. If you do not receive interest on the proceeds of the short sales, then the $1200 you receive will not be invested but will simply be returned to you. The proceeds from the strategy in part (b) are now negative: an arbitrage opportunity no longer exists.

	CF Now	CF in 6 months
Buy futures	0	$S_T - 1{,}218$
Sell shares	1,200	$-S_T - 15$
Place $1,200 in margin account	−1,200	1,200
Total	0	−33

d. If we call the original futures price F_0, then the proceeds from the long-futures, short-stock strategy are:

	CF Now	CF in 6 months
Buy futures	0	$S_T - F_0$
Sell shares	1,200	$-S_T - 15$
Place $1,200 in margin account	−1,200	1,200
Total	0	$1{,}185 - F_0$

Therefore, F_0 can be as low as 1,185 without giving rise to an arbitrage opportunity. On the other hand, if F_0 is higher than the parity value (1,221), then an arbitrage opportunity (buy stocks, sell futures) will exist. There is no short-selling cost in this case. Therefore, the no-arbitrage range is:

$$1{,}185 \leq F_0 \leq 1{,}221$$

4. a. Call p the fraction of proceeds from the short sale to which we have access. Ignoring transaction costs, the lower bound on the futures price that precludes arbitrage is the following usual parity value (except for the factor p):

$$S_0 (1 + r_f p) - D$$

The dividend (D) equals: $0.012 \times 1{,}350 = \$16.20$

The factor p arises because only this fraction of the proceeds from the short sale can be invested in the risk-free asset. We can solve for p as follows:

$$1{,}350 \times (1 + 0.022p) - 16.20 = 1{,}351 \Rightarrow p = 0.579$$

b. With p = 0.9, the no-arbitrage lower bound on the futures price is:

$$1,350 \times [1 + (0.022 \times 0.9)] - 16.20 = 1,360.53$$

The actual futures price is 1,351. The departure from the bound is therefore 9.53. This departure also equals the potential profit from an arbitrage strategy. The strategy is to short the stock, which currently sells at 1,350. The investor receives 90% of the proceeds (1,215) and the remainder (135) remains in the margin account until the short position is covered in 6 months. The investor buys futures and lends 1,215:

	CF Now	CF in 6 months
Buy futures	0	$S_T - 1,351$
Sell shares	$1350 - 135$	$135 - S_T - 16.20$
Lend	$-1,215$	$1,215 \times 1.022 = 1,241.73$
Total	0	9.53

The profit is: $9.53 \times \$250$ per contract $= \$2,382.50$

5. a. By spot-futures parity:

$$F_0 = S_0 \times (1 + r_f) = 185 \times [1 + (0.06/2)] = 190.55$$

b. The lower bound is based on the reverse cash-and-carry strategy.

Action Now	CF in $	Action at period-end	CF in $
Buy one TOBEC index futures contract	0	Sell one TOBEC index futures contract	$\$100 \times (F_1 - F_0)$
Sell spot TOBEC index	$+\$18,500$	Buy spot TOBEC index	$-\$100 \times S_1$
Lend $18,500	$-\$18,500$	Collect loan repayment	$\$18,500 \times 1.03 = +\$19,055$
		Pay transaction costs	$-\$15.00$
Total	0	Total	$-\$100F_0 + \$19,040$

(Note that $F_1 = S_1$ at expiration.)
The lower bound for F_0 is: $19,040/100 = 190.40$

6. a. You should be short the index futures contracts. If the stock value falls, you need futures profits to offset the loss.

b. Each contract is for $250 times the index, currently valued at 1,350. Therefore, each contract controls stock worth: $\$250 \times 1,350 = \$337,500$
In order to hedge a $13.5 million portfolio, you need:

$$\frac{\$13,500,000}{\$337,500} = 40 \text{ contracts}$$

c. Now, your stock swings only 0.6 as much as the market index. Hence, you need 0.6 as many contracts as in (b): $0.6 \times 40 = 24$ contracts

7.   If the beta of the portfolio were 1.0, she would sell \$1 million of the index. Because beta is 1.25, she should sell \$1.25 million of the index.

8.   a. $1,200 \times 1.01 = 1,212$

      b.   \$12 million $/(\$250 \times 1,200) = 40$ contracts short

      c. $40 \times 250 \times (1,212 - S_T) = 12,120,000 - 10,000 S_T$

      d.   The expected return on a stock is:

$$\alpha + r_f + \beta[E(r_M) - r_f]$$

The CAPM predicts that $\alpha = 0$. In this case, however, if you believe that $\alpha = 2\%$ (i.e., 0.02), then you forecast a portfolio return of:

$$r_P = 0.02 + 0.01 + 1.0 \times (r_M - 0.01) + \varepsilon = 0.03 + [1 \times (r_M - 0.01)] + \varepsilon$$

where ε is diversifiable risk, with an expected value of zero.

      e.   Because the market is assumed to pay no dividends:

$$r_M = (S_T - 1,200)/1,200 = (S_T/1,200) - 1$$

The rate of return can also be written as:

$$r_P = 0.03 + \left(1 \times [(S_T/1,200) - 1 - 0.01]\right) + \varepsilon$$

The *dollar* value of the stock portfolio as a function of the market index is therefore:

\$12 million $\times (1 + r_P) =$

\$12 million $\times [0.03 + (S_T/1,200) - 0.01 + \varepsilon] =$

$\$240,000 + 10,000 S_T + (\$12$ million $\times \varepsilon)$

The dollar value of the short futures position will be (from part c):

$12,120,000 - 10,000 S_T$

The total value of the portfolio plus the futures proceeds is therefore:

$[240,000 + 10,000 S_T + (12$ million $\times \varepsilon)] + [12,120,000 - 10,000 S_T] =$

$\$12,360,000 + (\$12$ million $\times \varepsilon)$

The payoff is independent of the value of the stock index. Systematic risk has been eliminated by hedging (although firm-specific risk remains).

      f.   The portfolio-plus-futures position cost \$12 million to establish. The expected end-of-period value is \$12,360,000. The rate of return is therefore 3%.

g. The beta of the hedged position is 0. The fair return should be $r_f = 1\%$. Therefore, the alpha of the position is $(3\% - 1\%) = 2\%$, the same as the alpha of the portfolio. Now, however, one can take a position on the alpha without incurring systematic risk.

9. You would short $0.50 of the market index contract and $0.75 of the computer industry stock for each dollar held in IBM.

10. a. The strategy would be to sell Japanese stock index futures to hedge the market risk of Japanese stocks, and to sell yen futures to hedge the currency exposure.

    b. Some possible practical difficulties with this strategy include:
    - Contract size on futures may not match size of portfolio.
    - Stock portfolio may not closely track index portfolios on which futures trade.
    - Cash flow management issues from marking to market.
    - Potential mispricing of futures contracts (violations of parity).

11. The dollar is depreciating relative to the euro. To induce investors to invest in the U.S., the U.S. interest rate must be higher.

12. a. From parity: $F_0 = E_0 \times \dfrac{1 + r_{US}}{1 + r_{UK}} = 1.60 \times \dfrac{1.04}{1.08} = 1.541$

    b. Suppose that $F_0 = \$1.58/\pounds$. Then dollars are relatively too cheap in the forward market, or equivalently, pounds are too expensive. Therefore, you should borrow the present value of £1, use the proceeds to buy pound-denominated bills in the spot market, and sell £1 forward:

Action Now	CF in $	Action at period-end	CF in $
Sell £1 forward for $1.58	0	Collect $1.58, deliver £1	$1.58 − $E_1
Buy £1/1.08 in spot market; invest at the British risk-free rate	−1.60/1.08 = −$1.481	Exchange £1 for $E_1	$E_1
Borrow $1.481	$1.481	Repay loan; U.S. interest rate = 4%	−$1.540
Total	0	Total	$0.04

13. a. Lend in the U.K.

   b. Borrow in the U.S.

   c. Borrowing in the U.S. offers a 4% rate of return. Borrowing in the U.K. and covering interest rate risk with futures or forwards offers a rate of return of:

$$r_{US} = \left[(1 + r_{UK}) \times \frac{F_0}{E_0} \right] - 1 = \left[1.07 \times \frac{1.58}{1.60} \right] - 1 = 0.0566 = 5.66\%$$

   It appears advantageous to borrow in the U.S., where rates are lower, and to lend in the U.K. An arbitrage strategy involves simultaneous lending and borrowing with the covering of interest rate risk:

Action Now	CF in $	Action at period-end	CF in $
Borrow $1.60 in U.S.	$1.60	Repay loan	$-$1.60 \times 1.04$
Convert borrowed dollars to pounds; lend £1 pound in U.K.	$-$1.60	Collect repayment; exchange proceeds for dollars	$1.07 \times E_1$
Sell forward £1.07 at $F_0 = 1.58	0	Unwind forward	$1.07 \times (\$1.58 - E_1)$
Total	0	Total	$0.0266

14. a. The hedged investment involves converting the $1 million to foreign currency, investing in that country, and selling forward the foreign currency in order to lock in the dollar value of the investment. Because the interest rates are for 90-day periods, we assume they are quoted as bond equivalent yields, annualized using simple interest. Therefore, to express rates on a per quarter basis, we divide these rates by 4:

	Japanese government	Swiss government
Convert $1 million to local currency	$\$1,000,000 \times 133.05 =$ ¥133,050,000	$\$1,000,000 \times 1.5260 =$ SF1,526,000
Invest in local currency for 90 days	¥133,050,000 × [1 + (0.076/4)] = ¥135,577,950	SF1,526,000 × [1 + (0.086/4)] = SF1,558,809
Convert to $ at 90-day forward rate	135,577,950/133.47 = $1,015,793	1,558,809/1.5348 = $1,015,643

   b. The results in the two currencies are nearly identical. This near-equality reflects the interest rate parity theorem. This theory asserts that the pricing relationships between interest rates and spot and forward exchange rates must make covered (that is, fully hedged and riskless) investments in any currency equally attractive.

   c. The 90-day return in Japan is 1.5793%, which represents a bond-equivalent yield of 1.5793% × 365/90 = 6.405%. The 90-day return in Switzerland is 1.5643%, which represents a bond-equivalent yield of 1.5643% × 365/90 = 6.344%. The estimate for the 90-day risk-free U.S. government money market yield is in this range.

15. The investor can buy X amount of pesos at the (indirect) spot exchange rate, and invest the pesos in the Mexican bond market. Then, in one year, the investor will have:

$$X \times (1 + r_{MEX}) \text{ pesos}$$

These pesos can then be converted back into dollars using the (indirect) forward exchange rate. Interest rate parity asserts that the two holding period returns must be equal, which can be represented by the formula:

$$(1 + r_{US}) = E_0 \times (1 + r_{MEX}) \times (1/F_0)$$

The left side of the equation represents the holding period return for a U.S. dollar-denominated bond. If interest rate parity holds, then this term also corresponds to the U.S. dollar holding period return for the currency-hedged Mexican one-year bond. The right side of the equation is the holding period return, in dollar terms, for a currency-hedged peso-denominated bond. Solving for r_{US}:

$$(1 + r_{US}) = 9.5000 \times (1 + 0.065) \times (1/9.8707)$$

$$(1 + r_{US}) = 1.0250$$

$$r_{US} = 2.50\%$$

Thus $r_{US} = 2.50\%$, which is the as the yield for the one-year U.S. bond.

16. a. From parity: $F_0 = E_0 \times \left(\dfrac{1 + r_{US}}{1 + r_{Japan}}\right)^{0.5} = 124.30 \times \left(\dfrac{1.0010}{1.0380}\right)^{0.5} = 122.06453$

b.

Action Now	CF in $	Action at period-end	CF in ¥
Borrow $1,000,000 in U.S.	$1,000,000	Repay loan	$-(\$1,000,000 \times 1.035^{0.25}) =$ $-\$1,008,637.45$
Convert borrowed dollars to yen; lend ¥124,300,000 in Japan	$-\$1,000,000$	Collect repayment in yen	$¥124,300,000 \times 1.005^{0.25} =$ ¥124,455,084.52
Sell forward $1,008,637.45 at $F_0 = ¥123.2605$	0	Unwind forward	$-(1,008,637.45 \times ¥123.2605) =$ $-¥124,325,156.40$
Total	0	Total	¥129,928.12

The arbitrage profit is: ¥129,928.12

17. The farmer must sell forward:

$$100,000 \times (1/0.90) = 111,111 \text{ bushels of yellow corn}$$

This requires selling: $111,111/5,000 = 22.2$ contracts

18. Municipal bond yields, which are below T-bond yields because of their tax-exempt status, are expected to close in on Treasury yields. Because yields and prices are inversely related, this means that municipal bond prices will perform poorly compared to Treasuries. Therefore you should establish a spread position, buying Treasury-bond futures and selling municipal bond futures. The net bet on the general level of interest rates is approximately zero. You have simply made a bet on relative performances in the two sectors.

19. The closing futures price will be: $100 - 5.20 = 94.80$
The initial futures price was 94.9825, so the loss to the long side is 18.25 basis points or:

$$18.25 \text{ basis points} \times \$25 \text{ per basis point} = \$456.25$$

The loss can also be computed as:

$$0.001825 \times \tfrac{1}{4} \times \$1,000,000 = \$456.25$$

20. Suppose the yield on your portfolio increases by 1.5 basis points. Then the yield on the T-bond contract is likely to increase by 1 basis point. The loss on your portfolio will be:

$$\$1 \text{ million} \times \Delta y \times D^* = \$1,000,000 \times 0.00015 \times 4 = \$600$$

The change in the futures price (per $100 par value) will be:

$$\$95 \times 0.0001 \times 9 = \$0.0855$$

This is a change of $85.50 on a $100,000 par value contract. Therefore you should sell:

$$\$600/\$85.50 = 7 \text{ contracts}$$

21. She must sell: $\$1 \text{ million} \times \dfrac{8}{10} = \$0.8$ million of T-bonds

22. If yield changes on the bond and the contracts are each 1 basis point, then the bond value will change by:

$$\$10,000,000 \times 0.0001 \times 8 = \$8,000$$

The contract will result in a cash flow of:

$$\$100,000 \times 0.0001 \times 6 = \$60$$

Therefore, the firm should sell: $8,000/60 = 133$ contracts
The firm sells the contracts because you need profits on the contract to offset losses as a bond issuer if interest rates increase.

23. $F_0 = S_0(1 + r_f)^T = 580 \times 1.05 = 609$

If $F_0 = 620$, you could earn arbitrage profits as follows:

	CF Now	CF in 1 year
Buy gold	−580	S_T
Short futures	0	$620 - S_T$
Borrow $580	580	−609
Total	0	11

The forward price must be 609 in order for this strategy to yield no profit.

24. If a poor harvest today indicates a worse than average harvest in future years, then the futures prices will rise in response to today's harvest, although presumably the two-year price will change by less than the one-year price. The same reasoning holds if corn is stored across the harvest. Next year's price is determined by the available supply at harvest time, which is the actual harvest plus the stored corn. A smaller harvest today means less stored corn for next year which can lead to higher prices.

Suppose first that corn is never stored across a harvest, and second that the quality of a harvest is not related to the quality of past harvests. Under these circumstances, there is no link between the current price of corn and the expected future price of corn. The quantity of corn stored will fall to zero before the next harvest, and thus the quantity of corn and the price in one year will depend solely on the quantity of next year's harvest, which has nothing to do with this year's harvest.

25. The required rate of return on an asset with the same risk as corn is:

$$1\% + 0.5(1.8\% - 1\%) = 1.4\% \text{ per month}$$

Thus, in the absence of storage costs, three months from now corn would sell for:

$$\$2.75 \times 1.014^3 = \$2.867$$

The future value of 3 month's storage costs is:

$$\$0.03 \times FA(1\%, 3) = \$0.091$$

where FA stands for the future value factor for a level annuity with a given interest rate and number of payments. Thus, in order to induce storage, the expected price would have to be:

$$\$2.867 + \$0.091 = \$2.958$$

Because the expected spot price is only $2.94, you would not store corn.

26. a. Delsing should sell stock index futures contracts and buy bond futures contracts. This strategy is justified because buying the bond futures and selling the stock index futures provides the same exposure as buying the bonds and selling the stocks. This strategy assumes high correlation between the bond futures and the bond portfolio, as well as high correlation between the stock index futures and the stock portfolio.

b. The number of contracts in each case is:

   i. $5 \times \$200,000,000 \times 0.0001 = \$100,000$

   $\$100,000/97.85 = 1022$ contracts

   ii. $\$200,000,000/(\$1,378 \times 250) = 581$ contracts

27. Situation A. The market value of the portfolio to be hedged is $20 million. The market value of the bonds controlled by one futures contract is \$63,330. If we were to equate the market values of the portfolio and the futures contract, we would sell:

$$\$20,000,000/\$63,330 = 315.806 \text{ contracts}$$

However, we must adjust this "naive" hedge for the price volatility of the bond portfolio relative to the futures contract. Price volatilities differ according to both the duration and the yield volatility of the bonds. In this case, the yield volatilities may be assumed equal, because any yield spread between the Treasury portfolio and the Treasury bond underlying the futures contract is likely to be stable. However, the duration of the Treasury portfolio is less than that of the futures contract. Adjusting the naive hedge for relative duration and relative yield volatility, we obtain the adjusted hedge position:

$$315.806 \times \frac{7.6}{8.0} \times 1.0 = 300 \text{ contracts}$$

Situation B. Here, the treasurer seeks to hedge the purchase price of the bonds; this requires a long hedge. The market value of the bonds to be purchased is:

$$\$20 \text{ million} \times 0.93 = \$18.6 \text{ million}$$

The duration ratio is 7.2/8.0, and the relative yield volatility is 1.25. Therefore, the hedge requires the treasurer to take a long position in:

$$\frac{18,600,000}{63,330} \times \frac{7.2}{8.0} \times 1.25 = 330 \text{ contracts}$$

28. a.   % change in T-bond price = modified duration × change in YTM

$$= 7.0 \times 0.50\% = 3.5\%$$

b.   When the YTM of the T-bond changes by 50 basis points, the predicted change in the yield on the KC bond is 1.22 × 50 = 61 basis points. Therefore:

% change in KC price = modified duration × change in YTM

$$= 6.93 \times 0.61\% = 4.23\%$$

29. If the exchange of currencies were structured as three separate forward contracts, the forward prices would be determined as follows:

Forward exchange rate × $1 million euros = dollars to be delivered

Year 1:   1.20 × (1.05/1.04) × $1 million euros = $1.2115 million

Year 2:   1.20 × (1.05/1.04)^2 × $1 million euros = $1.2232 million

Year 3:   1.20 × (1.05/1.04)^3 × $1 million euros = $1.2349 million

Instead, we deliver the same number of dollars (F*) each year. The value of F* is determined by first computing the present value of this obligation:

$$\frac{F^*}{1.05^1} + \frac{F^*}{1.05^2} + \frac{F^*}{1.05^3} = \frac{1.2115}{1.05^1} + \frac{1.2232}{1.05^2} + \frac{1.2349}{1.05^3} = 3.3300$$

F* equals $1.2228 million per year.

30. a.   The swap rate moved in favor of firm ABC. ABC should have received 1% more per year than it could receive in the current swap market. Based on notional principal of $10 million, the loss is:

0.01 × $10 million = $100,000 per year.

b.   The market value of the fixed annual loss is obtained by discounting at the current 7% rate on 3-year swaps. The loss is:

$100,000 × Annuity factor (7%, 3) = $262,432

c.   If ABC had become insolvent, XYZ would not be harmed. XYZ would be happy to see the swap agreement cancelled. However, the swap agreement ought to be treated as an asset of ABC when the firm is reorganized.

31. The firm receives a fixed rate that is 2% higher than the market rate. The extra payment of (0.02 × $10 million) has present value equal to:

$200,000 × Annuity factor (8%, 5) = $799,542

CHAPTER 24: PORTFOLIO PERFORMANCE EVALUATION

1. a. Arithmetic average: $\bar{r}_{ABC} = 10\%$; $\bar{r}_{XYZ} = 10\%$

   b. Dispersion: $\sigma_{ABC} = 7.07\%$; $\sigma_{XYZ} = 13.91\%$

   Stock XYZ has greater dispersion.
   (Note: We used 5 degrees of freedom in calculating standard deviations.)

   c. Geometric average:

   $$r_{ABC} = (1.20 \times 1.12 \times 1.14 \times 1.03 \times 1.01)^{1/5} - 1 = 0.0977 = 9.77\%$$

   $$r_{XYZ} = (1.30 \times 1.12 \times 1.18 \times 1.00 \times 0.90)^{1/5} - 1 = 0.0911 = 9.11\%$$

   Despite the fact that the two stocks have the same arithmetic average, the geometric average for XYZ is less than the geometric average for ABC. The reason for this result is the fact that the greater variance of XYZ drives the geometric average further below the arithmetic average.

   d. In terms of "forward looking" statistics, the arithmetic average is the better estimate of expected rate of return. Therefore, if the data reflect the probabilities of future returns, 10% is the expected rate of return for both stocks.

2. a. Time-weighted average returns are based on year-by-year rates of return:

Year	Return = (capital gains + dividend)/price
1998 − 1999	[($120 − $100) + $4]/$100 = 24.00%
1999 − 2000	[($90 − $120) + $4]/$120 = −21.67%
2000 − 2001	[($100 − $90) + $4]/$90 = 15.56%

   Arithmetic mean: (24% − 21.67% + 15.56%)/3 = 5.96%

   Geometric mean: $(1.24 \times 0.7833 \times 1.1556)^{1/3} - 1 = 0.0392 = 3.92\%$

   b.

Date	Cash Flow	Explanation
1/1/98	−$300	Purchase of three shares at $100 each
1/1/99	−$228	Purchase of two shares at $120 less dividend income on three shares held
1/1/00	$110	Dividends on five shares plus sale of one share at $90
1/1/01	$416	Dividends on four shares plus sale of four shares at $100 each

Date: 1/1/98   1/1/99   1/1/00   1/1/01

−228

−300

Dollar-weighted return = Internal rate of return = −0.1607%

3.

Time	Cash flow	Holding period return
0	3(−$90) = −$270	
1	$100	(100–90)/90 = 11.11%
2	$100	0%
3	$100	0%

a. Time-weighted geometric average rate of return =

$$(1.1111 \times 1.0 \times 1.0)^{1/3} - 1 = 0.0357 = 3.57\%$$

b. Time-weighted arithmetic average rate of return = (11.11% + 0 + 0)/3 = 3.70%

The arithmetic average is always greater than or equal to the geometric average; the greater the dispersion, the greater the difference.

c. Dollar-weighted average rate of return = IRR = 5.46%
[Using a financial calculator, enter: n = 3, PV = –270, FV = 0, PMT = 100. Then compute the interest rate.] The IRR exceeds the other averages because the investment fund was the largest when the highest return occurred.

4.　a.　The alphas for the two portfolios are:

$$\alpha_A = 12\% - [5\% + 0.7(13\% - 5\%)] = 1.4\%$$

$$\alpha_B = 16\% - [5\% + 1.4(13\% - 5\%)] = -0.2\%$$

Ideally, you would want to take a long position in Portfolio A and a short position in Portfolio B.

b.　If you will hold only one of the two portfolios, then the Sharpe measure is the appropriate criterion:

$$S_A = \frac{12-5}{12} = 0.583$$

$$S_B = \frac{16-5}{31} = 0.355$$

Using the Sharpe criterion, Portfolio A is the preferred portfolio.

5.

a.

		Stock A	Stock B
(i)	Alpha = regression intercept	1.0%	2.0%
(ii)	Information ratio = $\alpha_P /\sigma(e_P)$	0.0971	0.1047
(iii)	*Sharpe measure = $(r_P - r_f)/\sigma_P$	0.4907	0.3373
(iv)	**Treynor measure = $(r_P - r_f)/\beta_P$	8.833	10.500

* To compute the Sharpe measure, note that for each stock, $(r_P - r_f)$ can be computed from the right-hand side of the regression equation, using the assumed parameters $r_M = 14\%$ and $r_f = 6\%$. The standard deviation of each stock's returns is given in the problem.

** The beta to use for the Treynor measure is the slope coefficient of the regression equation presented in the problem.

b.　(i) If this is the only risky asset held by the investor, then Sharpe's measure is the appropriate measure. Since the Sharpe measure is higher for Stock A, then A is the best choice.

(ii) If the stock is mixed with the market index fund, then the contribution to the overall Sharpe measure is determined by the appraisal ratio; therefore, Stock B is preferred.

(iii) If the stock is one of many stocks, then Treynor's measure is the appropriate measure, and Stock B is preferred.

6. We need to distinguish between market timing and security selection abilities. The intercept of the scatter diagram is a measure of stock selection ability. If the manager tends to have a positive excess return even when the market's performance is merely "neutral" (i.e., has zero excess return), then we conclude that the manager has on average made good stock picks. Stock selection must be the source of the positive excess returns.

Timing ability is indicated by the curvature of the plotted line. Lines that become steeper as you move to the right along the horizontal axis show good timing ability. The steeper slope shows that the manager maintained higher portfolio sensitivity to market swings (i.e., a higher beta) in periods when the market performed well. This ability to choose more market-sensitive securities in anticipation of market upturns is the essence of good timing. In contrast, a declining slope as you move to the right means that the portfolio was more sensitive to the market when the market did poorly and less sensitive when the market did well. This indicates poor timing.

We can therefore classify performance for the four managers as follows:

	Selection Ability	Timing Ability
A.	Bad	Good
B.	Good	Good
C.	Good	Bad
D.	Bad	Bad

7. a. Bogey: $(0.60 \times 2.5\%) + (0.30 \times 1.2\%) + (0.10 \times 0.5\%) = 1.91\%$
    Actual: $(0.70 \times 2.0\%) + (0.20 \times 1.0\%) + (0.10 \times 0.5\%) = \underline{1.65\%}$
    $\textit{Under}$performance: 0.26%

    b. Security Selection:

Market	(1) Differential return within market (Manager – index)	(2) Manager's portfolio weight	(3) = (1) × (2) Contribution to performance
Equity	–0.5%	0.70	–0.35%
Bonds	–0.2%	0.20	–0.04%
Cash	0.0%	0.10	0.00%
		Contribution of security selection:	–0.39%

c. Asset Allocation:

Market	(1) Excess weight (Manager – benchmark)	(2) Index Return	(3) = (1) × (2) Contribution to performance
Equity	0.10%	2.5%	0.25%
Bonds	−0.10%	1.2%	−0.12%
Cash	0.00%	0.5%	0.00%
	Contribution of asset allocation:		0.13%

Summary:

Security selection	−0.39%
Asset allocation	0.13%
Excess performance	−0.26%

8. a. Manager return: $(0.30 \times 20) + (0.10 \times 15) + (0.40 \times 10) + (0.20 \times 5) = 12.50\%$
Benchmark (bogey): $(0.15 \times 12) + (0.30 \times 15) + (0.45 \times 14) + (0.10 \times 12) = \underline{13.80\%}$

Added value: −1.30%

b. Added value from country allocation:

Country	(1) Excess weight (Manager – benchmark)	(2) Index Return minus bogey	(3) = (1) × (2) Contribution to performance
U.K.	0.15%	−1.8%	−0.27%
Japan	−0.20%	1.2%	−0.24%
U.S.	−0.05%	0.2%	−0.01%
Germany	0.10%	−1.8%	−0.18%
	Contribution of country allocation:		−0.70%

c. Added value from stock selection:

Country	(1) Differential return within country (Manager – Index)	(2) Manager's country weight	(3) = (1) × (2) Contribution to performance
U.K.	8%	0.30%	2.4%
Japan	0%	0.10%	0.0%
U.S.	−4%	0.40%	−1.6%
Germany	−7%	0.20%	−1.4%
	Contribution of stock selection:		−0.6%

Summary:

Country allocation	−0.70%
Stock selection	−0.60%
Excess performance	−1.30%

9. *Support*: A manager could be a better performer in one type of circumstance than in another. For example, a manager who does no timing, but simply maintains a high beta, will do better in up markets and worse in down markets. Therefore, we should observe performance over an entire cycle. Also, to the extent that observing a manager over an entire cycle increases the number of observations, it would improve the reliability of the measurement.

    Contradict: If we adequately control for exposure to the market (i.e., adjust for beta), then market performance should not affect the relative performance of individual managers. It is therefore not necessary to wait for an entire market cycle to pass before evaluating a manager.

10. The use of universes of managers to evaluate relative investment performance does, to some extent, overcome statistical problems, as long as those manager groups can be made sufficiently homogeneous with respect to style.

11. a. The manager's alpha is: $10\% - [6\% + 0.5(14\% - 6\%)] = 0$

    b. From Black-Jensen-Scholes and others, we know that, on average, portfolios with low beta have historically had positive alphas. (The slope of the empirical security market line is shallower than predicted by the CAPM.) Therefore, given the manager's low beta, performance might actually be sub-par despite the estimated alpha of zero.

12. a. <u>Manager A</u>
    Strength. Although Manager A's one-year total return was somewhat below the international index return (–6.0 percent versus –5.0 percent), this manager apparently has some country/security return expertise. This large local market return advantage of 2.0 percent exceeds the 0.2 percent return for the international index.

    Weakness. Manager A has an obvious weakness in the currency management area. This manager experienced a marked currency return shortfall, with a return of –8.0 percent versus –5.2 percent for the index.

    <u>Manager B</u>
    Strength. Manager B's total return exceeded that of the index, with a marked positive increment apparent in the currency return. Manager B had a –1.0 percent currency return compared to a –5.2 percent currency return on the international index. Based on this outcome, Manager B's strength appears to be expertise in the currency selection area.

    Weakness. Manager B had a marked shortfall in local market return. Therefore, Manager B appears to be weak in security/market selection ability.

b. The following strategies would enable the fund to take advantage of the strengths of each of the two managers while minimizing their weaknesses.

   1. *Recommendation:* One strategy would be to direct Manager A to make no currency bets relative to the international index and to direct Manager B to make only currency decisions, and no active country or security selection bets.

   Justification: This strategy would mitigate Manager A's weakness by hedging all currency exposures into index-like weights. This would allow capture of Manager A's country and stock selection skills while avoiding losses from poor currency management. This strategy would also mitigate Manager B's weakness, leaving an index-like portfolio construct and capitalizing on the apparent skill in currency management.

   2. *Recommendation:* Another strategy would be to combine the portfolios of Manager A and Manager B, with Manager A making country exposure and security selection decisions and Manager B managing the currency exposures created by Manager A's decisions (providing a "currency overlay").

   Justification: This recommendation would capture the strengths of both Manager A and Manager B and would minimize their collective weaknesses.

13. a. Indeed, the one year results were terrible, but one year is a poor statistical base from which to draw inferences. Moreover, the board of trustees had directed Karl to adopt a long-term horizon. The Board specifically instructed the investment manager to give priority to long term results.

b. The sample of pension funds had a much larger share invested in equities than did Alpine. Equities performed much better than bonds. Yet the trustees told Alpine to hold down risk, investing not more than 25% of the plan's assets in common stocks. (Alpine's beta was also somewhat defensive.) Alpine should not be held responsible for an asset allocation policy dictated by the client.

c. Alpine's alpha measures its risk-adjusted performance compared to the market:

$$\alpha = 13.3\% - [7.5\% + 0.90(13.8\% - 7.5\%)] = 0.13\% \text{ (actually above zero)}$$

d. Note that the last 5 years, and particularly the most recent year, have been bad for bonds, the asset class that Alpine had been encouraged to hold. Within this asset class, however, Alpine did much better than the index fund. Moreover, despite the fact that the bond index underperformed both the actuarial return and T-bills, Alpine outperformed both. Alpine's performance *within* each asset class has been superior on a risk-adjusted basis. Its overall disappointing returns were due to a heavy asset allocation weighting towards bonds, which was the Board's, not Alpine's, choice.

e.   A trustee may not care about the time-weighted return, but that return is more indicative of the manager's performance. After all, the manager has no control over the cash inflows and outflows of the fund.

14. a.   Method I does nothing to separately identify the effects of market timing and security selection decisions. It also uses a questionable "neutral position," the composition of the portfolio at the beginning of the year.

     b.   Method II is not perfect, but is the best of the three techniques. It at least attempts to focus on market timing by examining the returns for portfolios constructed from bond market *indexes* using actual weights in various indexes versus year-average weights. The problem with this method is that the year-average weights need not correspond to a client's "neutral" weights. For example, what if the manager were optimistic over the entire year regarding long-term bonds? Her average weighting could reflect her optimism, and not a neutral position.

     c.   Method III uses net purchases of bonds as a signal of bond manager optimism. But such net purchases can be motivated by withdrawals from or contributions to the fund rather than the manager's decisions. (Note that this is an open-ended mutual fund.) Therefore, it is inappropriate to evaluate the manager based on whether net purchases turn out to be reliable bullish or bearish signals.

15. Treynor measure = $(17 - 8)/1.1 = 8.182$

16. Sharpe measure = $(24 - 8)/18 = 0.888$

17. a.   Treynor measures
          Portfolio X: $(10 - 6)/0.6 = 6.67$
          S&P 500: $(12 - 6)/1.0 = 6.00$
          Sharpe measures
          Portfolio X: $(10 - 6)/18 = 0.222$
          S&P 500: $(12 - 6)/13 = 0.462$

          Portfolio X outperforms the market based on the Treynor measure, but underperforms based on the Sharpe measure.

     b.   The two measures of performance are in conflict because they use different measures of risk. Portfolio X has less systematic risk than the market, as measured by its lower beta, but more total risk (volatility), as measured by its higher standard deviation. Therefore, the portfolio outperforms the market based on the Treynor measure but underperforms based on the Sharpe measure.

18. Geometric average $= (1.15 \times 0.90)^{1/2} - 1 = 0.0173 = 1.73\%$

19. Geometric average $= (0.91 \times 1.23 \times 1.17)^{1/3} - 1 = 0.0941 = 9.41\%$

20. Internal rate of return $= 7.5\%$

21. d.

22. Time-weighted average return $= (15\% + 10\%)/2 = 12.5\%$

    To compute dollar-weighted rate of return, cash flows are:

    $CF_0 = -\$500,000$

    $CF_1 = -\$500,000$

    $CF_2 = (\$500,000 \times 1.15 \times 1.10) + (\$500,000 \times 1.10) = \$1,182,500$

    Dollar-weighted rate of return $= 11.71\%$

23. b.

24. a.

25. a. Each of these benchmarks has several deficiencies, as described below.

    Market index:

    - A market index may exhibit survivorship bias. Firms that have gone out of business are removed from the index, resulting in a performance measure that overstates actual performance had the failed firms been included.
    - A market index may exhibit double counting that arises because of companies owning other companies and both being represented in the index.
    - It is often difficult to exactly and continually replicate the holdings in the market index without incurring substantial trading costs.
    - The chosen index may not be an appropriate proxy for the management style of the managers.
    - The chosen index may not represent the entire universe of securities. For example, the S&P 500 Index represents 65% to 70% of U.S. equity market capitalization.
    - The chosen index (e.g., the S&P 500) may have a large capitalization bias.
    - The chosen index may not be investable. There may be securities in the index that cannot be held in the portfolio.

Benchmark normal portfolio:

- This is the most difficult performance measurement method to develop and calculate.
- The normal portfolio must be continually updated, requiring substantial resources.
- Consultants and clients are concerned that managers who are involved in developing and calculating their benchmark portfolio may produce an easily-beaten normal portfolio, making their performance appear better than it actually is.

Median of the manager universe:

- It can be difficult to identify a universe of managers appropriate for the investment style of the plan's managers.
- Selection of a manager universe for comparison involves some, perhaps much, subjective judgement.
- Comparison with a manager universe does not take into account the risk taken in the portfolio.
- The median of a manager universe does not represent an "investable" portfolio; that is, a portfolio manager may not be able to invest in the median manager portfolio.
- Such a benchmark may be ambiguous. The names and weights of the securities constituting the benchmark are not clearly delineated.
- The benchmark is not constructed prior to the start of an evaluation period; it is not specified in advance.
- A manager universe may exhibit survivorship bias; managers who have gone out of business are removed from the universe, resulting in a performance measure that overstates the actual performance had those managers been included.

b.   i.   The Sharpe ratio is calculated by dividing the portfolio risk premium (i.e., actual portfolio return minus the risk-free return) by the portfolio standard deviation:

$$\text{Sharpe ratio} = (r_P - r_f)/\sigma_P$$

The Treynor measure is calculated by dividing the portfolio risk premium (i.e., actual portfolio return minus the risk-free return) by the portfolio beta:

$$\text{Treynor measure} = (r_P - r_f)/\beta_P$$

Jensen's alpha is calculated by subtracting the market risk premium, adjusted for risk by the portfolio's beta, from the actual portfolio excess return (risk premium). It can be described as the difference in return earned by the portfolio compared to the return implied by the Capital Asset Pricing Model or Security Market Line:

$$\alpha_P = r_P - [r_f + \beta_P (r_M - r_f)]$$

ii. The Sharpe ratio assumes that the relevant risk is total risk, and it measures excess return per unit of total risk. The Treynor measure assumes that the relevant risk is systematic risk, and it measures excess return per unit of systematic risk. Jensen's alpha assumes that the relevant risk is systematic risk, and it measures excess return at a given level of systematic risk.

26. i. The statement is incorrect. Valid benchmarks are unbiased. Median manager benchmarks, however, are subject to significant survivorship bias, which results in several drawbacks, including the following:
    - The performance of median manager benchmarks is biased upwards.
    - The upward bias increases with time.
    - Survivor bias introduces uncertainty with regard to manager rankings.
    - Survivor bias skews the shape of the distribution curve.

    ii. The statement is incorrect. Valid benchmarks are unambiguous and able to be replicated. The median manager benchmark, however, is ambiguous because the weights of the individual securities in the benchmark are not known. The portfolio's composition cannot be known before the conclusion of a measurement period because identification as a median manager can occur only after performance is measured.

    Valid benchmarks are also investable. The median manager benchmark is not investable. That is, a manager using a median manager benchmark cannot forego active management and, taking a passive/indexed approach, simply hold the benchmark. This is a result of the fact that the weights of individual securities in the benchmark are not known.

    iii. The statement is correct. The median manager benchmark may be inappropriate because the median manager universe encompasses many investment styles and, therefore, may not be consistent with a given manager's style.

27. a. Sharpe ratio = $(r_P - r_f)/\sigma_P$

    Williamson Capital: Sharpe ratio = $(22.1\% - 5.0\%)/16.8\% = 1.02$

    Joyner Asset Management: Sharpe ratio = $(24.2\% - 5.0\%)/20.2\% = 0.95$

    Treynor measure = $(r_P - r_f)/\beta_P$

    Williamson Capital: Treynor measure = $(22.1\% - 5.0\%)/1.2 = 14.25$

    Joyner Asset Management: Treynor measure = $(24.2\% - 5.0\%)/0.8 = 24.00$

    b. The difference in the rankings of Williamson and Joyner results directly from the difference in diversification of the portfolios. Joyner has a higher Treynor measure (24.00) and a lower Sharpe ratio (0.95) than does Williamson (14.25 and 1.202, respectively), so Joyner must be less diversified than Williamson. The Treynor measure indicates that Joyner has a higher return per unit of systematic risk than does Williamson, while the Sharpe ratio indicates that Joyner has a lower return per unit of total risk than does Williamson.

CHAPTER 25: INTERNATIONAL DIVERSIFICATION

1. Initial investment = 2,000 × $1.50 = $3,000

    Final value = 2,400 × $1.75 = $4,200

    Rate of return = ($4,200/$3,000) − 1 = 0.40 = 40%

2. a.

3. c.

4. a. $10,000/2 = £5,000

    £5,000/£40 = 125 shares

    b. To fill in the table, we use the relation:

    $$1 + r(US) = [(1 + r(UK)]\frac{E_1}{E_0}$$

Price per Share (£)	Pound-Denominated Return (%)	Dollar-Denominated Return (%) for Year End Exchange Rate		
		$1.80/£	$2.00/£	$2.20/£
£35	-12.5%	-21.25%	-12.5%	-3.75%
£40	0.0%	-10.00%	0.0%	10.00%
£45	12.5%	1.25%	12.5%	23.75%

    c. The dollar-denominated return equals the pound-denominated return when the exchange rate is unchanged over the year.

5. The standard deviation of the pound-denominated return (using 3 degrees of freedom) is 10.21%. The dollar-denominated return has a standard deviation of 13.10% (using 9 degrees of freedom), greater than the pound-denominated standard deviation. This is due to the addition of exchange rate risk.

6.   a.   First we calculate the dollar value of the 125 shares of stock in each scenario. Then we add the profits from the forward contract in each scenario.

| Price per | | Dollar Value of Stock at Given Exchange Rate | | |
Share (£)	Exchange Rate:	$1.80/£	$2.00/£	$2.20/£
£35		7,875	8,750	9,625
£40		9,000	10,000	11,000
£45		10,125	11,250	12,375
Profits on Forward Exchange:		1,500	500	-500
$[=5000(2.10-E_1)]$				

| Price per | | Total Dollar Proceeds at Given Exchange Rate | | |
Share (£)	Exchange Rate:	$1.80/£	$2.00/£	$2.20/£
£35		9,375	9,250	9,125
£40		10,500	10,500	10,500
£45		11,625	11,750	11,875

Finally, calculate the dollar-denominated rate of return, recalling that the initial investment was $10,000:

| Price per | | Rate of return (%) at Given Exchange Rate | | |
Share (£)	Exchange Rate:	$1.80/£	$2.00/£	$2.20/£
£35		-6.25%	-7.50%	-8.75%
£40		5.00%	5.00%	5.00%
£45		16.25%	17.50%	18.75%

   b.   The standard deviation is now 10.24%. This is lower than the unhedged dollar-denominated standard deviation, and is only slightly higher than the standard deviation of the pound-denominated return.

7.   Currency Selection

EAFE: [0.30 × (−10%)] + (0.10 × 0%) + (0.60 × 10%) = 3.0%

Manager: [0.35 × (−10%)] + (0.15 × 0%) + (0.50 × 10%) = 1.5%

Loss of 1.5% relative to EAFE.

Country Selection

EAFE: (0.30 × 20%) + (0.10 × 15%) + (0.60 × 25%) = 22.50%

Manager: (0.35 × 20%) + (0.15 × 15%) + (0.50 × 25%) = 21.75%

Loss of 0.75% relative to EAFE.

Stock Selection

[(18% − 20%) × 0.35] + [(20% − 15%) × 0.15] + [(20% − 25%) × 0.50] = − 2.45%

Loss of 2.45% relative to EAFE.

8. $1 + r(US) = [1 + r_f(UK)] \times (F_0/E_0) = 1.08 \times (1.85/1.75) = 1.1417 \Rightarrow r(US) = 14.17\%$

9.   You can now purchase: $\$10,000/\$1.75 = £5,714.29$

This will grow with 8% interest to £6,171.43. Therefore, to lock in your return, you would sell forward £6,171.43 at the forward exchange rate.

10. a.   The primary rationale is the opportunity for diversification. Factors that contribute to low correlations of stock returns across national boundaries are:
         i.   imperfect correlation of business cycles
         ii. imperfect correlation of interest rates
         iii. imperfect correlation of inflation rates
         iv. exchange rate volatility

     b.   Obstacles to international investing are:
         i.   <u>Availability of information</u>, including insufficient data on which to base investment decisions. Interpreting and evaluating data that is different in form and/or content than the routinely available and widely understood U.S. data is difficult. Also, much foreign data is reported with a considerable lag.
         ii. <u>Liquidity</u>, in terms of the ability to buy or sell, in size and in a timely manner, without affecting the market price. Most foreign exchanges offer (relative to U.S. norms) limited trading, and experience greater price volatility. Moreover, only a (relatively) small number of individual foreign stocks enjoy liquidity comparable to that in the U.S., although this situation is improving steadily.
         iii. <u>Transaction costs</u>, particularly when viewed as a combination of commission plus spread plus market impact costs, are well above U.S. levels in most foreign markets. This, of course, adversely affects return realization.
         iv. <u>Political risk</u>.
         v.   <u>Foreign currency risk</u>, although to a great extent, this can be hedged.

     c.   The asset-class performance data for this particular period reveal that non-U.S. dollar bonds provided a small incremental return advantage over U.S. dollar bonds, but at a considerably higher level of risk. Each category of fixed income assets outperformed the S&P 500 Index measure of U.S. equity results with regard to both risk and return, which is certainly an unexpected outcome. Within the equity area, non-U.S. stocks, represented by the EAFE Index, outperformed U.S. stocks by a considerable margin with only slightly more risk. In contrast to U.S. equities, this asset category performed as it should relative to fixed income assets, providing more return for the higher risk involved.

         Concerning the Account Performance Index, its position on the graph reveals an aggregate outcome that is superior to the sum of its component parts. To some extent, this is due to the beneficial effect on performance resulting from multi-market diversification and the differential covariances involved. In this case, the portfolio manager(s) (apparently) achieved an on-balance positive alpha, adding to total portfolio return by their actions. The addition of international (i.e., non-U.S.) securities to a portfolio that would otherwise have held only domestic (U.S.) securities clearly worked to the advantage of this fund over this time period.

11. The return on the Canadian bond is equal to the sum of:

coupon income +

gain or loss from the premium or discount in the forward rate relative to the spot exchange rate +

capital gain or loss on the bond.

Over the six-month period, the return is:

Coupon + forward premium/discount + capital gain =

$$\frac{7.50\%}{2} + (-0.75\%) + \text{Price change in } \% = 3.00\% + \% \text{ capital gain}$$

The expected semiannual return on the U.S. bond is 3.25%. Since the U.S. bond is selling at par and its yield is expected to remain unchanged, there is no expected capital gain or loss on the U.S. bond. Therefore, in order to provide the same return, the Canadian bond must provide a capital gain of 0.25% (i.e., 1/4 point relative to par value of 100) over and above any expected capital gain on the U.S. bond.

12. a. We exchange $1 million for foreign currency at the current exchange rate and sell forward the amount of foreign currency we will accumulate 90 days from now. For the yen investment, we initially receive:

1 million/0.0119 = ¥84.034 million

Invest for 90 days to accumulate:

¥84.034 × [1 + (0.0252/4)] = ¥84.563 million

(Note that we divide the quoted 90-day rate by 4 because quoted money market interest rates typically are annualized using simple interest, assuming a 360-day year.)

If we sell this number of yen forward at the forward exchange rate of 0.0120¥//dollar, we will end up with:

84.563 million × 0.0120 = $1.0148 million

The 90-day dollar interest rate is 1.48%.

Similarly, the dollar proceeds from the 90-day Canadian dollar investment will be:

$$\frac{\$1 \text{ million}}{0.7284} \times \left(1 + \frac{0.0674}{4}\right) \times 0.7269 = \$1.0148 \text{ million}$$

The 90-day dollar interest rate is 1.48%, the same as that in the yen investment.

b. The dollar-hedged rate of return on default-free government securities in both Japan and Canada is 1.48%. Therefore, the 90-day interest rate available on U.S. government securities must also be 1.48%. This corresponds to an APR of 5.92%, which is greater than the APR in Japan, and less than the APR in Canada. This result makes sense, as the relationship between forward and spot exchange rates indicates that the U.S. dollar is expected to depreciate against the yen and appreciate against the Canadian dollar.

13. a. Incorrect. There have been periods of strong performance despite weak currencies. It is also possible that an appreciating currency could enhance performance.

b. Correct.

c. Correct.

d. Incorrect. Correlations are not stable over time. Also, the portfolio can move dramatically away from the efficient frontier from one period to the next.

14. a. The following arguments could be made in favor of active management:

Economic diversity: the diversity of the Otunian economy across various sectors may offer the opportunity for the active investor to employ "top down" sector timing strategies.

High transaction costs: very high transaction costs may discourage trading activity by international investors and lead to inefficiencies that may be exploited successfully by active investors.

Good financial disclosure and detailed accounting standards: good financial disclosure and detailed accounting standards may provide the well-trained analyst an opportunity to perform fundamental research analysis in order to identify inefficiently priced securities.

Capital restrictions: restrictions on capital flows may discourage foreign investor participation and serve to segment the Otunian market, thus creating exploitable market inefficiencies for the active investor.

Developing economy and securities market: developing economies and markets are often characterized by inefficiently priced securities and by rapid economic change and growth. The active investor may exploit these characteristics.

Settlement problems: long delays in settling trades by non-residents may serve to discourage international investors, leading to inefficiently priced securities which may be exploited by active management.

The following arguments could be made in favor of indexing:

Economic diversity: economic diversity across a broad sector of industries implies that indexing may provide a diverse representative portfolio that is not subject to the risks associated with concentrated sectors.

High transaction costs: indexing would be favored by the implied lower levels of trading activity and costs.

Settlement problems: indexing would be favored by the implied lower levels of trading activity and settlement requirements.

Financial disclosure and accounting standards: wide public availability of reliable financial information presumably leads to greater market efficiency, reducing the value of both fundamental analysis and active management, and favoring indexing.

Restrictions of capital flows: indexing would be favored by the implied lower levels of trading activity and thus smaller opportunity for regulatory interference.

b.   A recommendation for active management would focus on short-term inefficiencies in, and long term prospects for, the developing Otunian markets and economy, inefficiencies and prospects which would not generally be found in more developed markets.

A recommendation for indexing would focus on the factors of economic diversity, high transaction costs, settlement delays, capital flow restrictions, and lower management fees.

CHAPTER 26: INVESTMENT POLICY AND
THE FRAMEWORK OF THE CFA INSTITUTE

1. a. i. Return Requirement: IPS Y has the appropriate language. Since the Plan is currently under-funded, the primary objective should be to make the pension fund financially stronger. The risk inherent in attempting to maximize total returns would be inappropriate.

   ii. Risk Tolerance: IPS Y has the appropriate language. Because of the fund's under-funded status, the Plan has limited risk tolerance; should the fund incur a substantial loss, payments to beneficiaries could be jeopardized.

   iii. Time Horizon: IPS Y has the appropriate language. Although going-concern pension plans usually have a long time horizon, the Acme plan has a shorter time horizon because of the reduced retirement age and the relatively high median age of the workforce.

   iv. Liquidity: IPS X has the appropriate language. Because of the early retirement feature starting next month and the age of the work force (which indicates an increasing number of retirees in the near future), the Plan needs a moderate level of liquidity in order to fund monthly benefit payments.

   b. The current portfolio is the most appropriate choice for the pension plan's asset allocation. The current portfolio offers:
   i. An expected return that exceeds the Plan's return requirement;
   ii. An expected standard deviation that only slightly exceeds the Plan's target; and,
   iii. A level of liquidity that should be sufficient for future needs.

   The higher expected return will ameliorate the Plan's under-funded status somewhat, and the change in the fund's risk profile will be minimal. The portfolio has significant allocations to U.K. bonds (42 percent) and large-cap equities (13 percent) in addition to cash (5 percent). The availability of these highly liquid assets should be sufficient to fund monthly benefit payments when the early retirement feature takes effect next month, particularly in view of the stable income flows from these investments.

   The Graham portfolio offers:
   i. An expected return that is slightly below the Plan's requirement;
   ii. An expected standard deviation that is substantially below the Plan's target; and,
   iii. A level of liquidity that should be more than sufficient for future needs.

   Given the Plan's under-funded status, the portfolio's level of risk is unacceptable.

The Michael portfolio offers:

i.   An expected return that is substantially above the Plan's requirement;
ii. An expected standard deviation that far exceeds the Plan's target; and
iii. A level of liquidity that should be sufficient for future needs.

Given the Plan's under-funded status, the portfolio's level of risk is unacceptable.

2.   c.   Liquidity

3.   b.   Organizing the management process itself.

4.   a.   An approach to asset allocation that GSS could use is the one detailed in the chapter. It consists of the following steps:

1. Specify asset classes to be included in the portfolio. The major classes usually considered are the following:

> Money market instruments (usually called cash)
> Fixed income securities (usually called bonds)
> Stocks
> Real estate
> Precious metals
> Other

2. Specify capital market expectations. This step consists of using both historical data and economic analysis to determine your expectations of future rates of return over the relevant holding period on the assets to be considered for inclusion in the portfolio.

3. Derive the efficient portfolio frontier. This step consists of finding portfolios that achieve the maximum expected return for any given degree of risk.

4. Find the optimal asset mix. This step consists of selecting the efficient portfolio that best meets your risk and return objectives while satisfying the constraints you face.

b.   A guardian investor typically is an individual who wishes to preserve the purchasing power of his assets. Extreme guardians would be exclusively in AAA short term credits. GSS should first determine how long the time horizon is and how high the return expectations are. Assuming a long time horizon and 8-10% return (pretax) expectations, the portfolio could be allocated 30-40% bonds, 30-40% stocks, and modest allocations to each of the other asset groups.

5.   a.   OBJECTIVES

1. *Return*

The required total rate of return for the JU endowment fund is the sum of the spending rate and the expected long-term increase in educational costs:

Spending rate = $126 million (current spending need)

divided by

($2,000 million current fund balance less $200 million library payment)

= $126 million/$1,800 million = 7 percent

The expected educational cost increase is 3 percent. The sum of the two components is 10 percent. Achieving this relatively high return would ensure that the endowment's real value is maintained.

2. *Risk*

Evaluation of risk tolerance requires an assessment of both the ability and the willingness of the endowment to take risk.

Ability: Average Risk

- Endowment funds are long-term in nature, having infinite lives. This long time horizon by itself would allow for above-average risk.
- However, creative tension exists between the JU endowment's demand for high current income to meet immediate spending requirements and the need for long-term growth to meet future requirements. This need for a spending rate (in excess of 5 percent) and the university's heavy dependence on those funds allow for only average risk.

Willingness: Above Average Risk

- University leaders and endowment directors have set a spending rate in excess of 5 percent. To achieve their 7 percent real rate of return, the fund must be invested in above-average risk securities. Thus, the 7 percent spending rate indicates a willingness to take above-average risk.
- In addition, the current portfolio allocation, with its large allocations to direct real estate and venture capital, indicates a willingness to take above-average risk.

Taking both ability and willingness into consideration, the endowment's risk tolerance is best characterized as "above average."

CONSTRAINTS

1. *Time Horizon.*

A two-stage time horizon is needed. The first stage recognizes short-term liquidity constraints ($200 million library payment in eight months). The second stage is an infinite time horizon (endowment funds are established to provide permanent support).

2. *Liquidity*.

Generally, endowment funds have long time horizons, and little liquidity is needed in excess of annual distribution requirements. However, the JU endowment requires liquidity for the upcoming library payment in addition to the current year's contribution to the operating budget. Liquidity needs for the next year are:

Library Payment	+$200 million
Operating Budget Contribution	+$126 million
<u>Annual Portfolio Income</u>	<u>−$29 million</u>
Total	+$297 million

Annual portfolio income =

$(0.04 \times \$40 \text{ million}) + (0.05 \times \$60 \text{ million}) + (0.01 \times \$300 \text{ million})$

$+ (0.001 \times \$400 \text{ million}) + (0.03 \times \$700 \text{ million}) = \$29 \text{ million}$

3. *Taxes*. U.S. endowment funds are tax-exempt.

4. *Legal/Regulatory*.

U.S. endowment funds are subject to predominantly state (but some federal) regulatory and legal constraints, and standards of prudence generally apply. Restrictions imposed by Bremner may pose a legal constraint on the fund (no more than 25 percent of the initial Bertocchi Oil and Gas shares may be sold in any one-year period).

5. *Unique Circumstances*.

Only 25 percent of donated Bertocchi Oil and Gas shares may be sold in any one-year period (constraint imposed by donor). A secondary consideration is the need to budget the one-time $200 million library payment in eight months.

b. U.S. Money Market Fund: 15% (Range: 14% - 17%)

Liquidity needs for the next year are:

Library payment	+$200 million
Operating budget contribution	+$126 million
<u>Annual portfolio income</u>	<u>−$29 million</u>
Total	+$297 million

Total liquidity of at least $297 million is required (14.85 percent of current endowment assets). Additional allocations (more than 2 percent above the suggested 15 percent) would be overly conservative. This cushion should be sufficient for any transaction needs (i.e., mismatch of cash inflows/outflows).

Intermediate Global Bond Fund: 20% (Range: 15% - 25%)

To achieve a 10 percent portfolio return, the fund needs to take above average risk (e.g., 20 percent in Global Bond Fund and 30 percent in Global Equity Fund). An allocation below 15 percent would involve taking unnecessary risk that would put the safety and preservation of the endowment fund in jeopardy. An allocation in the 21 percent to 25 percent range could still be tolerated because the slight reduction in portfolio expected return would be partially compensated by the reduction in portfolio risk. An allocation above 25 percent would not satisfy the endowment fund return requirements.

Global Equity Fund: 30% (Range: 25% - 35%)

To achieve a 10 percent portfolio return, the fund needs to take above average risk (e.g., 30 percent in Global Equity Fund and 20 percent in Global Bond Fund). An allocation above 35 percent would involve taking unnecessary risk that would put the safety and preservation of the endowment fund in jeopardy. An allocation in the 25 percent to 29 percent range could still be tolerated, as the slight reduction in portfolio expected return would be partially compensated by the reduction in portfolio risk. An allocation below 25 percent would not satisfy the endowment fund return requirements.

Bertocchi Oil and Gas Common Stock: 15%

There is a single issuer concentration risk associated with the current allocation, and a 25 percent reduction ($100 million), which is the maximum reduction allowed by the donor, is required ($400 million − $100 million = $300 million remaining).

Direct Real Estate: 10%

Venture Capital: 10%

The suggested allocations (point estimates) would allow the JU endowment fund to meet the 10 percent return requirement, calculated as follows:

Asset	Suggested Allocation	Expected Return	Weighted Return
U.S. Money Market Fund	0.15	4.0%	0.60%
Intermediate Global Bond Fund	0.20	5.0%	1.00%
Global Equity Fund	0.30	10.0%	3.00%
Bertocchi Common Stock	0.15	15.0%	2.25%
Direct Real Estate	0.10	11.5%	1.15%
Venture Capital	0.10	20.0%	2.00%
Total	1.00		10.000%

The allowable allocation ranges, taken in proper combination, would also be consistent with the 10 percent return requirement.

6. a. *Overview.* Fairfax is 58 years old and has seven years until a planned retirement. She has a fairly lavish lifestyle but few money worries. Her large salary pays all current expenses, and she has accumulated $2 million in cash equivalents from savings in previous years. Her health is excellent, and her health insurance coverage will continue after retirement and is employer paid. While Fairfax's job is a high-level one, she is not well versed in investment matters and has had the good sense to connect with professional counsel to start planning for her investment future, a future that is complicated by ownership of a $10 million block of company stock that, while listed on the NYSE, pays no dividends and has a zero-cost basis for tax purposes. All salary, investment income (except interest on municipal bonds) and realized capital gains are taxed to Fairfax at a 35 percent rate; this tax rate and a 4 percent inflation rate are expected to continue into the future. Fairfax would accept a 3 percent real, after-tax return from the investment portfolio to be formed from her $2 million in savings ("the Savings Portfolio") if that return could be obtained with only modest portfolio volatility (i.e., less than a 10 percent annual decline). She is described as being "conservative in all things."

OBJECTIVES

- *Return Requirement.* Fairfax's need for portfolio income begins seven years from now, at the date of retirement. The investment focus for her Savings Portfolio should be on growing the portfolio's value in the interim in a way that provides protection against loss of purchasing power. Her 3% real, after-tax return preference implies a gross total return requirement of at least 10.8%, assuming her investments are fully taxable (as is the case now) and assuming 4% inflation and a 35 percent tax rate. For Fairfax to maintain her current lifestyle, then, at retirement, she would have to generate inflation-adjusted annual income of:

$$\$500,000 \times 1.04^7 = \$658,000$$

If the market value of Reston's stock does not change, and if she is able to earn a 10.8% return on the Savings Portfolio (or 7% nominal after-tax return), then, by retirement age, she should accumulate:

$$\$10,000,000 + (\$2,000,000 \times 1.07^7) = \$13,211,500$$

To generate \$658,000 per year, a 5.0% return on the \$13,211,500 would be needed.

- *Risk Tolerance.* The information provided indicates that Fairfax is quite risk averse; she does not want to experience a decline of more than 10% in the value of the Savings Portfolio in any given year. This would indicate that the portfolio should have below average risk exposure in order to minimize its downside volatility. In terms of overall wealth, Fairfax could afford to take more than average risk, but because of her preferences and the non-diversified nature of the total portfolio, a below-average risk objective is appropriate for the Savings Portfolio. It should be noted, however, that truly meaningful statements about the risk of Fairfax's total portfolio are tied to assumptions regarding both the volatility of Reston's stock (if it is retained) and when and at what price the Reston stock will be sold. Because the Reston holding constitutes 83% of Fairfax's total portfolio, it will largely determine the risk she actually experiences as long as this holding remains intact.

CONSTRAINTS

- *Time Horizon.* Two time horizons are applicable to Fairfax's life. The first time horizon represents the period during which Fairfax should set up her financial situation in preparation for the balance of the second time horizon, her retirement period of indefinite length. Of the two horizons, the longer term to the expected end of her life is the dominant horizon because it is over this period that the assets must fulfill their primary function of funding her expenses, as an annuity, in retirement.

- *Liquidity.* With liquidity defined either as income needs or as cash reserves to meet emergency needs, Fairfax's liquidity requirement is minimal. Five hundred thousand dollars of salary is available annually, health cost concerns are nonexistent, and we know of no planned needs for cash from the portfolio.

- *Taxes*. Fairfax's taxable income (salary, taxable investment income, and realized capital gains on securities) is taxed at a 35% rate. Careful tax planning and coordination with investment planning is required. Investment strategy should include seeking income that is sheltered from taxes and holding securities for lengthy time periods in order to produce larger after-tax returns. Sale of the Reston stock will have sizeable tax consequences because Fairfax's cost basis is zero; special planning will be needed for this eventuality. Fairfax may want to consider some form of charitable giving, either during her lifetime or at death. She has no immediate family, and we know of no other potential gift or bequest recipients.

- *Laws and Regulations*. Fairfax should be aware of, and abide by, any securities (or other) laws or regulations relating to her "insider" status at Reston and her holding of Reston stock. Although there is no trust instrument in place, if Fairfax's future investing is handled by an investment advisor, the responsibilities associated with the Prudent Person Rule will come into play, including the responsibility for investing in a diversified portfolio. Also, she has a need to seek estate planning legal assistance, even though there are no apparent gift or bequest recipients.

- *Unique Circumstances and/or Preferences*. The value of the Reston stock dominates the value of Fairfax's portfolio. A well-defined exit strategy needs to be developed for the stock as soon as is practical and appropriate. If the value of the stock increases, or at least does not decline before it is liquidated, Fairfax's present lifestyle can be maintained after retirement with the combined portfolio. A significant and prolonged setback for Reston Industries, however, could have disastrous consequences. Such circumstances would require a dramatic downscaling of Fairfax's lifestyle or generation of alternate sources of income in order to maintain her current lifestyle. A worst-case scenario might be characterized by a 50% drop in the market value of Reston's stock and sale of that stock to diversify the portfolio, where the sale proceeds would be subject to a 35% tax rate. In this scenario, the net proceeds of the Reston part of the portfolio would be:

$$\$10{,}000{,}000 \times 0.5 \times (1 - 0.35) = \$3{,}250{,}000$$

When added to the Savings Portfolio, total portfolio value would be $5,250,000. For this portfolio to generate $658,000 in income, a 12.5% return would be required.

Synopsis. The policy governing investment in Fairfax's Savings Portfolio will put emphasis on realizing a 3% real, after-tax return from a mix of high-quality assets with less than average risk. Ongoing attention will be given to Fairfax's tax planning and legal needs, her progress toward retirement, and the value of her Reston stock. The Reston stock holding is a unique circumstance of decisive significance in this situation. Developments should be monitored closely, and protection against the effects of a worst-case scenario should be implemented as soon as possible.

b. *Critique*. The Coastal proposal produces a real, after-tax expected return of approximately 5.18%, which exceeds the 3% level sought by Fairfax. The expected return for this proposal can be calculated by first subtracting the tax-exempt yield from the total current yield: 4.9% − 0.55% = 4.35%

Next, convert this to an after-tax yield: 4.35% × (1 − 0.35) = 2.83%

The tax exempt income is then added back to the total: 2.83% + 0.55% = 3.38%

The appreciation portion of the return (5.8%) is then added to the after-tax yield to get the nominal portfolio return: 3.38% + 5.80% = 9.18%

Finally, the 4% inflation rate is subtracted to produce the expected real after-tax return: 9.18% − 4.0% = 5.18%

This result can also be obtained by computing these returns for each of the individual holdings, weighting each result by the portfolio percentage and then adding to derive a total portfolio result.

From the data available, it is not possible to determine specifically the inherent degree of portfolio volatility. Despite meeting the return criterion, the allocation is neither realistic nor, in its detail, appropriate to Fairfax's situation in the context of an investment policy usefully applicable to her. The primary weaknesses are the following:

• Allocation of Equity Assets. Exposure to equity assets will be necessary in order to achieve the return requirements specified by Fairfax; however, greater diversification of these assets among other equity classes is needed to produce a more efficient, potentially less volatile portfolio that would meet both her risk tolerance parameters and her return requirements. An allocation that focuses equity investments in U.S. large-cap and/or small-cap holdings and also includes smaller international and Real Estate Investment Trust exposure is more likely to achieve the return and risk tolerance goals. If more information were available concerning the returns and volatility of the Reston stock, an argument could be made that this holding is the U.S. equity component of her portfolio. But the lack of information on this issue precludes taking it into account for the Savings Portfolio allocation and creates the need for broader equity diversification.

• Cash allocation. Within the proposed fixed-income component, the 15% allocation to cash is excessive given the limited liquidity requirement and the low return for this asset class.

• Corporate/Municipal Bond Allocation. The corporate bond allocation (10 percent) is inappropriate given Fairfax's tax situation and the superior after-tax yield on municipal bonds relative to corporate (5.5% vs. 4.9% after-tax return).

• Venture Capital Allocation. The allocation to venture capital is questionable given Fairfax's policy statement indicating that she is quite risk averse. Although venture capital may provide diversification benefits, venture capital returns historically have been more volatile than other risky assets such as U.S. large- and small-cap stocks. Hence, even a small percentage allocation to venture capital may be inappropriate.

• Lack of Risk/Volatility Information. The proposal concentrates on return expectations and ignores risk/volatility implications. Specifically, the proposal should have addressed the expected volatility of the entire portfolio to determine whether it falls within the risk tolerance parameters specified by Fairfax.

c.　i. Fairfax has stated that she is seeking a 3% real, after-tax return. Table 26G provides nominal, pre-tax figures, which must be adjusted for both taxes and inflation in order to ascertain which portfolios meet Fairfax's return objective. A simple solution is to subtract the municipal bond return component from the stated return, then subject the resulting figure to a 35% tax rate, and then add back tax-exempt municipal bond income. This produces a nominal, after-tax return. Finally, subtract 4% percent inflation to arrive at the real, after-tax return. For example, Allocation A has a real after-tax return of 3.4%, calculated as follows:

$$\{[0.099 - (0.072 \times 0.4)] \times (1\text{-}0.35)\} + (0.072 \times 0.4) - 0.04 = 3.44\%$$

Alternatively, this can be calculated as follows: multiply the taxable returns by their respective allocations, sum these products, adjust for the tax rate, add the result to the product of the nontaxable (municipal bond) return and its allocation, and deduct the inflation rate from this sum. For Allocation A:

$$[(0.045 \times 0.10) + (0.13 \times 0.20) + (0.15 \times 0.10) + (0.15 \times 0.10) + (0.10 \times 0.10)] \times$$
$$(1 - 0.35) + [(0.072 \times 0.4)] - 0.04 = 3.46\%$$

Return Measure	Allocation				
	A	B	C	D	E
Nominal Return	9.9%	11.0%	8.8%	14.4%	10.3%
Real After-Tax Return	3.5%	3.1%	2.5%	5.3%	3.5%

Table 26G also provides after-tax returns that could be adjusted for inflation and then used to identify those portfolios that meet Fairfax's return guidelines.

Allocations A, B, D, and E meet Fairfax's real, after-tax return objectives.

ii. Fairfax has stated that a worst case return of –10% in any 12-month period would be acceptable. The expected return less two times the portfolio risk (expected standard deviation) is the relevant risk tolerance measure. In this case, three allocations meet the criterion: A, C, and E.

Parameter	Allocation				
	A	B	C	D	E
Expected Return	9.9%	11.0%	8.8%	14.4%	10.3%
Exp. Std. Deviation	9.4%	12.4%	8.5%	18.1%	10.1%
Worst Case Return	–8.9%	–13.8%	–8.2%	–21.8%	–9.9%

d.　i. The Sharpe Ratio for Allocation D, using the cash equivalent rate of 4.5 percent as the risk-free rate, is: $(0.144 - 0.045)/0.181 = 0.547$

ii. The two allocations with the best Sharpe Ratios are A and E; the ratio for each of these allocations is 0.574.

e.   The recommended allocation is A. The allocations that meet both the minimum real, after-tax objective and the maximum risk tolerance objective are A and E. These allocations have identical Sharpe Ratios and both of these allocations have large positions in municipal bonds. However, Allocation E also has a large position in REITs, whereas the comparable equity position for Allocation A is a diversified portfolio of large and small cap domestic stocks. Because of the diversification value of the large and small stock positions in Allocation A, as opposed to the specialized or non-diversified nature of REIT stocks and their limited data history, one would have greater confidence that the expectational data for the large- and small- cap stock portfolios will be realized than for the REIT portfolio.

7.   a.   The key elements that should determine the foundation's grant-making (spending) policy are:
1. Average expected inflation over a long time horizon;
2. Average expected nominal return on the endowment portfolio over the same long horizon; and,
3. The 5%-of-asset-value payout requirement imposed by tax authorities as a condition for ongoing U.S. tax exemption, a requirement that is expected to continue indefinitely.

To preserve the real value of its assets and to maintain its spending in real terms, the foundation cannot pay out more, on average over time, than the real return it earns from its investment portfolio, since no fund-raising activities are contemplated. In effect, the portion of the total return representing the inflation rate must be retained and reinvested if the foundation's principal is to grow with inflation and, thus, maintain its real value and the real value of future grants.

b.   OBJECTIVES

Return Requirement: Production of current income, the committee's focus before Mr. Franklin's gift, is no longer a primary objective, given the increase in the asset base and the Committee's understanding that investment policy must accommodate long-term as well as short-term goals. The need for a minimum annual payout equal to 5% of assets must be considered, as well as the need to maintain the real value of these assets. A total return objective (roughly equal to the grant rate plus the inflation rate, but not less than the 5% required for maintenance of the foundation's tax-exempt status) is appropriate.

Risk Tolerance: The increase in the foundation's financial flexibility arising from Mr. Franklin's gift and the committee's spending policy change have increased the foundation's ability to assume risk. The organization has a more or less infinite expected life span and, in the context of this long-term horizon, has the ability to accept the consequences of short-term fluctuations in asset values. Moreover, adoption of a clear-cut spending rule will permit cash flows to be planned with some precision, adding stability to annual budgeting and reducing the need for precautionary liquidity. Overall, the foundation's risk tolerance is above average and oriented to long-term considerations.

CONSTRAINTS

Liquidity Requirements: Liquidity needs are low, with little likelihood of unforeseen demands requiring either forced asset sales or immense cash. Such needs as exist, principally for annual grant-making, are known in advance and relatively easy to plan for in a systematic way.

Time Horizon: The foundation has a virtually infinite life; the need to plan for future as well as current financial demands justifies a long-term horizon with perhaps a five year cycle of planning and review.

Taxes: Tax-exempt under present U.S. law if the annual minimum payout requirement (currently 5% of asset value) is met.

Legal and Regulatory: Governed by state law and Prudent Person standards; ongoing attention must be paid to maintaining the tax-exempt status by strict observance of IRS and any related Federal regulations.

Unique Circumstances: The need to maintain real value after grants is a key consideration, as is the 5% of assets requirement for tax exemption. The real return achieved must meet or exceed the grant rate, with the 5% level a minimum requirement.

Narrative: Investment actions shall take place in a long-term, tax-exempt context, reflect above average risk tolerance, and emphasize production of real total returns, but with at least a 5% nominal return.

c. To meet requirements of this scenario, it is first necessary to identify a spending rate that is both sufficient (i.e., 5% or higher in nominal terms) and feasible (i.e., prudent and attainable under the circumstances represented by the Table 26H data and the empirical evidence of historical risk and return for the various asset classes). The real return from the recommended allocation should be shown to equal or exceed the minimum payout requirement (i.e., equal to or greater than 5% in nominal terms).

The allocation philosophy will reflect the foundation's need for real returns at or above the grant rate, its total return orientation, its above average risk tolerance, its low liquidity requirements, and its tax exempt status. While the Table 26H data and historical experience provide needed inputs to the process, several generalizations are also appropriate:

1. Allocations to fixed income instruments will be less than 50% as bonds have provided inferior real returns in the past, and while forecasted real returns from 1993 to 2000 are higher, they are still lower than for stocks. Real return needs are high and liquidity needs are low. Bonds will be included primarily for diversification and risk reduction purposes. The ongoing cash flow from bond portfolios of this size should easily provide for all normal working capital needs.

2. Allocations to equities will be greater than 50%, and this asset class will be the portfolio's "work horse asset." Expected and historical real returns are high, the horizon is long, risk tolerance is above average, and taxes are not a consideration.

3. Within the equity universe there is room in this situation for small-cap as well as large-cap issues, for international as well as domestic issues and, perhaps, for

venture capital investment as well. Diversification will contribute to risk reduction, and total return could be enhanced. All could be included.

4. Given its value as an alternative to stocks and bonds as a way to maintain real return and provide diversification benefits, real estate could be included in this portfolio. In a long term context, real estate has provided good inflation protection, helping to protect real return production.

An example of an appropriate, modestly aggressive allocation is shown below. Table 26H contains an array of historical and expected return data which was used to develop real return forecasts. In this case, the objective was to reach a spending level in real terms as close to 6% as possible, a level appearing to meet the dual goals of the committee and that is also feasible. The actual expected real portfolio return is 5.8%.

	Intermediate Term Forecast of Real Returns	Recommended Allocation	Real Return Contribution
Cash (U.S.) T bills	0.7%	*0%	
Bonds:			
Intermediate	2.3	5	0.115%
Long Treasury	4.2	10	0.420
Corporate	5.3	10	0.530
International	4.9	10	0.490
Stocks:			
Large Cap	5.5	30	1.650
Small Cap	8.5	10	0.850
International	6.6	10	0.660
Venture Capital	12.0	5	0.600
Real Estate	5.0	10	0.500
Total Expected Return		100%	5.815%

*No cash is included because ongoing cash flow from the portfolio should be sufficient to meet all normal working capital needs.

8. You would advise them to exploit all available retirement tax shelters, such as 403b, 401k, Keogh plans and IRAs. Since they will not be taxed on the income earned from these accounts until they withdraw the funds, they should avoid investing in tax-preferred instruments like municipal bonds. If they are very risk-averse, they should consider investing a large proportion of their funds in inflation-indexed CDs, which offer a riskless real rate of return.

9. a. The Maclins' overall risk objective must consider both willingness and ability to take risk.

        Willingness: The Maclins have a below-average willingness to take risk, based on their unhappiness with the portfolio volatility in recent years and their desire to avoid shortfall risk in excess of −12 percent return in any one year in the value of the investment portfolio.

        Ability: The Maclins have an average ability to take risk. While their large asset base and a long time horizon would otherwise suggest an above-average ability to take risk, their living expenses (£74,000) are significantly greater than Christopher's after-tax salary (£48,000), causing them to be very dependent on projected portfolio returns to cover the difference, and thereby reducing their ability to take risk.

        Overall: The Maclins' overall risk tolerance is below average, as their below-average willingness to take risk dominates their average ability to take risk in determining their overall risk tolerance.

    b. The Maclins' return objective is to grow the portfolio to meet their educational and retirement needs as well as to provide for ongoing net expenses. The Maclins will require annual after-tax cash flows of £26,000 (calculated below) to cover ongoing net expenses, and they will need £2 million in 18 years to fund their children's education and their own retirement. To meet this objective, the Maclins' pre-tax required return is 7.38 percent, which is calculated below.

        The after-tax return required to accumulate £2 million in 18 years, beginning with an investable base of £1,235,000 (calculated below) and with annual outflows of £26,000, is 4.427 percent. When adjusted for the 40 percent tax rate, this results in a 7.38 percent pretax return: $4.427\%/(1 − 0.40) = 7.38\%$

Annual Cash Flow = −£26,000	
Christopher's Annual Salary	80,000
Less: Taxes (40%)	−32,000
Living Expenses	−74,000
Net Annual Cash Flow	−£26,000

Asset Base = £1,235,000	
Inheritance	900,000
Barnett Co. Common Stock	220,000
Stocks and Bonds	160,000
Cash	5,000
Subtotal	£1,285,000
Less One-time Needs:	
Down Payment on House	−30,000
Charitable Donation	−20,000
Total Assets	£1,235,000

Note: No inflation adjustment is required in the return calculation because increases in living expenses will be offset by increases in Christopher's salary.

c. The Maclins' investment policy statement should include the following constraints:

i. Time horizon: The Maclins have a two-stage time horizon because of their changing cash flow and resource needs. The first stage is the next 18 years. The second stage begins with their retirement and the university education years for their children.

ii. Liquidity requirements: The Maclins have one-time immediate expenses (£50,000) that include the deposit on the house they are purchasing and the charitable donation in honor of Louise's father.

iii. Tax concerns: The U.K. has a 40 percent marginal tax rate on both ordinary income and capital gains. Therefore there is no preference for investment returns from taxable dividends or interest over capital gains. Taxes will be a drag on investment performance because all expenditures will be after tax.

iv. Unique circumstances: The large holding of the Barnett Co. common stock (representing 18 percent of the Maclins' total portfolio) and the resulting lack of diversification is a key factor to be included in evaluating the risk of the Maclins' portfolio and in the future management of the Maclins' assets. The Maclins' desire not to invest in alcohol and tobacco stocks is another constraining factor, especially in the selection of any future investment style or manager.

10. a. 1. The cash reserve is too high.
   - The 15 percent (or £185,250) cash allocation is not consistent with the liquidity constraint.
   - The large allocation to a low-return asset contributes to a shortfall in return relative to required return.

2. The 15 percent allocation to Barnett Co. common stock is too high.
   - The risk of holding a 15 percent position in Barnett stock, with a standard deviation of 48, is not appropriate for the Maclins' below-average risk tolerance and −12 percent shortfall risk limitation.
   - The large holding in Barnett stock is inconsistent with adequate portfolio diversification.

3. Shortfall risk exceeds the limitation of −12 percent return in any one year.
   - The Maclins have stated that their shortfall risk limitation is −12 percent return in any one year. Subtracting 2 times the standard deviation from the portfolio's expected return, we find:

   $$6.70 \text{ percent} - (2 \times 12.40 \text{ percent}) = -18.10 \text{ percent}$$

   This is below their shortfall risk limitation.

4. The expected return is too low (the allocation between stocks and bonds is not consistent with return objective).
   - The portfolio's expected return of 6.70 percent is less than the return objective of 7.38 percent.

b.   Note: The Maclins have purchased their home and made their charitable contribution.

Cash: 0% to 3%
The Maclins do not have an ongoing need for a specific cash reserve fund.
Liquidity needs are low and only a small allocation for emergencies need be
considered. Portfolio income will cover the annual shortfall in living expenses.
Therefore the lowest allocation to cash is most appropriate.

U.K. Corporate Bonds: 50% to 60%
The Maclins need significant exposure to this less volatile asset class, given their
below-average risk tolerance. Stable return, derived from current income, will also
be needed to offset the annual cash flow shortfall. Therefore the highest allocation
to U.K. Corporate Bonds is most appropriate.

U.S. Equities: 20% to 25%
The Maclins must meet their return objective while addressing their risk tolerance.
U.S. Equities offer higher expected returns than bonds and also offer international
diversification benefits. The risk/return profile is also relatively more favorable
than it is for either U.K. Bonds or Barnett stock. Therefore the highest allocation to
U.S. Equities is most appropriate.

Barnett Co. Common Stock: 0% to 5%
The Maclins' below average risk tolerance includes a shortfall risk limitation of −12
percent return in any one year, and the Barnett stock is very volatile. There is too
much stock-specific (non-systematic) risk in this concentrated position for such an
investor. They also have "employment risk" with Barnett. Therefore the lowest
allocation to Barnett stock is most appropriate.

The following sample allocations are provided to illustrate that selected ranges
meet the return objective.

Sample allocation 1:

Asset Class	Weight (%)	Return (%)	Weighted Return (%)
Cash	1	1.0	0.01
U.K. Corporate Bonds	55	5.0	2.75
U.K. Small-capitalization	10	11.0	1.10
U.K. Large-capitalization	10	9.0	0.90
U.S. Equities	20	10.0	2.00
Barnett Co. Common Stock	4	16.0	0.64
Portfolio Expected Return			7.40

Sample allocation 2:

Asset Class	Weight (%)	Return (%)	Weighted Return (%)
Cash	1	1.0	0.01
U.K. Corporate Bonds	50	5.0	2.50
U.K. Small-capitalization	10	11.0	1.10
U.K. Large-capitalization	10	9.0	0.90
U.S. Equities	24	10.0	2.40
Barnett Co. Common Stock	5	16.0	0.80
		Portfolio Expected Return	7.71

11. a. George More's expected accumulation at age 65:

	n	i	PV	PMT		FV
Fixed income	25	3%	$100,000	$1,500	$\Rightarrow$	FV = $264,067
Common stocks	25	6%	$100,000	$1,500	$\Rightarrow$	FV = $511,484

b. Expected retirement annuity:

	n	i	PV	FV		PMT
Fixed income	15	3%	$264,067	0	$\Rightarrow$	PMT = $22,120
Common stocks	15	6%	$511,484	0	$\Rightarrow$	PMT = $52,664

c. In order to get a fixed-income annuity of $30,000 per year, his accumulation at age 65 would have to be:

	n	i	PMT	FV		PV
Fixed income	15	3%	$30,000	0	$\Rightarrow$	PV = $358,138

His annual contribution would have to be:

	n	i	PV	FV		PMT
Fixed income	25	3%	$100,000	-$358,138	$\Rightarrow$	PMT = $4,080

This is an increase of $2,580 per year over his current contribution of $1,500 per year.

12. a. The least risky asset for a person investing for her child's college tuition is an account denominated in units of college tuition. Such an account is the College Sure CD offered by the College Savings Bank of Princeton, New Jersey. A unit of this CD pays, at maturity, an amount guaranteed to equal or exceed the average cost of a year of undergraduate tuition, as measured by an index prepared by the College Board.

b. The least risky asset for a defined benefit pension fund with benefit obligations that have an average duration of ten years is a bond portfolio with a duration of ten years and a present value equal to the present value of the pension obligation. This is an immunization strategy that provides a future value equal to (or greater than) the pension obligation, regardless of the direction of change in interest rates. Note that, as discussed in Chapter 16, immunization requires periodic rebalancing of the bond portfolio.

c. The least risky asset for a defined benefit pension fund that pays inflation-protected benefits is a portfolio of immunized Treasury Inflation-Indexed Securities with a duration equal to the duration of the pension obligation (i.e., in this scenario, a duration of ten years). (Note: These securities are also referred to as Treasury Inflation-Protected Securities, or TIPS.)

13. a. The answer to this question depends on the assumptions made about the investor's effective income tax rates for the period of accumulation and for the period of withdrawals. First, we assume that (i) tax rates remain constant throughout the entire time horizon; and, (ii) the investor's taxable income remains relatively constant throughout. Consequently, the investor's effective tax rate does not change, and we find that the Roth IRA and the conventional IRA provide the same after-tax benefits.

Alternatively, we might consider a scenario in which a household has a low income early in the accumulation period and higher income later in the accumulation period and during the withdrawal period. If tax rates are constant throughout the time horizon, then the investor's effective tax rate would be lower throughout the accumulation period than during the withdrawal period, and, as a result, the Roth IRA would provide higher after-tax benefits. This is a consequence of the fact that an investor's Roth IRA contributions during the accumulation period are taxed at the lower rate, while withdrawals from a conventional IRA would be taxed at the higher rate. Similarly, the conventional IRA provides higher after-tax benefits in the event that the effective tax rate is higher during the accumulation period than it is during the period of withdrawals.

Clearly, each of the scenarios described here represents an extremely unrealistic simplification. The issue becomes more complex if we consider the many possible changes, both in tax law and in the investor's individual circumstances, that can have an impact on the effective tax rate.

b.   For the Roth IRA, contributions are made with after-tax dollars, so the tax rate is known (and taxes are paid) during the accumulation period; the tax rate for withdrawals at retirement from a Roth IRA is zero, and is therefore also known with certainty. On the other hand, contributions to a conventional IRA during the accumulation period are tax-free, but the tax rate for withdrawals is not known until the withdrawals are made at retirement. This tax rate uncertainty for a conventional IRA has two sources. First, the investor is unable to anticipate legislated changes in future tax rates; and, second, even if tax rates were to remain constant, the investor cannot determine her future tax bracket because she cannot accurately forecast her taxable income at retirement. Consequently, the Roth IRA provides protection against tax-rate uncertainty, while the conventional IRA subjects the investor to substantial tax rate uncertainty.

CHAPTER 27:
THE THEORY OF ACTIVE PORTFOLIO MANAGEMENT

1. Student exercise- answers will vary.

2. Student exercise- answers will vary.